DIPLOMACY IN
ANCIENT GREECE

ASPECTS OF GREEK AND ROMAN LIFE

General Editor: Professor H. H. Scullard

DIPLOMACY IN ANCIENT GREECE

Sir Frank Adcock

D. J. Mosley

St. Martin's Press   New York

For information, write:
St. Martin's Press, Inc., 175 Fifth Avenue,
New York, N.Y.   10010

Printed in Great Britain

Library of Congress Catalog Card No:
74-30066

First published in the United States of
America in 1975

12-19-78

CONTENTS

Part Two

PREFACE

IT WAS THE INTENTION of the late Professor Adcock to write a book on Ancient Greek and Roman Diplomacy for this series, and by the time of his death he had assembled notes and typescript in preparation. His aim was to produce a progressive narrative of events and institutions on the lines of the first part of this book. At the same time I had an interest in writing an analytical account of the forms and institutions of Ancient Greek Diplomacy. Consequently Professor Scullard suggested that a single book be prepared, in two parts, bearing this title. In the first part I have attempted to include as much as possible of what Professor Adcock had prepared, and the form, if not the chapter headings, is as he envisaged. For the second part I must accept the chief responsibility.

It is hoped that the contrast in the style of the two authors will not be found too stark, for Adcock had an inimitably brief, clear and lucid style which disguised the effort, care and time expended in composition. I have been concerned, however, to finish the work as quickly as possible in order that his association with the book should not be diminished by the passage of time.

I should like to acknowledge my debt to Mr G. T. Griffith, who sorted through Professor Adcock's papers and sent the relevant material to me, to Professor R. A. Crossland, sometime Fellow of King's College, Cambridge, and to Professor R. J. Hopper for their encouragement. The patience too of Thames and Hudson and Professor Scullard, the General Editor of the series, cannot pass without mention.

But, both first and last, tribute must be paid to F. E. Adcock, who, in addition to his academic distinction, displayed many human virtues and was always quick to encourage others. I was not one of his pupils, but from my undergraduate days he took the initiative in offering help and encouragement, and not long before his death he issued an invitation for a weekend, which was spent in reading and commenting on manuscript which has subsequently been incorporated in this book and other publications.

D. J. Mosley

University of Sheffield
Autumn 1974

GENERAL EDITOR'S NOTE

Since this book embodies the last piece of Sir Frank Adcock's work that is likely to be published, it is appropriate here to refer to the account of his life and work in the *Proceedings of the British Academy*, Liv (1968; published 1970), 425ff. and to the shorter notice and the bibliography of his published writings in the fifty-sixth volume (1966) of the *Journal of Roman Studies* which was dedicated to him on his eightieth birthday.

Knowing that I echo the feelings of many generations of ancient historians, I want to record the inspiration and encouragement that Professor Adcock has always provided. For me this has lasted for over forty years, from my undergraduate days of the mid 1920s down to our talks about the scope of the book that he agreed to write on diplomacy.

I also want to thank Dr Mosley for undertaking a difficult task. With characteristic modesty he has glossed over too lightly the great effort he has put into a skilful attempt to make available in the first part of this book the somewhat scattered material which he inherited.

H.H.S.

Part I

CHAPTER I

THE TRADITION OF GREEK DIPLOMACY

A PART OF THE SELF-CONSCIOUSNESS of the Greeks was their Heroic Age as revealed to them by the Epic poems, which enshrined for them their own distant past. But even before their Heroic Age began Greeks did exist, although what they did and suffered was largely unknown to their classical successors, just as it is to us. Less is known of the Greeks before the Heroic Age than of contemporary oriental monarchies, which have left us some of their own material records. For example, the Second Hittite Empire has left documents which reveal the character of Hittite diplomacy. The Hittites possessed a highly developed political instinct, a lively consciousness of their neighbours and a precocious ability to induce them to act in a way which suited Hittite interests.

The authority of the Hittites over their vassals is recorded in treaties which show a skilful adaptation of the formulae of diplomacy as early as the fourteenth and thirteenth centuries BC.[1] And what was true of this Hittite Empire was in a measure true of Egypt. An approach to what may be called a comity of nations can be detected, but the rise of the Assyrians, who wielded a heavy hand, crushed such promising developments in diplomacy. It was later to be said of the Athenians that they were willing neither to live at peace themselves nor to allow others to do so. With even greater truth could that be said of the Assyrians, for their vassals were left without even the shadow of independence.

It is hardly too much to say that diplomacy vanished in the storms which swept through the oriental world. The result was that when at last Greek diplomacy began the city-states did not have before them the lessons of the distant past. What they did have before them was what their epic presented as a literary background, and of that they remained conscious. For instance Odysseus remained, in the Epic and later traditions, the mirror of a diplomatist, eloquent and resourceful.

In the Heroic Age we begin to see episodes, sporadic though they are, in the interaction of communities, but above all the central event of the age was the expedition of many Greek communities led by Agamemnon against Troy. The great adventure which took the heroes to the plains of Troy enlisted many chieftains, bound by a long-standing oath to recover Helen for her husband and to leave their homes if that were necessary in order to keep their word. It was reserved for Thucydides to comment in the fifth century that the Greek chieftains followed Agamemnon for the same reasons that in his own day the lead of Athens was followed by her allies.[2] Nevertheless the Greeks attributed to the Heroic Age a form of internationalism like that of medieval chivalry, participation in a common adventure as in a medieval Crusade.

The forerunner of the expedition was the embassy of the Greeks to Priam of Troy and its voice was heard in the eloquence of Odysseus, whose words 'fell fast like snowflakes in winter'.[3] Odysseus too was employed as envoy to persuade the sulking hero Achilles to rejoin the Greek forces. After the Trojan War Odysseus returned to Ithaca to test the fidelity of his wife Penelope. Narrating his travels it was said of him that he spoke many words that were false but sounded like truth, and indeed it was that very phrase which was applied in later times to Isaeus, one of the subtlest of the Athenian orators. For the Greeks diplomacy involved a special application of the skills of the orator, that command of words and thought which made oratory the 'artificer of persuasion'. Such was the case in the Heroic Age and so it remained in historical times.

Neither in the Heroic Age nor in the early historical periods can we trace a formal and systematic development of the institutions or arts of diplomacy. The age of the chieftains whose will dominated their communities was followed by the rise of the republican city-states, where monarchy was replaced by aristocracies which guided the common will of the citizens at large. Greece was then composed of a multiplicity of inward-looking communities. The city-states were essentially self-centred and unbureaucratic, and the political instincts of their citizens were absorbed in their domestic affairs. The aristocracies which prevailed in the early city-states had little need to practise diplomacy, for they were willing not to impose their will on their neighbours if they could be confident that no neighbour would impose its will on them. It is roughly true that if an early Greek community could live as though it had no neighbours it was content to do so. It was not likely to seek fusion with a neighbouring state but rather an independent, autonomous co-existence, of which conflict in war was an interruption. Two factors, however, helped to mitigate the self-centred nature of the Greek communities. Ties existed between rulers and men of social standing in their respective communities. Such ties between families or individuals involved the courtesies of hospitality and induced reciprocal services. In time such practices found an institution in *proxenia*, in which the ties of *xenia*, guest-friendship between individuals, were extended to communities or their visiting representatives. The second factor which applied in some cases was the tie of religion, loyalty and sentiment which subsisted between colonies and their mother cities.

The simple unbureaucratic structure of early Greek states did not encourage the provision in advance of institutions directed to the initiation and systematic practice of diplomacy. In their concentration upon their internal affairs they were apprehensive of taking measures which might limit their freedom of action and they were slow to enter upon obligations which might extend beyond their means and their needs. In a later age they found freedom of action in a choice between competing obligations, but the day was still distant when active diplomacy was to create opportunities. In view of the natural reluctance, or even need, to come to terms with a neighbour the prime reason for doing so was the imminence of war, and the earliest word that denoted alliance or co-operation between states was *symmachia*, comradeship in arms. Naturally alliance for war brought communities to co-operate in making treaties and preserving peace, for it was irrational for one city to be at peace and for the other to remain at war. To take account of their several interests required negotiation between allies before negotiation with the enemy.

To confirm peace required a sanction admitted by both parties to a dispute, and the natural sanction was to be found in religion. For so far as diplomacy is a form of persuasion, it will seek something to which it can appeal in order to find some common ground for agreement. The natural appeal was to religion, partly because it implied a sanction independent of material force, partly because religion transcended the limits of the several city-states.

The making of peace had to begin with the cessation of hostilities and the formal establishment of a truce. That procedure was similar to the means which were regularly employed to provide a peaceful background to the religious festivals in which many states took part. Rivalry in the games at those festivals was a homeopathic remedy for rivalry elsewhere in war, and the prestige won in victory was matched by the leadership in war conferred upon the state which led a successful campaign.

It is rash to assert, as has been done by some, that war was the permanent characteristic of all Greek communities. If peace was worth attaining, it was worth preserving and common interests were likely to encourage a continuance of relations in time of peace. In early times often a period was fixed during which peace should endure, but it could be argued that such a practice did not so much limit as confirm the durability of inter-state agreements. The cities were highly conscious of their individuality, but they learned to recognize and respect the individuality of their friends and enemies. That led them to engage in, as far as possible, peaceful co-existence, a term which may describe their normal relationship. That relationship led them to associate for longer periods to avoid strife, which was more likely to bring them loss than to confer gain.

Therein lay the origin of diplomatic activity and the need of skilful negotiations to isolate and remove the causes of tension and hostility by persuasion, which is the prime duty of a diplomat. So far as diplomacy is a skill in that art, it was bound to attract to itself men of experience in affairs and men who possessed a cool appreciation of problems. Such men of natural authority were to be found in the aristocratic councils, which tended to be the place where foreign policy was determined by the Elders, men of admitted wisdom. It is not without significance that Greek envoys came into being without a technical term to denote them. The first word used to denote envoys was the word for elders (*presbeis*), men whose wisdom, authority and experience surpassed that of their fellows. They conducted their discussions in the council, which was the natural forum for informed debate and advice on all matters. There was no continuing institution or organ of government which was solely devoted to the discovery and formulation of a definite foreign policy. Rightly the Greeks were slow to believe that logical prevision could count upon logical fulfilment, for the course of events was wayward and capricious under the impulses of chance and accident, and few aspects of government required arcane knowledge or peculiarly distinctive skills.

It remains at least half true that the determination of policy, of which diplomacy is a kind of ectoplasm, is affected by the character of a community and the working of its institutions. Diplomacy is thus to be studied by its manifestations and origins together with the light which they shed on each other. In what follows it will be found useful to bear in mind particularly the relation of diplomacy to the states from which it proceeds. The study of Greek diplomacy in its earlier phases is based on deductions rather than on substantial direct evidence, but from the sixth century BC the personalities concerned in political activity begin to be visible, and that may not only add to the interest of the study but also help in the interpretation of what happened and why it did so. In the sixth and following two centuries strategy is a key determinant in the making of policy and that too requires interpretation. For strategy and material force increasingly become factors in diplomacy, both in cause and in effect.

Diplomacy does not exist in a vacuum: it is the work of men who see events from a particular angle of vision. In so far as diplomacy is conditioned by institutions, those have to be elucidated and placed in their historical setting. Consequently what is presented in the first half of this book is an attempt to shed light on men and events by estimating the degree in which the historical events and their bearing upon diplomacy may have a reciprocal influence. The second half of the book is an attempt to move beyond a chronological survey or history of foreign policy and to discuss in more detail the peculiar forms and institutions which the Greeks adopted and evolved in their diplomacy.

CHAPTER II

THE PELOPONNESE AND THE GROWTH OF SPARTAN POWER

SPARTAN DIPLOMATIC ACTIVITY begins to repay study from about the middle years of the sixth century, for by that time there had come into existence durable interactions of the Lacedaemonian state with its neighbours in the Peloponnese, and before the century ended the complex of city-states which described itself as the 'Lacedaemonians and their allies', commonly known as the Peloponnesian League, came into existence.

The efforts of Spartan diplomacy were primarily deployed to meet the needs of internal security, for the Spartans lived as a minority greatly outnumbered by the subordinate elements of the population of their state. Spartans could not feel safe so long as any neighbouring state could vie for influence in the vicinity. Consequently their military and diplomatic efforts were designed to secure regional supremacy within the Peloponnese, and so successful were they that influential powers and leading military states of the age of Agamemnon were far eclipsed by Sparta. Her position within the Peloponnese established her base as the principal military power in Greece for almost two centuries. Domestic problems, however, limited the consistent exploitation of her acknowledged supremacy outside the Peloponnese.

An early period of expansion by conquest had made the Spartans the inheritors of a subjugated population whose subordinate status was reflected in the name helots. The attempts of the latter to liberate themselves in the eighth and seventh centuries were decisively defeated. In addition to the helots a peripheral population, akin to the Spartans and described as *perioeci*, had become subordinate to the warrior caste of a homogeneous community contained in the valley of the Eurotas, with its centre at a group of villages which became the city of Sparta. From the middle of the sixth century Sparta entered into inter-state relations with her neighbours. The latter remained autonomous, living their own lives and enjoying their own local institutions, but united with the Spartans by a bond of reciprocal defence in time of need. Of course the most likely cause which the Spartans envisaged for invoking a treaty was a revolt of the helots. In the event of such a revolt the allies of Sparta were pledged to send her all the help they could. In return, each of the allies might look to Sparta for help against external attack. The original area within which the alliance operated was, at least to begin with, the Peloponnese, and the whole complex now bears the conventional name of the 'Peloponnesian League'.

The first act which clearly can be called diplomatic was the renunciation of aggression against the warlike city of Tegea in return for her adhesion to alliance with Sparta.[4] That step meant passing from war to the pledge of peaceful co-existence and to active co-operation. The agent of that transition was the Spartan sage Cheilon, who as ephor and general was brigaded with King Anaxandridas. The Spartan operations against Tegea (c. 560–550) had not been successful, and the men of Tegea won a victory which diminished the prestige of the Spartan army. Subsequently Sparta and Tegea were content to become allies and Sparta inaugurated a policy that was to lead to the formation of the Peloponnesian League.

During the next half-century Sparta had a hand in the fall of tyrannies in various cities in Greece. It was the pride of the Spartans that no tyrant had ruled over them.[5] Sparta had kings and provided a good example of the adaptation of an aristocratic monarchy to the needs of both its external and internal policy, but whatever her kings were they were not usurpers. In that age the converse of tyranny was aristocracy, and so far as the cities of the Peloponnesian League had a characteristic constitution, it was aristocracy. Typical of the Peloponnesian states in which a lineage of tyrants had become established was Sicyon. Cheilon of Sparta encompassed the overthrow of the tyranny there and so enhanced with the mantle of a liberator Sparta, the state where so many were held in subjection. With cool calculation, as tyrannies in some half dozen cities were ripe for overthrow by their aristocratic opponents, Sparta hastened their fall and secured the good will which that process engendered.

The climax of that policy was reached when the Spartans gave help to the Athenian Cleisthenes who c. 510 successfully planned the overthrow of the Peisistratid tyranny at Athens at a time when Hippias, the son and successor of Peisistratus, forfeited by his harsh and suspicious attitude the goodwill which his father had enjoyed. The Spartan king, Cleomenes I, who did not claim to be the dis-

interested champion of freedom, expected to secure by such a move
an aristocratic ally beyond the boundaries of the Peloponnese. He
had already, by a diplomatic stroke worthy of a Bismarck, sowed
enmity between Athens and Boeotia to preclude any possibility of
their combined hegemony north of the Isthmus of Corinth. Yet a
further opportunity occurred in 508 for Sparta to consolidate her
influence on Athenian affairs, for in the course of a sharp rivalry
at Athens between Cleisthenes and Isagoras, another aristocrat, the
latter invoked Spartan help to confirm his control of Athens. In the
face of that threat there was one source of power to which Cleisthenes
could turn, and that was the common people of Attica, for, according
to the historian Herodotus, he enlisted the *demos* as his partisans and
so became the first 'aristodemocrat' in an Athens which broke away
from the Spartan alliance.[6] King Cleomenes called together the contingents of the Peloponnesian League and set himself to invade Attica
in order to restore Hippias to his tyranny as a friend of Sparta in 506.
But the allies of Sparta had come to accept that the tradition of their
alliance was to maintain freedom from tyrants and they refused to
depart from that tradition to assist the policy of a Spartan king. Thus
there was exposed a practical limitation of the Peloponnesian League
– it was difficult to take the field without the proper co-operation of
members, although Sparta could have every reason to suppose that
she would receive support without question in dealing with any
uprising of her subject population in Laconia.

How Sparta's institutions adapted themselves to serve the general
direction of her external policy is an intricate problem. A partial
answer may be found in an occasional shift in the internal balance
of power induced by emergencies as they arose. A resolute king
fortified by military success could give a lead which might for a
time be autocratic. Such a king was Cleomenes in the heyday of his
power after he had inflicted a crushing defeat upon the Argives at the
battle of Sepeia in 494.[7] Not long afterwards dissensions between the
Spartan kings led to interventions by the ephors both for and against
Cleomenes. Powerful as was the elected college of five ephors within
its traditional limits, its membership changed annually and was not
necessarily united in its outlook or policy. Consequently a king who

tried to use the ephors for his own purposes was on difficult ground and Spartan foreign policy, when not dictated by fear of the helots, could suffer a variation which might seem the more irrational because of the secrecy which obscured both it and the motives that guided it from time to time.

The functions of the *Gerousia*, a council of Elders, linked with the monarchy by the membership of the kings, are not readily discerned. The most distinguishing feature was the age of its members, whose membership normally continued to the end of their life, and they constituted what was more certainly a judicial than a purely political body, rather in the manner of the Athenian Council of the Areopagus at certain periods of its existence. They represented an element of continuity and hesitance, qualities for which Sparta became noted and which partly disguised her guile and subtlety. The *Apella*, the gathering of the whole enfranchised Spartiate community, had an especial responsibility for the declaration of war and it had an especial relation with the ephors, because it was the First Ephor of the year who presided over it. Nevertheless the *Apella* was not a forum for open debate nor was it a body from which leadership emerged, for its task was to give constitutional approval to propositions placed before it. Consequently the policy of Sparta tended not to be decided by open discussion in a deliberative body.

It was a characteristic of the Spartans to trust to particular skills. That was the secret of their military efficiency, and the processes of their diplomacy were guided by men who understood that art just as Spartan generals understood the art of war. Thus there arose a kind of enduring diplomatic skill which is attested again and again through Spartan history. That diplomatic skill was the more needed because the army of Sparta, though supreme in its aptitude and training, was based on a static or declining population for much of her history. As it was a professional standing army it had the advantage that it could take the field at a time when neighbouring communities were preoccupied with the harvest, but it was dangerous for that army to leave Sparta with no remaining force adequate to supervise the helots. Furthermore the advantage of surprise was denied them if their operations were on a scale which required the presence of their allies. For the supply of allied contingents could not be secured until a conference had been held to discuss allied policy and requirements. The Spartan army had to win victories, and substantial, not Pyrrhic, victories, because even minor losses of men in defeat could not be tolerated by the small Spartiate community from which the core of army was recruited. For Sparta to take the field in strength it was necessary to draw upon the *perioeci*, and so Sparta was bound to make sure of them by engaging their loyalty through concessions. For to be engaged in operations against both helots and *perioeci* was a great strain, as became clear at the time of the great revolt which erupted *c.* 464 when elements among the *perioeci* assisted the uprising of the helots. Not only were *perioeci* given political concessions and full military training but also the Sciritai, who came from a district near the Arcadian frontier, were given a place of honour in the line of battle.

As we have seen Sparta's diplomacy reflected her internal needs and difficulties. She was intent upon securing the adhesion of her Peloponnesian neighbours and was reluctant to deploy her forces far afield. She attempted to influence affairs outside the Peloponnese by non-military means, for example by sowing the seeds of enmity between Athens and Thebes and ensuring that Athens was preoccupied nearer home with the threat posed to her security by the island of Aegina which lay off the coast of Attica. Consequently the concentration of Sparta in the Peloponnese meant that Spartan military power overshadowed that of other states in the Peloponnese, of which we know comparatively little. It is, however, worthwhile noting that other states of some general importance were present within the Peloponnese and that Sparta did not rule the Peloponnesian roost entirely in her own way.

Significant among those states was Argos, with a proud historical memory going back to the days of Agamemnon and Mycenaean greatness. It was the focal point of power in the north-east of the Peloponnese until the challenge of Sparta. Early in the seventh century Argos assumed a position of supremacy in Greece under Pheidon, a powerful king. His rule witnessed the defeat of Sparta early in the seventh century and he presided over the Olympic Games.[8] Thereafter, although the power of Argos declined, her past history made it impossible for her to acknowledge the hegemony of Sparta and outbreaks of hostilities tended to erupt between them in each generation. Militarily she could not carry the day against Sparta any longer but enemies of Sparta from outside the Peloponnese found it useful to exploit the situation. Consequently the Athenians and others attempted to weaken the strategic position of Sparta by enlisting Argive support against her in 461, 420 and 395. Consequently the Spartans were quite content if they could ensure Argive neutrality at times of crisis. Argos, for example, remained neutral in 480/79 during the Persian invasion of Greece[9] and maintained her neutrality in Greece according to the terms of the Thirty Year Peace with Sparta from c. 451/0 to the end of the Archidamian War, when it expired.[10]

Argive power was diminished not only by Sparta but also by events in another Peloponnesian city, Corinth. That city, centred on the defensible point of Acro-Corinth, occupied a strategic position at the Peloponnesian end of the Isthmus which separated the Peloponnese from the rest of the Greek mainland, and had access to the sea on both sides of the Isthmus. Corinth had developed in early times as a naval power and had established links with the Western Greeks from the eighth century during which she had settled communities in Corcyra (Corfu) and Syracuse. In the seventh century the tyranny of Cypselus saw the decline of Argive influence in Corinth and an era of considerable economic prosperity. Under such conditions Corinth did not encroach upon the territory of her independent neighbours and tended to favour negotiation as a way out of diplomatic disputes. For not only did she mediate between Cleomenes of Sparta and Athens, but also between Athens and Thebes over Plataea in 519 and between Gela and Syracuse in 491. A signal instance of Corinth's willingness to live and let live was the uninterrupted independence of her smaller western neighbour Sicyon. For although the military and naval strength of Corinth was much greater, she made no attempt to encroach upon Sicyon's territory. Corinth, however, was gradually drawn into enmity with Athens in the fifth century. As Athens attempted to strengthen her southern flank against the Peloponnese and made the alliance with Argos in 461, Corinth saw her military and naval position open to challenge by Athens. Nevertheless Corinth in 439 managed to prevail upon the Spartans to refrain from measures against Athens when she was besieging her dissident ally, Samos. Corinthian forbearance, though, was ill-rewarded for she came into dispute with the growing naval power of Athens at Corcyra in 433 and in Potidaea in 432. As a result she organized a diplomatic campaign in the Peloponnese and prevailed upon the Spartans to declare war on Athens.[11]

Another Peloponnesian neighbour of Corinth, Megara, occupied a position of considerable strategic importance on the Isthmus along the littoral of the Corinthian and Saronic Gulfs. Between the eighth and sixth centuries she spread her influence wide with the establishment of settlements in Sicily, on the Bosporus at Chalcedon and Byzantium, and elsewhere. Domestic strife, however, weakened her influence and advantage was taken of that by Corinth, which annexed the Peraea Chora in the west, and by Athens, which took over the strategically sited island of Salamis in the bay of Eleusis. Just before that, *c.* 600, a tyranny had been established in Megara and the tyrant Theagenes married his daughter to an Athenian nobleman, Cylon, whom he attempted to have installed as tyrant in Athens.[12]. That attempt to establish a dynastic combination was defeated by resistance led by the Athenian noble clan of the Alcmaeonids. In Athens the affair caused a natural suspicion of Megara, which, after the overthrow of tyranny, was the more inclined to lean to alliance with Sparta. Nevertheless Megara as a weak power in a strategic position was subject to influence and pressure from both sides. Athenian activity *c.* 460 made Corinth so nervous as to apply pressure to Megara, causing the latter temporarily to go over to Athens.[13] Then before the outbreak of the Peloponnesian War in 431 the Athenians applied a strict blockade upon Megara in order to compel her to desert from the Peloponnesian alliance.[14]

Sparta was the dominant power in the Peloponnese by the beginning of the fifth century and at heart she was content to remain just that. She had made treaties with others in Asia Minor but when the Ionian Greeks there, in revolt from Persia, sent an urgent appeal for help from Sparta they met with a bleak response. The tale is told of how Aristagoras of Miletus visited Cleomenes in 498 and attempted to persuade him with eloquent pleas and promises of the capture of immense wealth at the Persian capital of Susa. Cleomenes deferred his answer until the third day and then asked Aristagoras how many days' journey it was from the Ionian Sea to the Persian capital. The reply was that it was a three months' journey and so Cleomenes bade the Milesian to depart from Sparta before sunset for he spoke no agreeable language to the Spartans in wishing to lead them a three months' journey from the sea.[15] It is, however, difficult for a powerful state to confine itself to the limits which it sets for itself. Sparta was to receive yet another appeal for help, for the Athenians and others had given help to the Ionians. Then after the failure of the revolt the Persians directed a punitive expedition against Athens and Eretria in 490. The Spartans promised that they would send aid after the end of celebrations for the festival of Apollo Carneius, but by then the Athenians had led their allies to a resounding victory at the battle of Marathon.[16]

In spite of the reluctance of the Spartans to move against the Persians in defence of Greeks, the Greek community invited the Spartans to assume command of the combined Greek forces both by land and by sea to meet the renewed Persian invasion of King Xerxes in 480.[17] King Leonidas led a heroic stand with a small Spartan force at Thermopylae but after its loss and in view of the lack of Greeks willing and able to offer resistance to Persia in central Greece the Spartans advocated a strategy of making a final stand at the Isthmus of Corinth. As it would have left the Peloponnese as the last bastion of Greek resistance with no outer defence, that strategy was unacceptable to Athens and especially her leader Themistocles, who had been responsible for developing her naval power. Consequently he and the Spartan commander Eurybiades organized a naval battle at Salamis, in which the Greeks established their naval supremacy over the Persians. That shared success rendered fruitless the Persian attempts to detach Athens from alliance with Sparta and paved the way for the repulse of Persia in the following year. For in 479 the Spartans, under the leadership of the regent Pausanias, confirmed their military supremacy and reputation for heroism by routing the Persians at the battle of Plataea.

Thus for a period Sparta had been drawn into activity on a large scale outside the Peloponnese as the successful, if reluctant, champion of the Panhellenic cause. It was a role which she did not seek and for which she was ill-suited by reason of her internal situation and of her regional interests, but it was a role of which she was to be reminded and by which she was to be haunted in later generations.

After the repulse of the Persian invasions Sparta retired to her traditional sphere and role, leaving others under the leadership of Athens to pursue the cause against Persia. Initially, however, after a period of active leadership she found it hard to remain indifferent to what happened in the rest of Greece. Athens had used the prestige and diplomatic agility of Themistocles to rebuild her walls,[18] which left her in a strong position to resist any conceivable invasion by, for example, Sparta or which, as the Spartans argued in their protests, would constitute an effective strongpoint if they fell into the hands of an enemy of the Greek cause. The Thessalians, divided in sentiment, had offered no resistance to the Persian advance to Thermopylae and remained isolated after the Persian retreat which followed the Greek victory at Plataea. Sparta, therefore, took advantage of the political dissension in Thessaly to send an army there in support of her sympathisers, but the attempt was a failure and for twenty years Sparta left Greece north of the Isthmus to its own devices.

CHAPTER III

THE EMERGENCE OF
ATHENIAN POWER

IN THE EARLY SIXTH CENTURY, of the communities which lay to the
north of the Isthmus of Corinth Thessaly was the most powerful in
military terms and had a predominant voice in the affairs of the
Delphic Amphictyony, the religious association of twelve tribes of
north-east Greece. The early years of the century saw Athens loyally
following the lead of Thessaly in the campaign of the First Sacred
War. Athens at that time was by no means in the front rank of Greek
powers. Militarily she was inferior to Sparta and Thessaly and, in
terms of economic and naval resources, she was far outstripped by
Corinth.

During the sixth century many of the contacts established between
Athenians and other communities were designed less for the good of
the state than of individuals. Foremost among them was Peisistratus,
the tyrant who was responsible for resolving much of the social and
economic discontent in Athens. His career suffered varying fortunes
and it was at a time when he was in exile from Athens that he built
up with care connexions with a number of other communities. In the
years between 556 and 546 he exploited mineral resources in the
region between Macedon and Thrace and founded a community at
Rhaecelus on the Thermaic Gulf. Furthermore he obtained help from
the oligarchs in Thebes and Eretria and exploited ties by marriage in
Argos for the supply of men in addition to those which he received
from Lygdamis of Naxos.[19] After his restoration in 546 Peisistratus
further extended those external contacts, establishing his son at Sigeum
in the Troad as tyrant in place of the Mytileneans and purifying Delos,
the centre of Ionian religious activity, in accordance with the terms
of an oracle. Incidentally to serving his own welfare there is no doubt
that his activities strengthened Athens both economically and, in the
longer term, diplomatically by extending her trade and contacts at
a time when the westward movement of the Persians was creating
difficulty for the Greeks in the east and in Asia Minor.

In general, however, Athens was preoccupied with matters which affected her security nearer home. Early in the sixth century Athens secured a lasting title to the island of Salamis, which lay at the mouth of the Eleusinian Gulf and had been claimed by Aegina and Megara, and so greatly aided her security, for she had neighbours over whom she was not able to exercise the same degree of influence that Sparta was able to wield in the Peloponnese. Megara remained in the Peloponnesian sphere, Aegina long remained independent as the eye-sore of the Piraeus offering tactical opportunities to Athens' enemies, and the hand of Theban friendship offered to Peisistratus could not be relied upon at all times. Athens too, as we have seen, remained a prey for the political and military intervention of Sparta, who set Athens and Thebes against each other in 519 over Plataea and later under Cleomenes attempted to restore first Isagoras and then Hippias to Athens.

In 506 indeed Cleomenes concerted a campaign by the Pelopon-nesians, Boeotians, Chalcis and Aegina, in the face of which Athens sought alliance with Persia but broke off negotiations when the Persians named as their price the restoration of the tyrant Hippias, son of Peisistratus. Nevertheless Cleomenes withdrew as a result of pressures exerted in Sparta and Corinth, and the Athenians dealt a resounding defeat to the Chalcidians and Boeotians. Athens emerged as a power in her own right, a power worthy of the appeal of the Ionians for help in the revolt from Persia in 499, an appeal which she entertained by contrast with Sparta's aloofness.[20] From that time onwards the pretensions of Peisistratus to leadership of the Ionians were to assume significance and constitute an important factor in the changing patterns and distribution of power in Greece.

Her espousal of the Ionian cause, the superlative victory over the Persian invaders as a David against Goliath at Marathon in 490 and her vital role, through her naval skill and the guile of Themistocles, in the defeat of Xerxes' invasion of Greece in 480/79 brought Athens to the forefront of Greek affairs. The Greeks had not seen fit to award her a share in the command with Sparta against Xerxes, but Spartan insularity and the need of the Greeks for leadership presented Athens with an opportunity to emerge as the champion of the Greek cause, an opportunity for which she had both the inclination and the resources of statesmanship. In addition she had gathered by careful management new resources in the 490s and 480s.

The key to Athenian power and influence lay in her navy which was developed rapidly in the years between the two Persian invasions.

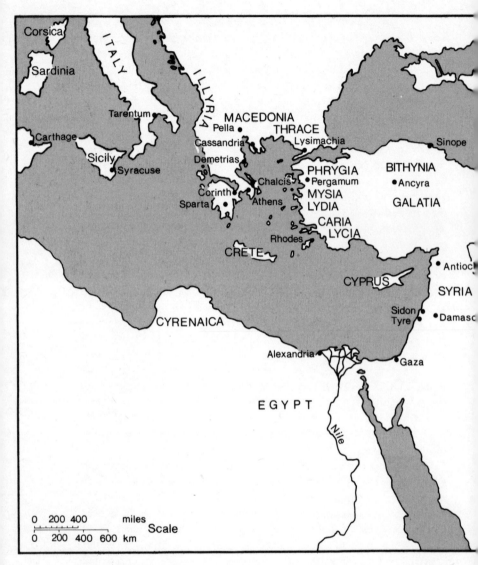

Map I Greece, the Aegean and Sicily

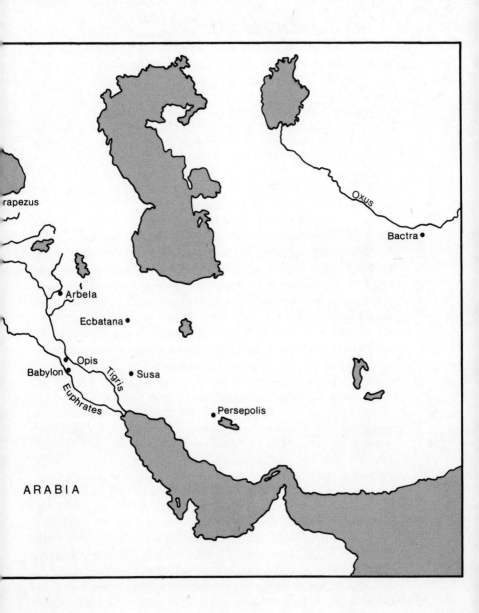

rapezus

Arbela

Ecbatana

Opis

Babylon

Euphrates

Tigris

Susa

Persepolis

ARABIA

Oxus

Bactra

But to equip and maintain a fleet with its crews and paraphernalia was much more expensive than to keep a corresponding number of men with simple equipment under arms for short periods. Silver had been produced from early times in the district of Laurium; exploitation was increased under Peisistratus and now a rich new lode was discovered at Maronea. This was a timely stroke of luck but the Athenians were wise enough to exploit the new resources for the public benefit. Themistocles thus was responsible not only for the development of the sheltered port and dockyards at the Piraeus from 493 but also for the increase in the size of the Athenian navy from seventy to two hundred triremes from 483.[21]

The year which brought about a transformation of the role and power of Athens also saw radical changes in the internal political structure, changes which also helped to influence the direction of Athenian external policy in the years after the Persian invasions. In the political struggles at the close of the sixth century Cleisthenes appealed to the Athenian masses for support against Isagoras, who had the backing of the Spartan King Cleomenes. To win and retain that support, and perhaps for no other reason, he carried into effect social and political changes which had the effect of giving the last if not the first word in policy to the Athenian commons. From then onwards Athenian diplomacy was apt to implement the purposes of the Athenian commons so far as those could be discerned.

It may be said at once that the new political order under the democracy at Athens was not without its defects. The Council of Five Hundred established by Cleisthenes, which drafted proposals on policy, consisted of men who were elected annually and its composition was so contrived as to reflect popular opinion of the moment. The sovereign assembly, which all citizens were entitled, and theoretically obliged, to attend, was highly changeable in mood and the attendance might well vary from meeting to meeting. The Athenian democracy prided itself on the equal opportunity to speak which any citizen might claim, and it can be assumed that the Athenians were as quick-witted as could be expected when the affairs in debate fell within their knowledge, but that knowledge might be less evident in dealing with foreign affairs. Indeed in matters of finance and external affairs the Athenians were in greater need of expert guidance than in other matters. The temper of the Athenians fluctuated between hopes and fears, and great force of character and eloquence were needed to guide their deliberations. The praise of the historian Thucydides for the capabilities of Pericles,[22] who bestrode the political arena from *c*. 460 until 429, reflects the need of more firm guidance than could be guaranteed by democratic practices. For he wrote that whenever Pericles saw the Athenians unseasonably and insolently elated, he would with a word reduce them to alarm; on the other hand, if they fell victims to a panic, he could at once restore them to confidence.

There is no clear evidence of how long Cleisthenes guided the *Demos* that his institutions promoted to power, and if the young democracy faced its enemies with courage and success there is little evidence for his diplomatic skill. The devices whereby Themistocles in the period of the Persian invasions could deceive both the friends and enemies of Athens were a measure of his intellectual resourcefulness but did not inspire trust in the longer term. Consequently he and Pausanias, the Spartan hero of the Battle of Plataea, who was also discredited, played little part in the events after the campaigns which they had helped to win.

The greatest achievement of the ensuing phase of Athenian history was the creation and management of what is now called the Delian League, and the man of the hour was the Athenian statesman Aristides, whose reputation for probity and fair dealing earned him the description as Aristides the Just. It was a rare moment in Greek history when so many states had combined to set aside their differences and offer united opposition to the Persian invasions in 481/0. After the repulse of the Persians the Greeks would, if they had followed their traditional inclinations, have resumed the pursuit of their several interests. Athens, however, had borne the full brunt of two Persian invasions and devastation of her territory, which left her fully alive to the danger of further Persian measures for revenge. Furthermore her fleet and the nature of her domestic and regional interests left her in a better capacity than Sparta to frame her policy accordingly. The Ionian states, which had risen against Persia, needed unity and mutual trust, without which their earlier revolt at the beginning of the century had ended in disaster. Those qualities Aristides could inspire once the Greek naval victories, first at Salamis and then at Mycale, had offered the prospect of freedom from Persia and the defence of liberty. Aristides also could promise the help of the Athenian fleet and its guidance by a resourceful and tactful admiral, Cimon.

Athens acceded to the request of the allies to lead a new alliance, which was based initially on the island of Delos, the centre of Ionian religious activity, which the Athenian tyrant Peisistratus had purified. The alliance drew its members principally from the Ionian communities of the west coast of Asia Minor, the Hellespont and the Propontis, and from the islands of the Aegean. The confederates cast ingots into the sea and swore their oaths to prosecute the war against the barbarians from Persia.[23]

The allies did not sit back to prepare their defences against the next invasion but actively carried the war against the enemy. Successful campaigns swept the Persians out of Thrace and the Chersonese, and the Greeks established themselves as masters of the south and west coasts of Asia Minor. In the wake of that success new members joined the League and brought its numbers up to about two hundred states. The immediate possibility of any Persian reprisal directed against the Greeks was effectively removed c. 466, for Cimon led two hundred Athenian and allied ships and destroyed a powerful assemblage of Persian forces by land and by sea at the mouth of the Eurymedon.[24]

The value of the Athenian navy was, as it were, underlined by that great victory over the Persians, which must have induced a sense of security throughout the Confederacy and, among many, a readiness to see its forces serve the interests of Athens. The hour of victory is at any time apt to be the moment of strain and dissension between allies. Even when they do not squabble over the division of spoil they tend to relax their loyalty to an alliance when once its purpose has ostensibly been fulfilled. The Delian League was no exception and indeed the problems were magnified by the very multiplicity of the states; and the geographical conditions and the nature of their institutions exacerbated the difficulties inherent in any such alliance of free partners.

In the beginning the aims of policy were clear and their execution urgent. Policy was agreed by all members in the allied council which met at Delos and in which all states had an equal vote, and funds were kept in the treasury on Delos.[25] But just as the bureaucracy and formal administrative structure of most states was rudimentary, so we must understand that an inter-state bureaucracy was the less likely to be established, let alone put into successful operation. Consequently much of the responsibility for running the affairs of the alliance devolved upon the Athenians, who were able to supply the naval and political expertise and who constituted the major power of the alliance. The Athenians supplied annually the ten Hellenotamiai, or Stewards of Greece, and it was a triumph of tact and organization that Aristides was able to draw up the lists and quotas of subscriptions without arousing feelings of jealousy and resentment among the allies. Apart from Lesbos, Chios and Samos, which each had a tradition of naval enterprise, few states had the resources or expertise to construct ships for the common fleet. Therefore most contributed money which was then, for the most part, expended on their behalf by Athens. That was conducive to the operational success of the alliance but it both accentuated the Athenian domination of the alliance and of its resources and diminished the active participation of most states, for whom the increasing remoteness of military activity compounded the sheer physical impossibility of maintaining speedy and effective political consultation.

Occasional crises erupted in the League's affairs. Carystus in Euboea, which had afforded a base for the Persians, was compelled to join c. 472 and Naxos, which had performed a similar service for Persia, was obliged to accept dictated terms c. 467 following her attempt to secede.[26] Basically, however, the alliance proceeded smoothly with success accompanied by the acquiescence of Sparta. But within the Greek world there had been a decisive shift in the distribution and balance of power in favour of Athens, and by the late 460s it became increasingly difficult for the Athenians to establish their priorities in foreign policy. Cimon sought to prosecute the war against Persia while maintaining friendship with Sparta. Some contemplated the possibility of campaigns against both Persia and Sparta whilst others thought that the limits of likely success against Persia had been reached and sought to direct their attention to matters nearer home in the sphere of the Peloponnesian alliance. The choice lay partly with the Athenians, but not entirely, for events often conspire to make a mockery of the processes of rational decision, and the Athenians were obliged to react to events of which they were not the prime movers.

CHAPTER IV

THE CONFRONTATION OF ATHENS AND SPARTA

As WE HAVE SEEN in the previous chapter Sparta had acquiesced in the situation whereby Athens took over the leadership of the alliance against Persia. At the outset Sparta may not have foreseen the extent to which Athenian power would increase while her own position in the Peloponnese was merely maintained. There were, no doubt, latent apprehensions in Sparta about the situation, for immediately after the battle of Plataea the Spartans had protested at the construction of the defensive walls at Athens.

Athens' power extended in several ways, for not only did the membership of the Delian League increase, but also the size of her own fleet grew and the political grip which the Athenians exercised over the allies intensified. Attempts of allies to secede were met with military and political intervention and in Greece there gradually developed a degree of political polarization which led the democratic factions in communities to seek identity with Athens and eventually led oligarchic factions to gravitate towards Sparta in their loyalty. The tendency became more pronounced as time passed but it should not be imagined that there was a complete ideological schism in Greece any more than there was an ethnic cleavage created by the Spartan attempts to harness the loyalties of the Dorian communities and the Athenian pretension to primacy among the Ionian states. Eventually, however, diplomacy was able to exploit the hopes and fears of the appropriate political factions which existed in most communities.

The first sign of a clash between Sparta and Athens in her new capacity as leader of the Delian League probably occurred c. 465, at a time when Thasos, an island which possessed a fleet and considerable mineral resources in the north Aegean, attempted to secede from Athens.[27] There was no immediate danger of trouble from Persia but no end had been declared to the war against the barbarian and so Athens pursued a policy of holding the allies to their contract. In any case the immediate point at issue between Athens and Thasos was not the conduct of the Delian Confederacy but the Athenian attempts to exploit the timber, pitch and mineral resources on the Thracian coast in an area which Thasos regarded as her own sphere. The dispute between Athens and Thasos came to war, with Cimon guiding the attack on Thasos and the siege of its city by land and by sea. It is said that the Thasians turned to Sparta for help, making their appeal to the state which had so often posed as a champion of liberty, and that assistance was promised by 'those in authority' in the form of an invasion of Attica. Perhaps self-esteem and self-interest inclined Sparta to such a course, but no invasion occurred, and it is at this point that we see factors of internal political development affecting the diplomacy of the two states.

The Spartans may have been deflected at that juncture from their natural inclination by a sudden rising of the helots which was assisted by some of the *perioeci*.[28] Cimon returned to Athens in 463 after reducing Thasos to submission, whereupon he was impeached for failing to attack the Kingdom of Macedon and was exposed to the almost conventional accusation of being bribed. That may have been little more than the recrudescence of a feud between clans, to which the young Pericles gave formal support, but there may also have been differences over policy. Cimon, however, was acquitted and urged the despatch of an Athenian army in order to help to crush the helot revolt at Sparta, for he believed that such an act would match the interests and honour of Athens as the comrade-in-arms of Sparta in the defeat of the Persian invasion of Xerxes some twenty years before. Cimon set out with a force, as he had proposed, but was shortly presented with a Spartan rebuff, for the Spartans, as was within their rights, declared that they had no need of him and his army, and so he returned to Athens. Sparta presumably did not wish to humiliate her political friends in Athens, but was moved by calculation and fear of the revolutionary instincts of the Athenians. For during the absence of Cimon the political conflict had gone against the conservative interests and had resulted in the traditionally influential Council of the Areopagus being divested of political power. Consequently the Spartans had grounds to hope that Cimon and his army on their return might have induced the Athenians to reverse their disestablishment of the Council of the Areopagus. His opponents, however, skilfully turned against him the natural indignation of the *Demos* at Sparta's high-handed action. He might perhaps have saved himself by joining the outcry, but he was too scrupulous to take that easy way to popularity, and in spite of all his good services, especially his great victory at the Eurymedon, he was formally ostracized and went into exile in 461.

Cimon's departure left the leadership of Athenian policy in the hands of men who, as Cleisthenes had done a generation earlier, allied themselves with the Athenian *Demos*. The leader of that movement was a man of integrity and principle, Ephialtes, who was effectively supported by Pericles, for it may be assumed that the eloquence of the latter was already capable of dominating the Athenian assembly. Ephialtes then disappeared, murdered by a bravo from Boeotia who was never brought to book. Thus Pericles had greatness thrust upon him and the effect of the change in leadership quickly became apparent, for the Athenians were soon in alliance with two powers which had performed a role of no credit in the Persian Wars. Thessaly had in the past been a dominant military power in the north and the punitive Spartan campaign against Thessaly after the battle of Plataea left fertile ground for the Athenians to exploit, and the adhesion of Thessaly gave Athens a useful lever on the opposite frontier of her neighbour, Boeotia. In the south the renunciation of the comradeship in arms with Sparta was accompanied by the logical step of an alliance with Argos, the secular rival of Sparta in the Peloponnese. It is scarcely surprising that in the performance in Athens of his tragedy the *Eumenides* the playwright Aeschylus made the Argive hero, Orestes, on his acquittal by the jurors on the Areopagus proclaim a true and lasting alliance of his deliverers with Argos.[29] Perhaps, too, the play reflected a reconciliation between the ancient jurisdiction of the Areopagus and the transference of political power to the Athenian democratic assembly. From then onwards the guidance of Athenian foreign policy and its consequent diplomacy devolved upon Pericles, an aristocrat who saw in the *Demos* the foundation of a political influence which was to last almost unchallenged for nearly thirty years.

The irony of the situation which ensued was that whereas Athens had the resources to devote her attentions to meet either the Persians or the Peloponnesians, she proceeded to become embroiled simultaneously with both and to make peace with both within fifteen years.

Pericles is credited with the aphorism, uttered on the eve of the Peloponnesian War in 431, that success in war is most often achieved by good judgement and reserves of money.[30] In that context good judgement involves skilful strategy and wise diplomacy. This last ingredient was supplied by Pericles, as will be shown presently.

There were occasions when he was the skilful agent of his own diplomacy; at other times it can be assumed that he inspired the action of envoys. Athens had renounced her comradeship with Sparta and allied herself with Argos, but that action did not involve her in active war with Sparta and Sparta's allies; it only brought war nearer. Athens and the Confederacy of Delos were still at war with Persia, and an opportunity presented itself for harming Persia by assisting a revolt in the Satrapy of Egypt.[31] In 460 a fleet, partly allied, partly Athenian, was transferred from Cyprus along the Phoenician coast to the Nile delta. Cimon was by then in exile and lesser generals were in command. If the decision to send the expedition was taken at Athens then it can be argued that the Athenians committed an error of judgement in over-extending their resources, but the decision may have been taken by their generals in Cyprus on their own initiative. However strong Athens was at sea, Egypt could not be defended against a full-scale invasion by the royal army of Persia; and such an invasion occurred in due course. In addition to other military and strategic considerations the techniques for the defence of territory had not developed yet to the pitch which they reached in the middle of the fourth century. For a time all went well for the forces ranged against Persia, but then the Persian land power asserted its supremacy, and the Greeks were defeated and blockaded until, despite attempts to relieve them, they were forced to capitulate in 454. Many men were lost, for only a few escaped to Cyrene across the desert, and more than a hundred vessels were lost. It was a serious disaster, the worse because by then Athens was involved in warfare nearer home.

The Athenian alliances with Argos and Thessaly and the Spartan rebuff of the Athenian offer to help in quelling the revolt of the helots did not immediately cause war, but in the absence of the restraining hand of Cimon, who was now in exile, relations between Athens and Sparta steadily deteriorated until they were involved in full-scale conflict by 457. First Athens took in refugees from the Spartan campaign to restore order among the subject population. Next, and more seriously, Megara, feeling herself too closely constricted by Corinthian surveillance, attempted a change in her internal and external policies.[32] Her best chance of external support, in view of her strategic position, lay in an appeal to Athens, and so with the installation of a democratic régime she found accommodation in Athenian alliance. The adhesion of Megara provided Athens with a base at Pegae on the Gulf of Corinth and another at Nisaea on the Saronic Gulf. The Athenians further consolidated their new advantage by constructing from coast to coast

in the Megarid new defensive works which were capable of hindering
all movement by land to and from the Peloponnese. At about the
same time Athens took further steps to construct the Long Walls
uniting the city with the Piraeus and so made herself by 457 virtually
impregnable by land.[33] Of the Peloponnesians Corinth, Aegina and
Epidaurus were the most immediately affected by the Athenian
moves in Megara. All of those three states were also at risk from
Argos, now an ally of Athens and interposed between them and their
main ally, Sparta. The naval supremacy of Corinth in the Corinthian
gulf was also threatened for the first time by the Athenian base at
Pegae. The test of naval strength between the two groups occurred
in 458 at Cecryphalea; there the Peloponnesian fleet, to which Sparta
as a land power could contribute no more than sixteen ships, was
outnumbered and defeated by the Athenian ships. Thus in the first
trial of strength Athens was able to demonstrate her naval supremacy
in Greek waters, a supremacy which she immediately followed up
by defeating a Corinthian force on land and by launching operations
to eradicate the threat posed to her security by Aegina.[34]

So far Athens had turned the situation on her southern flank to
her advantage, but there remained the chronic problem of the long
land boundary with Boeotia and as yet Sparta had not been fully
involved against Athens, nor indeed had Athens' other principal
enemy, Persia. Yet Athens' activity resulted in casualties in many
places; a famous inscription set up early in 457 records the death on
active service of one hundred and seventy-seven men of one of the
ten Athenian tribes in Cyprus, Egypt, Phoenicia, Halieis, Aegina and
Megara.[35] In 457 a powerful Spartan force, whose main task was to
intervene in a dispute between Doris and Phocis, caused the Athenians
concern by its movement out of the Peloponnese.[36] The Athenians
attempted to weaken the lines of communication of the Peloponnesian
force and the Spartans, for their part, halted in the neutral territory
of Boeotia and intrigued with anti-democratic elements in Athens.
Those intrigues came to nothing, but the Spartan forces gained the
upper hand in the ensuing battle of Tanagra. The Athenians then
were able to establish their naval superiority and a position of impregnability in Attica, but they were not able to muster forces of the
requisite quantity or quality to establish their superiority on land.
It was easy to collect subscriptions for a fleet which was then equipped
and substantially manned by Athenians, but it was more difficult to
muster many small and disparate contingents of allied land forces.
The Spartans were not able or willing to press their advantage further

in 457 and so the Athenians were able to make more headway in Boeotia. An Athenian army intervened at Oenophyta to disband the Boeotian League, which was under Theban control, and set up sympathetic democratic régimes in place of the oligarchs. That move left the Athenians as the predominant land power in central Greece and enabled them to secure the important naval base of Naupactus at the western end of the Corinthian Gulf. At the same time the Athenians also took the opportunity to expand their contacts in western Greece by concluding an alliance with Segesta in Sicily and subsequently with Leontini and Rhegium.[37]

The Athenians then took advantage of their military position in central Greece and of their naval supremacy to harass the Peloponnesians and eradicate their naval reserves. But by 454 the Athenians had run into difficulties in Egypt and differences arose between them and some of their allies. Within the Peloponnese Argos could expect little direct help from Athens, Thessaly was unstable, and the democratic support for Athens in Megara and Boeotia was somewhat brittle. Consequently from 454 there was a lull in activities between Athens and Sparta which left both parties ready to conclude an agreement by 451.[38] By then a timely move by Athens had recalled Cimon from exile and he readily undertook his part in making a truce for five years between Athens and Sparta in 451, the year in which Sparta and Argos too concluded a treaty for thirty years.[39]

The temporary détente with Sparta left Athens free to concentrate on the affairs of the Delian League – or of the Athenian Empire as it was becoming ever more appropriate to call it. Increasingly the Delian League was used as an extension of Athenian power and policy. Its resources were used by Athens against Corinth and Aegina in action which bore little relation to common avowed aims against Persia. Perhaps one single event which was symbolic of the transition from League to Empire was the transfer of the treasury, a measure at some time proposed by Samos, from Delos to Athens in 454/3.[40] No doubt in the aftermath of the severe defeat of allied forces in Egypt in 454 the transfer was necessary on grounds of security, but just as the fleet paid for by the allies was treated as Athens' own so the allied treasury now passed into Athens' possession. The Athenians maintained the level of financial contributions levied from the allies both in times of war and of inactivity and used money from that source to subsidize the working of her democracy and eventually her public building programme, a policy which did not pass without protest even in Athens.[41] In the 450s financial contributions increased in number from some states, for whom it was convenient, if not compulsory, to contribute money rather than ships, and from others which had attempted to secede or whose loyalty was suspect. In such cases where Athens deemed it advisable she imposed or protected democratic régimes together with an apparatus of governors and commissioners. Instances are to be found at Miletus[42] and Erythrae.[43] After 450 Athenian settlers were installed on expropriated land in communities such as Naxos[44] where they fulfilled political and strategic functions. Only three communities, Lesbos, Chios[45] and Samos,[46] were left with the means of conducting a semblance of an independent foreign policy, for they alone of the allies retained their fleet. Even they were subject to the will of Athens, for so long as the council of the League met on Delos Athens could easily muster a majority of votes from the small states, and after it ceased to meet she needed to consult no one. Increasingly, resolutions were passed at Athens which restricted the internal and external rights of members in matters of jurisdiction and the use of Athenian standards of coinage, weights and measures.[47] Such measures were not part of a continuously harsh and oppressive interference in internal affairs, for the democratic factions in most states had a vested interest in involvement with Athens and were very slow to rise to the Spartan cry for revolt and liberty in the last three decades of the fifth century, but the Athenian measures were a serious infringement of a jealously guarded sovereignty.

In the year after Cimon had seen the conclusion of the five years' armistice with Sparta the Athenians turned their attention once more to Persian affairs. Cimon led a strong fleet to make good Athens' hold on Cyprus, and although he died in the course of the campaign, a victory by land and sea revived the memory of his earlier success over the Persians at the Eurymedon. The latest success created a situation which could be used to reach an accommodation with Persia, and that opportunity was capitalized for the Athenians by Cimon's brother-in-law, Callias, who led the negotiations which culminated c. 449 in the so-called Peace of Callias.[48] By it the Great King was induced to renounce any intention of attacking the Greeks by land or sea and they, conversely, set limits on their eastern operations. The safety won by the efforts of Athens and Sparta over several decades was then assured.

Now that the Persian problem had been disposed of by a full treaty of peace it might be thought that it was not a long step to the renewal of the friendship with Sparta which Athens had renounced in 461, but the transition from the armistice of 451 to the peace of 446 was not smooth, for Sparta, ever posing as the champion of liberty, and Athens espoused rival parties in trying to install their supporters at Delphi.[49] Consequently Pericles seized the diplomatic initiative by causing to be issued an invitation to all Greek cities, small or great, to send representatives to a Panhellenic conference at Athens.[50] The subjects to be discussed were suitable for discussion in the light of the Peace with Persia, namely the restoration of temples burned by the Persians, the freedom of the seas and the establishment of peace in Greece. The momentum of Athenian propaganda, however, was not maintained and the invitation lapsed, for probably many Athenian allies were not enthusiastic and no Peloponnesian state was willing to acknowledge Athenian pretensions by accepting.

Then in 447/6 the Athenian position in Boeotia deteriorated, for many of the oligarchs exiled ten years before began a concerted attempt at restoration. The Athenians were not able to contain the movement and suffered defeat in the field at the hands of Boeotians, Locrians and Euboeans at Coronea,[51] a battle which undid the work of Oenophyta. Furthermore a plot was hatched between Megara and the Chalcidians of Euboea, and it is possible that it was no secret to the Spartan authorities. Pericles attempted to deal with the situation in Euboea but found that the Megarians, assisted by Corinth, Sicyon and Epidaurus, had surprised and massacred Athenian garrisons in the Megarid.

The Peloponnesian forces, led by the Spartan King Pleistoanax, were joined by Boeotians in an assault on Attica through the plain of Eleusis. After initial Spartan success Pleistoanax did not venture to attack, or was dissuaded by his adviser, it may be because the Athenian defenders had some advantage of ground or possibly the use of a wall. The breathing space thus gained enabled Pericles to restore order in Euboea and so prevent any further secession of allies. Thereafter negotiations proceeded during the winter of 446/5 and the result was a compromise peace between Athens and Sparta with a term of thirty years.[52] Accused by the ephors, Pleistoanax went into voluntary exile: his adviser, Cleandridas, escaped the penalty of death by flight. He may have been bribed, if he was as easily tempted as was his son Gylippus a generation later. Archidamus, however, the senior king at Sparta, may have realized that peace conferred the greater advantage upon Sparta until the army could be strengthened by the growth of her population after a period of war, and it has been well said that peace is easily made by parties who cannot afford not to do so.

By the terms of the treaty Athens renounced her claims on territory over which she had established some measure of control. Of the land allies only Naupactus, through fear of Corinth, and Plataea, through fear of Boeotia, chose to maintain their association with Athens. Aegina remained in the Delian League but her autonomy was nominally recognized. The Peloponnesian allies and Boeotia, whose interests Sparta had not been able to guarantee, were drawn freely back into the Spartan fold. On the surface Athens gave ground, but what she lost was less valuable than what she gained. For what Athens lost was what she could not be sure of holding; what she gained was the Spartan acceptance of her control over her allies. Various other provisions were made for the inclusion of subsequently acquired allies in the treaty and for the freedom of navigation for trade. The Peace was the first instance of an agreement which aimed at securing a balance of power and made possible peaceful co-existence between Athens and Sparta. It is an axiom of statecraft that peace is more easily made and maintained when the contracting powers fear to fare worse and see little prospect of doing better. The foreign policy of Sparta had tended to be, on balance, defensive and the natural optimism of Athens was limited both by the events of 447/6 and by the shrewd judgement of Pericles. The danger of friction between the two states was reduced by the acceptance of areas within which each power was free to act without interference from the other. Provision for dealing with disputes as they became apparent was made by the agreement that arbitration should be the method of settlement.[53] The peace restored the position, if not the sentiment, which had existed between Athens and Sparta up to 461. For some fifteen years that desirable state of affairs persisted, and in later and more troubled times the period when Athens and Sparta exercised their joint hegemony in the Greek world was regarded almost as a golden age.

A period of peace allowed both sides to consolidate their position in their respective spheres, but eventually it proved harder to maintain those separate spheres than it had been to recognize them. The settlement lasted only until the Spartans were overcome by fear that Athens would impair their vital interest, the leadership of their Peloponnesian allies. That fear was to enable a belligerent ephor to override King Archidamus, the guest-friend of Pericles, in the Spartan Apella. It is of course likely that some Spartans never trusted in the efficacy of the Thirty Years' Peace. Naturally it was hard for all Spartans to trust the democratic institutions of Athens and they could not but contrast the obligations of Athens' allies with the autonomy of their own. As the Spartan army became stronger, the more they may have felt they had been outwitted by Pericles.

The first crisis in Athens after the conclusion of the Peace was a domestic dispute as to whether Athens might use the contribution of her allies to erect splendid buildings and in the process lavish money upon her own citizens and *metics*, or resident aliens. The expenditure was denounced by Thucydides, son of Melesias, who had much justice on his side. Against him the arguments which Pericles deployed were specious, but the Athenian *Demos* became hostile to Thucydides and indulged its hostility by the easy weapon of ostracism.[54] The ostracism of Thucydides left Pericles unchallenged in the Athenian assembly, where his authority was confirmed by his re-election to the board of ten generals year after year.

In 441 Pericles' gifts were tested by the revolt of Samos.[55] Athens believed herself to be entitled to intervene in a war between Samos and Miletus, both members of her alliance. Accordingly Pericles led out an Athenian squadron and established in Samos a democratic régime which could be trusted to comply with Athenian wishes. The oligarchical faction from Samos, however, hired mercenaries from the Persian satrap at Sardis, and after restoring itself to power prepared to defend its position. Pericles set out with a fleet of sixty ships, of which a detachment was sent to summon others from Chios and Lesbos and to watch for a possible naval attack by the Phoenician fleet, which was all that remained ready for action of the naval strength of Persia. The Samian fleet on its return from Miletus broke through a naval cordon but was blockaded upon the arrival of Athenian re-inforcements. Pericles thereupon divided his forces and sailed with sixty ships to Caunus on the normal route from Phoenicia to the Aegean. The Phoenician fleet did not appear, and we may assume that its admiral did not venture to risk a battle or to risk the displeasure of the Persian king. It may be surmised that Pericles and the Phoenician admiral presently met and in discussion came to terms, and that Pericles offered to leave Caria in the possession of Persia. The tribute of Caria was small and not easy to collect, and the implied bargain suited both sides. It was characteristic of Pericles to secure what mattered and to let go what did not. He returned to Samos, and the blockade was resumed until, after an eight-months' siege, the city surrendered. Pericles returned to Athens in triumph, but did not wage war on Pissuthnes, the satrap of Sardis, for such a course would have meant the end of the accord which existed between Athens and

Persia. The overwhelming strength of Athens at sea was proved
beyond all doubt. The walls of Samos were dismantled, the Samian
ships surrendered, and the costs of the expensive and protracted siege
were repaid partly in land and partly by instalments of money. The
oligarchic leaders were exiled and settled at Anaea on the coast
opposite, perhaps under Persian protection or control. In the wake
of events at Samos the city of Byzantium, which had also revolted,
likewise came to heel, and with that settlement at Samos only Lesbos
and Chios were left as independent allies of Athens in possession of a
fleet.

Some seven years later Corinthian envoys at Athens asserted that,
as a service rendered to Athens, they had voted against a proposal
of the Peloponnesian League to make war against her on behalf of
Samos.[56] That claim may be an invention and nothing more, but if
it has some foundation of truth what evidence does it supply for
Spartan policy at the time of the Samian revolt? Some twenty-five
years or so earlier the Thasians had appealed to Sparta and may have
obtained a promise of help which in fact did not materialize. It would
have been natural for the Samians to appeal to Sparta, for they had
nothing to lose and perhaps something to gain. The Corinthians
implied that Sparta had been in favour of war before the proposal
could have been brought to a vote at a conference of her allies, but
that is doubtful. The proposal could have originated elsewhere. For
Byzantium had revolted at the same time as Samos and might hope
to profit from a Spartan attack on Athens. The mother-city of
Byzantium was Megara and she may have appealed to Sparta, even
if Sparta had not contemplated taking the field. Sparta may have
summoned a conference merely in order to show loyalty to the
Thirty Years' Peace by voting against intervention, and Corinth
may have followed her example. Sparta was thus washing her clean
linen in public, and Corinth, for whatever reason, may have done
the same.

The attitude of Sparta is then interesting, for it suggests that Sparta,
five years after making peace with Athens, did not want a general
war such as would have followed an invasion of Attica. If Pericles
had had reason to fear a Spartan invasion, he would presumably have
remained in Athens and left the conduct of the siege to some other
general. Pericles' disposition, therefore, suggests that he trusted the
peaceful intentions of Sparta at that time. That interpretation makes
it easier to understand Athenian diplomacy at the time when seven
years after the events in Samos the Corinthian envoys arrived in

Athens. For in 433 Corcyra sent an appeal to Athens for an alliance and help in a dispute with its mother-city Corinth over Epidamnus, which was a jointly sponsored colony of the two states in dispute.[57] The Athenians were wary of becoming involved in the dispute, for if they took action against Corinth that would be a breach of the Thirty Years' Peace. Indeed earlier in the 430s they had risked incurring Corinthian suspicion by responding to an appeal from Acarnania and Amphilochia against settlers from Ambracia, a colony of Corinth, although none of those communities was covered by the terms of the Peace. In the debate at Athens in 433 the Athenians were at first inclined not to accede to the request of Corcyra, but on the second day they decided to conclude a defensive agreement. That they were not eager to be provocative was shown in the event when Athens initially sent only a token force of ten vessels before the battle between the two combatants. But the Athenians do seem to have been ready to listen to those who argued that an outbreak of hostilities between Athens and the Peloponnesians was more likely to occur than not. Observers would have been able to register the great increase in the size of the Corinthian fleet in the years up to 433, when it was able to count on additional naval support from Megara, Elis, Leucas, Ambracia and Anactorium. Consequently on the second day of the debate in the Athenian assembly the envoys of Corcyra found that their arguments fell on fertile ground, for they pointed out that there were two principal naval powers, Athens and Corinth, and that if the Athenians wished to maintain their superiority then it was of great moment to ensure that the powerful navy of Corcyra did not fall into Corinthian hands and so tilt the naval balance.

Athens took the decision which secured her the maximum benefit in crude calculation of power and which committed her minimally to an obligation. She was able to baulk Corinth without intervening as the aggressor and was able to act as if consistently with her professed tradition of assistance to suppliants who were the victims of aggression. After that exercise in skilful Athenian diplomacy Corinth yielded to her anger and did everything that she could to bring about a general war. When her colony of Potidaea revolted from alliance with Athens in 432, Corinth sent there a force of volunteers, a move which, according to Greek ideas, did not constitute a formal act of war. It may seem to us a distinction without a difference, but certainly Pericles had grounds for believing that at that time Sparta might wish to avoid a war with Athens especially if she could find a legalistic excuse for inaction.

Corinth approached those states in the region of the Peloponnese which had grievances and could not be denied the right to air them before the Spartans.[58] At that time the First Ephor, Sthenelaidas, was in favour of war. The competent body in Sparta to declare war was the Apella, and it was his right to summon it. King Archidamus could not prevent the assembly from meeting but he could address it, if only because in the event of war it was his task to conduct military operations.[59] Pericles at that point may have wished to postpone war, for a war postponed might be a war averted. The Thirty Years' Peace was still in force, and envoys whom the Athenians had sent to Sparta ostensibly on other business were able to present these arguments which reinforced Archidamus' advice of proceeding cautiously.[60] To have done less than that would have been poor diplomacy, and Pericles was not a deficient practitioner of the art. King Archidamus argued that the Athenians were unlikely to yield in the face of a threat of war and that in almost every respect the Athenian resources were superior or insuperable, whereas after the lapse of two or three years the growth of the Peloponnesian forces might enable a challenge to be issued.

There was, however, one topic on which Archidamus was on much firmer and more convincing ground – that the Thirty Years' Peace obliged both parties to refrain from war until disputes had been submitted to arbitration. That obligation, which might preclude or delay war, was taken up and stressed by Archidamus in his speech, and it could not be denied. So the debate stood when the presiding ephor called the Apella to order and in a short speech put the question for decision. In the speeches as they are set out by Thucydides the Athenian envoys had the best of the argument and naturally the ephor began by declaring that he did not understand them. The argument that followed resembled a sharp sword cutting the knot of dialectic and legalism. Sparta, he declared, had to be true to herself. Neither ought Athens to be left to become stronger nor ought Sparta to betray her allies. The assembly divided between those who believed that the Peace had been broken by the misconduct of the Athenians and those who did not, and the 'ayes' had it by a large majority. The decision was announced to the Peloponnesian allies and the conference dispersed.

After the decision an enquiry was made of the Delphic Oracle by the Spartans to ask whether it would be well with them if they went to war, to which the god is reported to have replied that if they made war with all their power victory would be theirs and he would be with them whether called upon or not. The god did not proclaim the justice of their cause, merely the prospect of success and his support. That was enough. But more was needed than divine favour, for a majority of the votes of the Peloponnesian allies was needed to involve the League in war. On that there was a second conference. The Corinthians urged the several cities to vote for war for fear that their colony Potidaea, an ally of Athens and now besieged by the Athenians for failure to expel Corinthian officials, might be destroyed before help could be given. The Corinthians spoke last and by their arguments tried to instil confidence in the resources and opportunities of the Peloponnesians and in the prospect of victory. They denounced Athens as a 'tyrant city', and proclaimed the slogan of freedom for the Greeks who were then 'enslaved'. The speech had a twofold purpose, to claim both that victory was possible and that their cause was just. A vote was taken and the majority was for war.[61]

Lack of military preparedness precluded an immediate declaration of war, but rather less than a year elapsed between the end of the conference and the first invasion of Attica. Within that period embassies were sent to Athens making such demands as would provide the greatest possible justification of their going to war if they were rejected.[62] Before the first of those embassies a new college of ephors had entered office and it may be conjectured that they were less belligerent than their predecessors; certainly King Archidamus, who was likely to command operations, was in no hurry to invade Attica before the following year at a time when the crops were ripe for burning. The first demand was aimed at Pericles. It was that the Athenians should drive out the curse of the goddess, for Pericles and his family were tainted with the sacrilegious bloodshed committed when, two centuries before, the Alcmaeonidae had slain the supporters of the tyrant Cylon although they had taken refuge at altars. It was answered by a similar demand on Sparta, and Pericles remained at Athens, pressing forward the Athenian preparations for war and explaining his plans and the prospects of his strategy. The next Spartan demands were more mundane and such as may be more easily understood by readers in a later age.[63] Athens was summoned to lift the siege of Potidaea, to leave Aegina autonomous, and above all else to repeal the recent decree which was directed to the exclusion of the Megarians from the harbours of the Athenian Empire as well as from the markets in Attica. It was announced that compliance with those demands would avert the outbreak of war. The first of those three demands was covered by the admitted right of Athens to prevent

secession within her alliance; the second may have been covered by
the terms of the capitulation of Aegina in 459/8, which probably
entitled Athens to maintain a garrison in Aegina in certain eventualities
of which Athens was to be the judge. The third demand challenged
the right of Athens to control the commerce of her allied cities. No
Athenian decree, as such, could prevent the Megarians from carrying
their wares across the seas; what Athens could decree was that her
subjects should so act as to deny to Megarian goods an entrance to
their harbours. What Athens herself did to close her land frontiers
was a matter of her municipal law, for all sovereign states could settle
such matters for themselves. It was apparent that if the allies of Athens
were independent sovereign states they could admit whatever they
wished into their territory by land or sea, and it was only if the allies
were not so that the decree could have effect. Athens had, or believed
that she had, grievances against Megara, but it could be argued that
it was not worth while to gratify them if the consequence was war.
Pericles, however, thought that war was in any case likely and that
Sparta was not merely intent on the satisfaction of her published
demands. Consequently he insisted that the decree should stand, and
he prevailed.

Then came the last set of envoys.[64] They declared that the Lacedaemonians wished peace to continue and asserted that it would do
so if the Athenians left the Greeks autonomous. Their message has
often been described as an ultimatum, but it may just as aptly be
described as a device to keep negotiations going. The statement that
the Lacedaemonians desired peace may have given a throb of hope
to many citizens, especially to those Athenians whose lands were
likely to suffer devastation, but Pericles was unyielding. The reply
which he dictated to the assembly after a masterly survey of negotiations and of the prospects of war has a logical coherence and subtlety
of the first order. The specific answer, 'We will leave the cities
autonomous, if we possessed them as autonomous when we made the
Peace, and we will submit to arbitration according to our agreements',
was a diplomatic *tour de force*.

CHAPTER V

THE TEN YEARS' WAR AND
THE PEACE OF NICIAS

BY THE SPRING IN 431 the conflict of interest and obligations between Athens and Sparta had come to a head, but, as so often happens, the war itself actually started elsewhere. For in March of that year the Thebans attempted to incorporate Plataea in the Boeotian League and the Plataeans both executed Theban hostages and secured the support of an Athenian garrison.

Both of the opposing alliances of Athens and Sparta were at the peak of their strength by 431 following an unusually long period of peace. The Athenians had begun to conserve their funds before war broke out in order to accumulate reserves and to provide resources for their fleet, and so began a classic confrontation of the supreme land power with the supreme naval power of the Greek world. The clash at Plataea brought in its train a flurry of diplomatic activity in which both sides tried to rally neutral states and non-Greeks to their cause, but there were no significant developments and Persia, whose intervention was to tip the scales in the years after 411, remained aloof for the time being.

In the early summer King Archidamus proceeded from Sparta with a Peloponnesian army through the Isthmus towards the frontier of Attica. Before attacking he sent a herald to Athens but the Athenians refused to grant him an audience, whereupon as the herald was being escorted away he remarked that that day would be the beginning of great misfortunes for the Greeks.[65] There ensued protracted, but not continuous, warfare from 431 to 404. The first period, often labelled the Ten Years' War or the Archidamian War, was concluded by the Peace of Nicias.

From the outset it appeared to the historian Thucydides that a momentous and unprecedentedly destructive war was beginning and accordingly he began to compile his notes of events as a contemporary observer and participant. Even he, however, could scarcely foretell the extent to which the war would leave both victor and vanquished alike weakened and cause in the balance of forces of the Greek world a change more radical than had been precipitated by the Persian Wars.

The war came as a surprise to no one. Each side had made its plans and devised its strategy. In the absence of military and diplomatic surprises the war in progress was to be a test of strategy, especially of Periclean strategy and of that wise judgement which leads to victory. There were accidents and instances of folly such as make a mockery of the calculation of wise men but it was not until after the Peace of Nicias that they were to assume critical proportions. The aim of Sparta was the dissolution of the Athenian Empire as well as the defeat of Athens. Sparta lacked naval resources but planned an enlarged fleet with which to assist the liberation of Athens' subjects. Sparta did, however, enjoy a decisive superiority on land and so aimed to provoke Athens into an open battle, or if that could not be managed, her plan was to organize constant raids to devastate the Athenian countryside. Pericles remembered well the contest which had been waged by land with the Peloponnesians in the period leading up to the Thirty Years' Peace and based his strategy accordingly. He realized that Athenian naval superiority was sufficient to guarantee the security of subjects and allies in the Aegean from subversion and that Athenian land forces were sufficient to enable the Athenians to retire behind their walled defences and maintain an impregnable base. At the outset, therefore, the chances were that the Spartans would be baffled in their aims and that the Athenians could not be defeated. Furthermore if the Athenians could restrain themselves from meeting direct Spartan attacks and maintain their own morale by choosing their opportunity to launch raids on Megara they would worry the Peloponnesians on that front, and if the Athenian fleet could sever links between the Peloponnese and sources of supply in Egypt and the West then the Athenian fleet would be able to harry at will Sparta's allies who were confined to the Peloponnese, and cause them to sue for terms.

In the first year of the war the Spartans invaded Attica and departed. The Athenians invaded Megara and their squadrons sailed out on raids and returned. All went according to plan, and at the end of the first season of warfare Pericles was chosen to deliver the Funeral Oration in praise of the dead, in which he spoke with eloquence of their sacrifice and of the blessings which they had helped to preserve.[66] In Athens there was confidence and there was no need to seek ways to peace; indeed Pericles had caused to be passed a resolution that once the enemy had marched no herald and embassy should be received for as long as the war should last.

There were, especially among the young at Athens, some who found it hard to acquiesce in an apparently defensive policy, but Pericles had said that he had plans which would be revealed when the time came to put them into effect. Now in 430 came the time for him to lead a strong armament against Epidaurus on the north-east coast of the Peloponnese. He may have hoped to win over the city before the Spartan army, now in Attica, could come to its aid. But in the summer of 430 there occurred one of those unforeseen events which belie the calculation of men, the Great Plague.[67] It afflicted the Athenians hard and repeatedly, causing loss of men and morale. Accordingly when news of the pestilence reached the Peloponnese Epidaurus held out, whilst the Athenians, dismayed by their sufferings, sent envoys to Sparta to treat for peace. The Spartans may have had reason to believe that the god Apollo indeed was keeping his promise, made at Delphi, to intervene if the Peloponnesians pressed on with the war. The Athenian envoys, therefore, returned empty-handed. So too did Pericles from operations at Epidaurus, undaunted by god or man, to face the Athenian assembly – with authority and eloquence – and prevailed. The Athenians rallied to their greatness in their finest hour. But their sufferings bit deep. Pericles was presently deposed from office as general and, justly or unjustly, was visited with a fine. The Athenians, however, repented, re-elected him general, and placed their affairs in his hands. No more envoys were sent to Sparta.

While the first visitation of the Plague, that in 430/29, lasted, the central control from Athens must have weakened, but generals still went out and did their best. The siege of Potidaea, the Corinthian colony which had seceded from Athenian alliance in 432, was maintained until in the winter of 430/29 the city surrendered on reasonable terms, and the heavy drain on Athenian finances eased.[68] The Athenians suffered yet another grievous blow in 429, for in the autumn of that year Pericles, their wise mentor for so many years, died from the effects of the Plague. Above all others he had formed a clear conception of the military and diplomatic strengths and weaknesses of Athens. In executing policy he was at times aggressive, at others cautious. In 429 there was no one capable of assuming his mantle and fully replacing him in the confidence of the Athenians. Consequently the younger politicians, optimists and men who had been irritated by his caution, gained in influence and sought opportunities to deviate from his policy.

Ever since Sparta had proclaimed her policy of liberating the Greeks there had been a remarkable dearth of Athenian allies or subjects who considered themselves as candidates for liberation. The first crisis to arise in the Athenian alliance since the outbreak of war occurred in 428 in the island of Lesbos. There Mytilene, which had been a favoured ally of Athens, planned secession and at the Olympic Festival appealed to the general feeling against the 'tyrant city'.[69] Mytilene was besieged and a timid Spartan admiral failed to relieve the city, which was starved into surrender. The demagogue Cleon, who had emerged more powerful in Athens after the death of Pericles, urged a general massacre of the disloyal Mytileneans, and an angry meeting of the assembly agreed with him. On the next day, however, a second meeting reversed that decision after their mood of repentance had been reinforced by a dexterous appeal to consider the fundamental public interest. Athens accordingly just succeeded in avoiding what would have been at once a crime and a blunder committed in pursuing to extreme lengths Pericles' policy of keeping the allies in hand.

In 427, the year that saw the surrender of Mytilene, the Athenians sent out a small fleet of twenty ships. Presumably the first phase of the Plague had weakened the naval potential of Athens and more ships could not be spared. The despatch of the ships ran contrary to Pericles' warning, made five years earlier, against engaging in such aggressive adventures while the war was in progress. But ever since the start of the war the Syracusans and virtually all the Dorian communities of Sicily had been included in the Spartan alliance, and now the Leontines and their allies were at war with Syracuse. An appeal was launched by the Leontines and their Ionian allies to Athens, who saw an opportunity for a useful strategic exercise. At a minimum the Athenians would be able to gain help in hindering the despatch of corn and other supplies from Sicily to their enemies, and any such help in Sicily would minimize the strategic dependence of Athens upon Corcyra, whose loyalty and internal stability was suspect, for control of the western approaches to Balkan Greece by sea. The historian Thucydides suspected that the Athenians were testing the possibility of bringing Sicily into subjection,[70] but operations remained on a small scale and were bound to disappoint the larger hopes of sanguine and unrealistic demagogues. For the moment, however, by engaging in a limited enterprise to encourage inter-state hostilities in the island the Athenians had forestalled Syracusan intervention in the war.

In 425 a fleet of forty ships was sent out from Athens first to restore Athenian control over Corcyra, now divided by civil strife, and then to join the Athenian forces in Sicilian waters. With the fleet went an enterprising officer, Demosthenes, who had in the previous year attempted in vain a significant departure from Periclean policy by conducting land operations in central Greece, where he had found insufficient support. In 425 he had a secret plan of his own, nothing less than to establish a strong-point on the western coast of the Peloponnese.[71] That he managed to achieve at Pylos with a few ships and repelled the attack of forces sent from the Peloponnesian army that was then in Attica. Meanwhile the rest of the Athenian fleet returned from Corcyra in time to attack the Peloponnesian fleet in the harbour of Pylos. The activity initiated by Demosthenes came the nearest yet to resolving the strategic and diplomatic stalemate. For the defeat of the Peloponnesian fleet at Pylos caused the isolation of four hundred and twenty Spartan hoplites on the island of Sphacteria, which was closely blockaded. Since there were among those troops Spartiates of rank and influence the arrival of the news of the events made 'those in authority' at Sparta act with notable speed and initiative. They arranged a local armistice, during which the Peloponnesian ships were to remain in the hands of the Athenians. Spartan envoys were sent to make proposals at Athens which, if accepted, would have not only ended the war but also altered the balance of power in Greece. The Spartan envoys proposed the negotiation of a peace which included a pact of amity between the chief belligerents, Athens and Sparta. The terms were to be privately agreed and their implementation was to be marked by the restoration to Sparta of the troops on Sphacteria. That offer may have seemed too good to be true. Certainly the Spartans suffered from a loss of confidence and there were those among them who regarded the latest events as divine retribution for their failure to resort to arbitration before launching the war. There were those at Athens who sensed their advantage and sought to press it home, and in any event the Athenians had heard in the recent performance of Aristophanes' *Acharnians* the denunciation of the Spartans as knowing neither altars nor oaths. The powerful demagogue Cleon sabotaged the proposals, and the Spartan envoys returned to the scene of the operations where the Athenians, with slight justification, refused to hand back the enemy fleet.

Then came a lull, and autumn gales, during which the blockade might not be maintained, approached. Cleon, full of boasts and promises, went off committed to capture the hoplites on the island within twenty days. Aided by the chance of a fire on the island and by the skill of Demosthenes, the attack succeeded and the Spartan survivors surrendered after a gallant defence. The surrender caused utter astonishment throughout Greece. The captives were brought to

Athens and Cleon was the man of the hour. A sign of his ascendant influence was that the Athenians decreed a reassessment of the tribute of the allies in order to replenish the dwindling funds of the State treasury, though, indeed, the reassessment was implemented only in part.

For some two years the war continued in a state of unstable equilibrium. Protected from invasion by the threat of killing the Spartan prisoners, the Athenians achieved some minor successes on and off the Peloponnesian coast, but in Boeotia they were chastened. The Athenian generals, encouraged by overtures from democratic factions in the Boeotian communities, judged that the time was suitable to intervene there, but their attempt to fortify and hold a strong-point in Boeotia resulted in defeat at the Battle of Delium (424).[72]

Meanwhile the Spartan Brasidas, a soldier of resource and enterprise, led an army through Thessaly to the peninsula of Chalcidice helped by the co-operation of the King of Macedon.[73] In that region Athenian diplomacy had not been sufficiently active to avert danger and so Brasidas was able to induce a number of cities to secede from the Athenians, above all, their highly prized possession of Amphipolis. Brasidas was not only 'a good orator for a Lacedaemonian'; he was also a shrewd diplomat, as appeared when on at least two occasions he declared that he was authorized to pledge his home government to respect the autonomy and freedom of whatever cities took his side.

The Spartans could now bargain from a position of relative strength and in the spring of 423 they initiated negotiations for a year's armistice with the aim of achieving a definitive peace.[74] To that task their representatives and those of Athens bent their energies. But the armistice, though carefully devised, was never fully observed, least of all by Brasidas, and it expired without achieving its purpose.

In Sicily the Athenian expedition sent in 427, though reinforced two years later, had been doomed to ultimate failure by the brilliant diplomacy of Hermocrates, a Syracusan statesman. In a conference held at Gela in the summer of 424 he maintained the thesis that Athens was a potential enemy against which the Sicilian cities must unite their strength, sacrificing their quarrels to the needs of a common defence.[75] The Athenian generals and their ships returned home, bringing with them at most some kind of understanding that the Sicilian cities would not intervene in the conflict with Sparta. That much was certainly worth securing, but the Athenians had hoped for more and vented their disappointment upon the generals. In the summer of 422 the Athenians sent Phaeax on a diplomatic mission to further their interests in Sicily and southern Italy, where he enjoyed only limited success; but by the time of his return in the following year there were other moves afoot to end the war.[76] Meanwhile on balance Athens might have been reasonably content, and Sicily, left to herself, was no serious danger to Athens.

When the Armistice which was made in 423 expired, Cleon persuaded the Athenians to send him with an army to restore Athenian control over Chalcidice. At first he had some promising successes, until, in an evil hour, he pressed forward in the hope of recapturing Amphipolis. When he came face to face with Brasidas he was out-generalled and defeated, but neither he nor Brasidas survived the battle. When Aristophanes wrote his *Peace* during the following winter he described them as the pestles with which war was grinding the Greeks to powder. Thucydides shared that judgement on the two protagonists, when he wrote that they stood for the continuation of war, Brasidas because it brought him honour and glory, Cleon because he feared that tranquillity would expose his malpractices and make men disbelieve his calumnies. With them Thucydides contrasted Pleistoanax, the Spartan king, and Nicias, the Athenian statesman and general, who from personal motives advocated peace.[77] There were also motives arising from diplomatic considerations elsewhere. The Thirty Years' Peace between Sparta and Argos, made in 451, was running out and there was a possibility that it would not be renewed. In both Athens and Sparta there were those who thought it desirable to anticipate that possibility and any consequential instability which might arise in the diplomatic situation, and no doubt those who were so inclined remembered the Spartan proposal of 425 to add to any treaty of peace an alliance between the two High Contracting Powers. In fact not long after the conclusion of peace in 421 there followed an alliance between Athens and Sparta.

By 421 the essential interests of both Athens and Sparta were intact and neither could gain a decisive advantage over the other. There was, therefore, little to be gained by protraction of the war. There were those in Sparta who had given close attention to preparing terms for peace in 425 and 423; similarly Nicias and his friends had been involved in exploring the possibilities from 423. Each side had many allies with their own private interests which could not be resolved to the satisfaction of everyone and so the terms of peace were not easy to prepare in spite of the long attention given to the diplomatic possibilities. Representatives of both Athens and Sparta met several times in conference before producing the terms for approval. A conference of the allies of Sparta met and accepted the

Peace, although four states, Boeotia, Corinth, Elis and Megara, did not agree 'for they were not content with what was being done'. Nevertheless the Spartans felt themselves able to speak for their allies as for themselves, as indeed the Athenians already had done for their allies. The terms were more numerous and complicated than in most treaties, and there was also an unusual clause which empowered Athens and Sparta to add, after due consultation, to the treaty such provisions as they might agree together 'if anything had been forgotten on either side'. That clause aroused suspicion and alarm, even if, as is possible, it was no more than an expression of the caution of weary negotiators.

The text of the treaty, [78] which was recorded at Athens and elsewhere, must have been the fruit of many hopes and the refutation of many fears. Ten years of internecine and demoralizing war were over and the diplomats had brought their protracted task to a close. As Pericles had promised his countrymen, Athens had survived the War. So far as the War had been an attack on the empire of Athens, the Peace acknowledged its failure. As the financial records show, the Athenian treasures on the Acropolis were running down by 421, but not to a greater extent than could be replenished by a decade of peace. The two remaining pillars of Athenian power, the linked fortress of the city and the Piraeus together with the Athenian fleet, were unchallenged, and there was the promise of the return of Amphipolis. Sparta had suffered no direct attack and her prisoners were returned. During the war Athens had not succeeded in detaching the Peloponnesian allies, but the allies of Sparta whose losses were not made good found their loyalty to Sparta strained too far by the terms. Nevertheless the dictum had been propounded in 425, that if Sparta and Athens were in agreement then no Greek state could challenge the result. The two powers now had the opportunity to confirm this, an opportunity whose chances of success appeared all the greater because the Peace of Nicias and the alliance which followed it contained a clause which made explicit the obligation to submit any dispute to arbitration.

Superficially the omens for guaranteeing an enduring peace in the Greek world may have seemed bright. But by 421 Argos had been released from the stipulations of her treaty of 451 and so the disappointed allies of Sparta might find some focus in their search for a new leader. It was that search and the possibilities of fresh alignments of states which overshadowed the diplomatic exchanges of the next few years.

CHAPTER VI

ATHENS SUCCUMBS TO SPARTA

THE PEACE OF NICIAS could have presented to Athens and Sparta the opportunity to re-create the stability and equilibrium which the Greeks had enjoyed for periods in their inter-state affairs after the Persian Wars and after the Thirty Years' Peace. But if such hopes were entertained they were soon belied, for the Peace of Nicias inaugurated a sequence of events which was marked by a degree of diplomatic chaos such as could scarcely have been anticipated or imagined. The accounts of ancient writers of history frequently strike the modern reader as a catalogue of wars and constitutions, but at this point all that the historian Thucydides has to offer is a catalogue of embassies, treaties and shifting combinations, the effect of which is to underline the political incompetence of so many statesmen in so many communities.

There were three main reasons why the Peace failed to last. Sparta had reached stalemate in the war with Athens and was glad to conclude terms which involved no loss to her, but the allies of Sparta had many grievances against Athens in 431 and ten years later those grievances were not yet assuaged. Therefore Sparta's allies stood to derive little satisfaction from the conclusion of a Peace in which they were not consulted and their interests were not considered adequately. In the second place the terms involved concessions by so many states, and unwilling states at that, that it was difficult for all parties to be convinced of the good faith of the rest. Finally there were those politicians in both Athens and Sparta who did not wish the Peace to become securely established, and in so far as one man above all was responsible for preventing the establishment of peace with security, that man was Alcibiades at Athens, a man who was to be involved in the direction of Athenian policies for good and ill almost until the conclusion of the War in 404.

The loyalties of Sparta's Peloponnesian allies had been subjected to too great a strain by Sparta's pacts with Athens. Boeotia, Megara and Corinth remained aloof from the Peace and did not accede to

Spartan pressure to recognize it. These states were so placed as to present Athens with a strategic problem on her frontiers, but without considerable Spartan assistance they were likely to achieve little in the field, and initially Spartan assistance was most unlikely for so long as Sparta was trying to preserve her treaties with Athens.

The Peace weakened Sparta in a way that both Cleon and Pericles had hoped or expected to achieve in war – by the detachment of her allies. Corinth seized the diplomatic initiative in the Peloponnese in an attempt to form a bloc of states which could secure their own interests independently of Athens and Sparta. Corinthian envoys persuaded the Argives to set up constitutional machinery which would ensure confidential negotiations with all Greek states which were willing to make defensive alliance, excluding Athens and Sparta.[79] Before long Argos and Corinth were joined by Elis and Mantinea, democratic states, but the movement did not include Megara and Boeotia, for they were reluctant to sever their ties with the Spartan oligarchy in favour of alliance with democracies.

Sparta was aware of those moves in the Peloponnese, but for the moment concentrated on trying to implement the terms for peace agreed with Athens without going so far as to damage her relations with the Peloponnesians beyond repair by invoking the alliance with Athens in order to deal with recalcitrants. The Spartans withdrew their forces from the Chalcidic peninsula, the Bottiaean cities and Amphipolis, but Athens was unable to gain possession of Amphipolis. Similarly, the Thracians, Corinthians and Boeotians refused to comply, while Sparta on the one hand threatened to join with Athens in compelling their compliance but on the other hand made no written undertaking. The Athenians had surrendered their prisoners, but regretting that concession they resolved to give up no other territory until there were positive signs of good faith on the other side. For the moment Athens declined to give up the base at Pylos but made a concession to Sparta by removing Messenians, helots and other such subversive elements from there.

By the winter of 421/0 elections had brought new ephors into office at Sparta, and they were men who had a different conception of Spartan priorities. They considered that Spartan freedom of action was more hindered both by the neutrality or hostility of Argos within the Peloponnese and by Athenian occupation of Pylos than it was enhanced by alliance with Athens. Consequently the new ephors privately encouraged Boeotian representatives to join the Argive alliance and then to combine with the Corinthians in bringing over

Argos into alliance with Sparta. They further asked the Boeotians to restore Panactum to Athens in accordance with the terms of peace in order that the Athenians might be induced to reciprocate by restoring Pylos.

The Boeotian envoys who had just received those proposals from Sparta happened to encounter on their way home two Argive officials who had been waiting for them. Those officials were evidently unaware of the confidential suggestions of the Spartan ephors and they too proposed that the Boeotians should join the Argive alliance to make peace or war, as they should decide, against Sparta or any other state. The chief officials of Boeotia were impressed by the possibility of complying with the requests of both Argos and Sparta and decided to make an alliance accordingly. What they could not do, however, was to take members of the Boeotian councils into their confidence to the extent of explaining the confidential exchanges with the Spartan ephors. Consequently the Boeotian councillors were needlessly apprehensive of offending Sparta by joining the Argive alliance and so failed to accept the proposals. For the moment Sparta was frustrated in her attempt to win over Argos to her side and Boeotian intransigence over Panactum brought her more clearly into antagonism with Athens. For Sparta realized that she must ensure the cession of Panactum to Athens in order to recover Pylos from Athens. The price to which the Boeotians adhered for that concession was the conclusion of a separate alliance between Sparta and Boeotia, which involved a clear breach of faith vis-à-vis Athens by Sparta.[80] The Spartans concluded that they had little realistic alternative but to accede. The Boeotians however first razed Panactum and the Athenians continued to hold Pylos until 409. And so ended the first year of peace – or rather the eleventh year of the war as Thucydides put it, for although the principal combatants refrained from attacks on each other's territory for six years and ten months the period of peace was merely a brief interruption of war.

In the field of diplomacy there was no slackening of the rivalry of the two sides, and most immediately Argos was the object of pursuit. For the moment, however, the Argives had failed to keep themselves abreast of events. They had worked to isolate Sparta, but so far were they from doing so that they themselves felt isolated. Boeotia had failed to follow up Argive overtures for alliance and now the Argives saw Boeotia in alliance with Sparta. Falsely they assumed that the alliance and the destruction of Panactum had occurred with the connivance of Athens and Sparta respectively, and so they immediately sent envoys to open negotiations for a treaty with Sparta. Meanwhile at Athens there was a vigorous debate. Nicias was prepared to keep options open, by attempting to put the agreed terms into effect and using the threat of an Athenian alliance with Argos to put pressure upon Sparta. Alcibiades, both for personal motives and for reasons of policy, was inclined to cause a breach with Sparta and bring the Argives into alliance with Athens,[81] for by that time the Thirty Years' Treaty between Sparta and Argos had run its course and there was nothing in the alliance between Athens and Sparta to preclude either or both of them from becoming allied to Argos. Alcibiades may well be described as a man who was more clever than wise and possessed of an excessive belief in his own diplomatic skills, but at this point he succeeded in undermining any residual goodwill and trust which may have persisted between Athens and Sparta, for he disabused the Argives of their fears of collusion between Athens, Sparta and Boeotia and discredited an embassy which had come from Sparta to Athens to attempt to settle points at issue. He pretended to take into his confidence the Spartan envoys, men of goodwill towards Athens, and abused that relationship to induce them to say one thing to the council and another to the assembly. Nicias went to Sparta in a despairing attempt to retrieve the situation but managed to secure, as a favour to himself, nothing but a renewal of the oaths. Consequently the Argives failed to pursue their overtures to Sparta and a treaty was concluded between Athens, Argos, Mantinea and Elis.[82] The first clause, apparently a minute recorded by the Secretary of the Assembly and set down by Thucydides, runs as follows: 'The Athenians, Argives, Mantineans and Eleans made a treaty for one hundred years on behalf of themselves and of the allies over whom either group of them rules, to be observed without fraud or injury on land or sea.' The period of one hundred years suggests the notion of permanence which is attached in modern times to a lease of ninety-nine years and it is to be noted that the influence of Athens and Argos over their respective allies is taken for granted in the clause quoted above. One significant and recent ally of Argos stayed aloof – Corinth. Corinth remained content with her original defensive alliance with Argos although the latter had proceeded to an offensive and defensive alliance with Elis and Mantinea, but as she had been unable to recover Sollium and Anactorium from Athens and had seen Athens join Argos, she turned her attention once more to Sparta.

For the time being Sparta was content to complete her internal recovery from the ten years of war. She was not as easily provoked into action against Argos as Alcibiades wished and so long as Argos constituted a counterpoise to her in the Peloponnese, Sparta was unlikely to attempt adventures far afield. Sparta did threaten to take the field on two occasions in response to Argive provocations in the Peloponnese but when her forces approached her frontier the omens conveniently were found to be unfavourable for departure. By 418, however, the situation changed. Ominously Alcibiades persuaded the Athenians to record below the inscribed text of their treaty with Sparta that the Spartans had not adhered to their oaths and he persuaded the Athenians to instal dissident helots once more on Pylos as a menace to Spartan security. Within the Peloponnese Corinth and Megara were driven by the trespasses of Argos to conclude that their interests lay ultimately in seeking the protection of the Peloponnesian League. Their return to the fold immediately opened up new prospects for Sparta for it reopened the direct access by land to Boeotia. Therefore if Sparta was able to deal a blow against Argos her strategic position in relation to Athens would be restored to what it had been in 431, and the threat of extension of democracy and Athenian intervention in the Peloponnese would recede. King Agis of Sparta seized the opportunity to summon allied contingents and gained the upper hand over the Argives in the Argolid.[83] To his credit he sought to complete his victory rather by diplomatic than by military means, and in so doing he exposed himself to serious criticism at home. Immediately after establishing a superior position in the field Agis received two Argives, one a general and the other the proxenos of Sparta, and negotiated a truce. At Argos there was considerable annoyance at the conclusion of a truce, but the pressure of Elis and Mantinea and the military and diplomatic encouragement of Alcibiades were of little use to Argos in the event, for Sparta demonstrated her clear military superiority over the confederates at the Battle of Mantinea in 418 and exploited the situation to bring over Argos and Mantinea into her alliance on skilfully contrived terms.

In the winter following the Battle of Mantinea the Spartans proceeded with a force to Tegea and then sent on to Argos proposals for peace, which Thucydides records in the Laconian original.[84] The first four clauses dealt with the restoration of hostages and the freedom of Epidaurus, which had been the object of Argive attacks. Then followed three clauses which proposed to guarantee the autonomy of all states within the Peloponnese and to provide for the common defence of their territories against invasion from outside that area. Furthermore the rights of the allies of Argos and Sparta outside the

Peloponnese were to be respected. A final clause provided for the announcement of the treaty to the allies of the two Contracting Powers. The Argives accepted the proposals as a basis for an agreement which was concluded in the form of an alliance for fifty years. The treaty guaranteed the traditional jurisdiction and autonomy of all states and stipulated that all disputes arising should be settled by fair and impartial arbitration. To add to the woes of the Athenians the Argives then requested them to withdraw their force from Epidaurus, and the Peloponnesians both renewed their Chalcidic contacts and invited King Perdiccas of Macedon to enter their alliance and thereby abandon his special relationship with Athens, a course of action which he was tempted to justify by the plea that his family was of Argive descent. Those skilfully contrived stipulations of the treaty barely concealed a dramatic shift in the balance of power in favour of Sparta, a shift which was presently confirmed by the substitution of oligarchic constitutions for the democracies in both Argos and Sicyon.

The situation then was that within the Peloponnese was a group of oligarchies, dominated by Sparta. The empire of Athens remained for the time being more or less intact, protected from external interference by the alliance which existed between Athens and Sparta. That state of affairs constituted an ingenious variation on the Thirty Years' Peace, but, from the Spartan point of view, security depended upon the maintenance of a sympathetic oligarchic régime in Argos. That régime, however, was overthrown by the resurgent democrats with the assistance of Alcibiades, who removed leading oligarchs from the territory. The Argive democrats then aimed to render themselves impregnable by land and accessible to Athenian supplies by sea, and so they began to build Long Walls on the Athenian model. Sparta, however, intervened to wreck the construction and when the Spartans captured the little Argive town of Hysiae they did not scruple to massacre its citizens. There were indeed further signs of incipient disunion within the Spartan alliance when Corinth refused to supply a contingent to help in restoring Sparta's hegemony over her allies.

Those events did not pass unobserved by the Athenians, who took advantage of Sparta's embarrassment to send an expedition in 416 to complete their command of the Aegean Sea by subjugating the old Spartan colony on the island of Melos. Melos, though sympathetic to Sparta, had striven to maintain her independence and neutrality since 431. Naval powers have ever been allergic to the independence of islands, for the Athenians had sought since 425 to enrol Melos in their empire. In 416 when the Athenians pressed their demands and sent envoys to the island they are reputed to have remarked to the Melian commissioners that continentals generally caused little alarm but that islanders such as the Melians, among others, were likely to take rash steps which would lead themselves and Athens into danger.[85]

In the situation of the moment the Athenian action needs no other explanation, however much it reveals a high-handed mood of aggression. Thucydides in his famous Melian Dialogue, when he purports to give the essential arguments of the Melian commissioners and of the Athenian envoys, is concerned to show by a striking example of realistic dialectic how vain were the arguments which the Melians could advance to justify their courageous resistance. They were brave self-confiding men and can claim admiration and pity when after the city was taken by treachery its defenders were put to death. But war had become a violent preceptor and the Athenians had judged the situation aright. As Thucydides wrote in the Dialogue the Spartans were most conspicuous in considering as honourable what was agreeable and as just what was expedient, and they could not, at that moment, afford to go to war against Athens. A Spartan threat to invade Attica if Melos was not spared might have saved the Melians. But that was too much to expect of the Spartans, who had the massacre at Hysiae upon what consciences they possessed.

Since 421 the Spartans had encountered difficulty with allies and enemies alike in the Peloponnese but the Athenians had been unable to use the situation decisively to their own advantage. Baulked in one direction but ever prone to vigorous activity, the Athenians were ready to turn their attention elsewhere and by 415 an opportunity was presented to them and they resolved to sail again to Sicily with a bigger armament than they had deployed before. According to Thucydides most Athenians were ignorant of the size of Sicily and of the number of its inhabitants, let alone of the fact that they were undertaking a war not much inferior to that which was waged against the Peloponnesians.[86] Ambitious of conquering the island and gaining control of Carthage and southern Italy they had, in the words of the historian, the specious design of helping their allies and kinsmen in the island. The invitation and direct pretext was the appeal of Segesta for help against her neighbour Selinus. Segesta did have a treaty with Athens but the obligations incurred were by no means as absolute as they were portrayed by the activists at Athens. The eloquent and convincing pleas of the Segestan envoys fell on fertile ground at Athens for they offered to supply ample funds for the war and invited Athens to send envoys to examine for themselves evidence of the wealth of Segesta. After they had heard from their envoys a report, as attractive as it was untrue, the Athenians voted a large expedition under the command of Alcibiades, Nicias and Lamachus. Nicias, a man as cautious as was Pericles, had argued that it would be folly to divert resources to distant theatres when the alliance with Sparta was in a parlous condition and not observed by many states. He was in favour of maintaining the treaty to give the longest possible period for restoring prosperity but argued that Sparta, who had concluded peace and alliance from a sense of necessity rather than of honour, might be more easily tempted to launch an attack upon the divided resources of Athens. As proxenos of Syracuse he was fully aware of the strong position which Syracuse had established for herself in recent years but concluded that Sicily under Syracusan hegemony would constitute little threat to Athens and little comfort to Sparta. In his judgement it was folly to send help to right the wrongs of Segesta when Athens had not managed to remedy the injustices which she herself was suffering from the failure to implement the Peace of Nicias. Furthermore the mere threat of Athenian intervention and a brief demonstration of force would have a greater effect upon Athens' friends and enemies alike than would a full campaign. Nevertheless when his diplomatic and strategic assessment of the situation patently failed to convince his fellow-citizens he gave them a full list of military and naval requirements, perhaps in the expectation of deterring them, but their enthusiasm for action was undiminished.

Alcibiades was represented as arguing that not only had the Athenians obligations by treaty in Sicily but that if those obligations were seen to be fulfilled then many communities would come over to join the Athenians and so weaken the position of Syracuse. With such influences and resources behind her the Athenians would have nothing to fear from Sparta. Alcibiades further reminded the Athenians of his diplomatic achievements in the Peloponnese, where he had been instrumental in turning Argos against Sparta. He is depicted as a man full of self-confidence and self-praise, sanguine about the relative strengths of Athens and of the Sicilian cities. At the very worst nothing seemed likely to prevent the safe return of the expedition and he could argue that whereas the spirit of adventure had made Athens great, inactivity was likely to herald the decay of her skills. The safest course was for a state to act in tune with its habits and institutions.

The expedition sailed amid great hopes and expectations in 415, but within two years there befell what Thucydides described as 'the most important event in the whole war . . . unequalled alike in the glory which it brought to the victors and in the catastrophe which it brought upon the vanquished . . . ships, army, everything was lost.'[87] A concatenation of accidents and decisions indicative of political and military incompetence afflicted the expedition. The enterprise was not entirely misconceived, in terms of the relative strength of the combatants, and the possibility of some limited success was not hard to imagine. But the skilled general Lamachus was killed and Nicias, the reluctant leader and a sick man, was left in sole command, for Alcibiades, the author of the expedition, fled as a deserter to the enemy rather than face charges of being implicated in a scandal which broke out on the eve of the departure of the expedition. What is now relevant to our theme is that the hopes which Alcibiades' diplomacy in Sicily might have rescued his advocacy in Sparta now destroyed.[88]

If the Athenians had undertaken risks in concentrating so much of their resources and endeavour upon Sicily, they compounded their rashness by observing a lack of caution in respect of Sparta. For Sparta and Corinth were the obvious resorts of Syracuse for help against Athens and their help was a decisive factor in the Athenian plight. They were the more ready to move since Athens had been provocative in the Peloponnese and by 414 bore a clear responsibility for breach of the agreements made in 421. Whereas Sparta had failed to respond to the challenge to arbitration in 431, Athens now failed to do so and at the request of Argos raided Laconian territory in the Peloponnese.[89]

The immediately obvious move was for Sparta to do what she had contemplated in 431 and in 422 and what she was now encouraged to do by Alcibiades, namely to fortify a strong point in Attica in order to rob the Athenians of the use of their territory and to cause loss of morale in the city. The other obvious move was to block Athenian supplies at their source and to organize a campaign of liberation of Athens' subjects now that the Athenian navy had been weakened. Syracuse blocked Athenian supplies from Italy, and Sparta soon tried similar tactics in the east. The disaster incurred in Sicily had seemed to herald the total defeat of Athens, but with characteristic resilience she held out. The hesitations between competing roads to victory made Sparta, as Thucydides wrote, 'the most convenient of enemies'.[90] Alcibiades soon outstayed his welcome in Sparta and found a refuge within easy reach of the Athenian fleet at Samos.

Off the coast of Asia Minor squadrons played hide and seek until the naval war gravitated to the area of the Hellespont, the lifeline of Athens. Now Persia, with her Phoenician fleet, was within reach if the Great King decided to intervene through the agency of his satraps on the western borders of his realm. Near the Hellespont there was the satrap Pharnabazus, resolutely and resourcefully loyal to his sovereign, and at Sardis Tissaphernes, whose family was descended from that Hydarnes who had helped to revive the Persian monarchy after the death of Cambyses a century or more earlier. Ultimately it was Persia which exerted a decisive influence on the outcome of the war. Both sides had sought to enlist Persian aid at the outset of the Ten Years' War and Athens did indeed secure a treaty with Persia in 424/3,[91] but that brought little concrete result. Evidently, however, by 412 the Persian king had concluded that the Athenians constituted a greater threat to his sovereignty than did Sparta. Accordingly Sparta became the beneficiary of Persian aid in 412 and an agreement was concluded at Miletus.[92] Persian policy was none the less difficult to interpret and co-ordinate for Pharnabazus and Tissaphernes acted independently and as rivals for Spartan support. Sparta chose not to support Pharnabazus, who wished to oust the Athenians from the Hellespont, but to fall in with Tissaphernes (now backed by the ubiquitous Alcibiades)[93] who wished to encourage those of the Chians and other islanders who wished to be freed from association with Athens. Nevertheless Sparta still moved with caution and made no rash assumptions when secret emissaries of factions approached her to seek aid for revolt and assured her of the eagerness and capacity of Athens' subjects for such action. In spite of Thucydides' statement that Athenian allies were eager beyond their capacity for revolt,[94] widespread defections did not result so much from the encouragement of Sparta as from the policy of the Athenian oligarchs of establishing oligarchies which turned out to be less loyal to that of Athens than to Sparta.

In 411 a political reaction against democracy at Athens created a new situation both within the city and outside. For Alcibiades, once regarded as an extreme democrat but now espousing the cause of oligarchy, was keeping a careful watch upon the situation. Both to him in exile and to others any change might have seemed a change for the better. Alcibiades had been cultivating the satrap Tissaphernes, who was less interested in supporting any particular Greek faction than in playing off one against another, and word was sent to Athens that if an oligarchy were to replace the democracy then Persian aid would be channelled to Athens. A combination of circumstances and interests then led to a temporary oligarchy at Athens, but whereas the leaders had let it be known that their aim was to promote the more efficient management of the war they immediately proceeded to make overtures – in vain – to Sparta for peace. Neither Persian aid nor peace with Sparta was forthcoming and the Athenian oligarchs failed to retain either credibility or power; and in the ensuing political confusion Alcibiades returned from exile both to prevent civil war and to prove that Athenian naval capacity was still able to win victories, if not to achieve victory. Twice, in 410[95] and 406,[96] after Athenian successes the Spartans were ready to negotiate a peace which would have enabled Athens at least to cut her losses and survive, and twice sanguine demagogues let the opportunity pass them by. For there was then no Pericles in Athens, nor even by 406 a clear-sighted Alcibiades, since the latter carried ultimate responsibility, but not blame, for a defeat at Notium in the spring of that year, and resumed his wanderings as an exile. Even from exile he warned the Athenians against concentrating their fleet in the Hellespont in a final attempt to win the war at Aegospotami, where they lost decisively the last round.[97] From 408 Spartan diplomacy had been far more successful in conciliating Persia, for in that year the Great King sent his son Cyrus to act as his viceroy in western Asia Minor. There he came, he saw, and was conquered by the dazzling personality of yet another extraordinary and energetic Spartan statesman and general, Lysander, a man worthy to follow in the steps of Brasidas. The relationship between Lysander and Cyrus,[98] who supplanted Tissaphernes, was decisive. With additional Persian support Sparta was able to resolve the strategic deadlock in the struggle between the land power and the sea power by defeating Athens, which had been steadily deprived of her resources and external sources of support, at sea. The empire of the Athenians vanished with their fleet, to reappear as a Spartan empire under the control of Lysander.

CHAPTER VII

THE ASCENDANCY OF SPARTA

'AT ATHENS IT WAS NIGHT when the *Paralus* sailed in with word of
the disaster at Aegospotami, and a voice of lament passed from the
Piraeus through the Long Walls to the city, as each man told the news
to his neighbour, so that in that night no one slept; not only did they
weep for those who had perished, but much more for themselves,
for they expected to suffer the fate which they had inflicted upon the
Melians . . . and many others of the Greeks.'[99] Such is the graphic
description of the historian Xenophon of the state of anxiety in which
the Athenians braced themselves to prepare a siege against the final
onslaught of Lysander, for they had neither command of the seas nor
even of their own territory. The Athenians were at the mercy of the
Spartans, and especially of Lysander, the very spirit of revenge. They
had no fleet, no allies, no food, but even though numbers of persons
in the city were dying of starvation there was no talk of peace.

When stocks of food were exhausted the Athenians made overtures
through King Agis of Sparta indicating their preparedness to join the
Spartan alliance provided that they were allowed to retain their Long
Walls. Sparta had never felt happy about the Athenian construction
of land defences since the Persian Wars and was certainly unwilling
to accept such terms in 405. The Athenians therefore sent Theramenes,
a resourceful politician and diplomat, to obtain the best terms which
he could from Lysander, and more than three months passed while
starvation pressed even harder upon them. At Sparta the Corinthians
and Thebans, among others, demanded the destruction of their great
enemy, but the Spartans refused to destroy 'a Greek city which had
such exploits to its credit in the great danger that had once beset
Greece'.[100]

The terms which Theramenes took back with him seemed to end
the power of Athens – the Long Walls and the fortifications of the
Piraeus were to be dismantled, all the warships but twelve to be surrendered and exiles to be allowed to return: the Athenians were to

have the same friends and enemies as the Lacedaemonians and to be under their hegemony by land and sea.[101] After a debate in the assembly the Athenians accepted the terms, whereupon Lysander sailed into the Piraeus, the exiles returned, and the walls were pulled down amid scenes of great enthusiasm and to the music of flute girls. That day was thought to be the beginning of freedom for Greece, and so ended the twenty-seven years of the greatest war which Greece had experienced up to that time.

Sparta in 404 was in a position such as no other community had attained, in control of her own alliance and of that of Athens, supreme by land and dominant by sea. Beyond the immediate vicinity of the Aegean she had the backing of the Sicilian Greeks in the west and of Persia in the east. Within Sparta resources and manifestations of material wealth were greater than ever before, for Lysander took back with him the prows of all captured ships, the triremes from the Piraeus, the crowns he had received as personal gifts, the balance of the tribute which Cyrus had given him amounting to four hundred and seventy talents, and everything else which had been appropriated in the war.

Incredibly, however, within thirty years Athens became once more the leading sea power and by 371 Thebes surprised the Greek world by administering a decisive defeat upon Sparta by land. Sparta had for long campaigned in the name of the liberty of the Greeks, but in 412 she had gained the support of the Persians by conceding to them recognition of sovereignty over the Greeks of Asia Minor. She had succeeded in liberating communities from Athenian control by working through sympathetic oligarchies, but such régimes by definition imply minority rule and have a habit of requiring more external support than democratic régimes. And the installation of garrisons to protect them was consonant neither with the appearance of liberty nor with the reserves of Spartan man-power. Even with Spartan assistance the oligarchy which seized control of Athens for a few months in 404 was unable to maintain its position, and there was considerable difficulty at Sparta in deciding whether or not to accept the course adopted by King Pausanias, namely of trying to reconcile the democratic and oligarchic factions. The excesses of the oligarchic régime caused many to withdraw into exile from Athens and significantly both Megara and Thebes, according to Xenophon, were full of refugees.[102] After all that had happened over the preceding decades it may seem strange that Athenian democratic refugees found a haven in the territory of apparently inveterate enemies, for the Thebans had pressed for the destruction of Athens as the penalty in defeat. Sparta's rejection of that course which was advocated in Thebes and Corinth served as a reminder that there were conflicting interests within the Peloponnesian alliance and that whereas an alliance could be an effective combination for a specific and immediate purpose a divergence of interest could easily result in a rapid diplomatic *volte-face*. Sparta failed to share out the spoils of war and it was not in her interest to allow the fall of Athens to be compensated by an increase in the power of Thebes and Corinth. Irrespective of whether or not Pausanias, the younger king at Sparta, did look further ahead to a degree of reconciliation and a return to the old dualism between Athens and Sparta, if Athens was to survive, technically as an ally of Sparta, there was every reason for those of Sparta's allies who so wished to keep their options open as to their future diplomatic course. If in fact the harbouring of refugees from Athens was a source of irritation to the Spartans then it served as a reminder that autonomous allies did have their own interests to consider and none of them could ignore the possibility that Athens might once again become a counterpoise to Sparta.

For almost a decade Sparta was supreme and without any serious challenge the arbiter of the fortunes of Aegean Greece, but her past and her Panhellenic pretensions caught up with her. For after her promises, made to Persia in 411, she sought to repair the discredit of making them by evading the discredit of keeping them. First she became involved in providing assistance to Cyrus, in return for his favours, in subversion against the Persian King, Artaxerxes, and then when Greek cities of Asia Minor appealed for help in defending their liberty against the satrap Tissaphernes Sparta was placed in a predicament, a predicament which was in no way eased by the despatch of Spartan forces under Thibron, who, in a typically Spartan fashion, succeeded equally in annoying friend and foe. There ensued a war with Persia largely compounded of operations in Asia Minor and alternating armistices. In 396 King Agesilaus, persuaded by Lysander, headed a major expedition to Asia Minor and departed in true Panhellenic fashion by staging a sacrifice at Aulis as Agamemnon had done before embarking for Troy.[103] Upon his arrival in Asia Minor he declared to Tissaphernes that he had come to see to it that the cities of Asia might be as free as those in the rest of Greece. Lysander's aim, however, was to shore up the oligarchies imposed under Spartan auspices since 411 by the reimposition of the decarchies, or colleges of ten commissioners, which had been installed to impose Sparta's will but which had with the acquiescence of the ephors for the most part been dissolved owing to their unpopularity.

Sparta's breach with Persia, thanks to whose aid she had emerged victorious by 405/4, was of critical importance in numbering her days as undisputed champion in the Greek world, for although there was before long a *rapprochement* between the two powers the breach was sufficiently long and serious to bring about the revival of Athens, now under a democracy which was wisely moderate and endowed with a generous readiness to forgive and forget excesses committed in the cause of revolution. Sparta's Panhellenic propaganda was not consistent with Lysander's activities, Sparta's allies had little to show for their efforts in the fifth century, and in Athens there were those who had a clear recollection of the Athenian role as it had been before the humiliation of Aegospotami. Such fertile ground was ready for exploitation by the Persians who encouraged opposition to Sparta and offered money to support it. In addition Spartan naval power, based upon only a brief tradition, and the ability to support her Aegean friends were severely curtailed by the operations of a Persian fleet under the command of Conon, an Athenian admiral who had been in exile since 405 and who now delivered a blow at Cnidos in 394 in revenge for his defeat at Aegospotami.[104] Persian subsidies and the activities of Conon brought about a resurgence of the Athenian navy and before long Athens was able to repair her land defences with the assistance of Thebans, for both Thebes and Corinth were drawn into a defensive alliance with Athens in order to protect their own interests.[105] Athens, however, did not so much actively seek out such an opportunity as act as the recipient of overtures from Thebes, where there predominated a faction more sympathetic than that which had the upper hand in 405/4. Spartan carelessness and Persian tactics brought about a change in the alignment of powers. As always, Greeks were quick to seek and accept Persian aid and were equally quick to blame their enemies for selling out to the barbarians, but Greek politicians did not have to be bribed to enter a coalition against Sparta. They readily accepted any Persian money which came their way, but only to help them to do what they would have done without it; they were in fact paid but not bought, just as English politicians in the seventeenth century did not scruple to accept French money while they did what they thought best for their party or their country.

From 395 it became increasingly apparent that no bond of loyalty existed between Persia and any group of Greek states; each was content to use the other as circumstances dictated. Thebes became involved in war against Sparta over a dispute between allies in central

Greece, and Athens was ready to be involved in order to encourage a powerful ally to keep Sparta out of central Greece, for Sparta began to concentrate her energies nearer home rather than in Asia Minor. In spite of the brave spirit which led Timolaus of Corinth to advocate a united assault on Sparta and action to set the nest on fire, as it were, while the wasps were still inside,[106] the Spartan forces were still formidable by land even if they could not demonstrate an overwhelming superiority in battle. The so-called Corinthian War dragged on, no decisive result was in prospect and the main beneficiary appeared to be Athens, who was in receipt of aid from Thebes and Persia and was using it to retrieve the losses which had been incurred both inside and outside Athens during the Peloponnesian War. Indeed her revival, which led to an increase in her navy, to the re-establishment of her control over the islands of Lemnos, Scyros and Imbros, staging posts on the corn-route from the Black Sea, and to contacts with both Salamis in Cyprus, nominally under Persian control, and other sensitive areas, gave Sparta some hope of convincing the Persian King that in the light of her past naval and imperialist tendencies which showed signs of recrudescence Athens constituted a greater menace.

The Spartans, in view of the fact that Persian money was being used to rebuild Athens' walls and fleet and to enable her to win over Greek cities in Asia Minor, thought that the time was ripe to point this out to the Persian King in an attempt to reach an accommodation with him. They resolved to send Antalcidas, a man skilled as an admiral and as a diplomat, to the satrap Tiribazus.[107] The satrap heard Antalcidas' proposals that the Persians should cease to spend money on supporting Sparta's enemies in return for a recognition of the King's sovereignty over the Greek communities in Asia Minor and a declaration that all of the other islands and cities should be independent. Naturally the Boeotians, Corinthians, Argives and especially the Athenians were opposed to such a settlement, but Tiribazus approved the idea and before going to his king to recommend the proposals he arrested Conon and secretly gave money to the Spartans. The Persian King, however, promptly dismissed Tiribazus for his advice and replaced him with Struthas, who supported the Athenians and their allies. But if in 392/1 there were divided counsels in Persia there was also a difference of opinion in Athens, for the Spartans maintained their initiative to reach a settlement among the Greeks. In Athens there were voices raised in favour of peace, and among them was Andocides, a man who had pursued a chequered political career but whose grandfather had helped negotiate the Thirty Years'

Peace with Sparta in 446/5 and whose maternal uncle, Epilycus, had helped to arrange the alliance with Persia in 424/3. He argued, according to a speech which survives in his name,[108] that Athens could hope to gain little from protracted war, especially if her ability to do so depended upon the fickle Persians and upon the dubious will and stamina of the Boeotians; that the Athenians stood to gain much in a peace which either implicitly or explicitly recognized the gains which they had made since the treaty of 404, for no one any longer questioned the right of Athens to maintain her navy and her Long Walls or her possession of Lemnos, Scyros and Imbros. After his embassy to Sparta he recommended peace but feeling against him in Athens was so strong that he and his colleagues were charged with misconduct and they fled in anticipation of a capital sentence.[109] For the moment the Athenians enjoyed security and friendship with their neighbours, they had Persian support, their naval and diplomatic standing was growing visibly, but it still remained short of what it had been in the 'normal' years of the preceding century. There was no immediately compelling need to come to terms, Sparta with her diminishing man-power and loss of social cohesion showed greater signs of strain, and for the ordinary Athenian there was greater prosperity than for many years, not least because naval security provided staple supplies of cereals at prices which were lower than they had been for several years.

Democracy can be wayward in its decisions, and few could accurately foretell what was likely to occur or when, but as it happened Antalcidas and Andocides were proved to have read the position more correctly than had the Persian King and Andocides' opponent Callistratus in 392/1. For a time all went well for Athens, who basked in the approval of the satrap Pharnabazus. The Athenian general Thrasybulus helped democracies back to power and above all won over Byzantium and Chalcedon, dominating the western and eastern shores respectively at the southern entrance to the Bosporus. But the Athenians caused annoyance to many communities by soliciting contributions for their enterprises, the Boeotians were in disarray and by 387 Antalcidas and Tiribazus had resumed their partnership. Antalcidas also obtained Syracusan naval support in spite of Athenian diplomacy in Syracuse, and with a shrewd eye for strategy he struck at the Dardanelles and threatened the Piraeus from Aegina, moves which terrified the Athenians who well remembered that they had been but recently starved into surrender by such tactics. Within the Peloponnese Argos, which to the discomfort of Sparta had joined with Corinth to form a democratic union, was no longer able to hold out confidently against Sparta, while Sparta herself was extended by her commitments. For she had to keep a wary eye upon her allies, in order, wrote Xenophon,[110] to prevent those whom she trusted from being ruined by the enemy and those whom she distrusted from seceding.

That was the situation when in 387 Antalcidas induced Tiribazus to summon envoys from all states which were willing in order that they might hear from him at Sardis the terms of peace which the Persian King stated in his rescript. The effect of the terms was to confirm Persia in control of her possessions in Asia Minor, together with the island of Cyprus, and to guarantee the Athenian claim to possess as of old the islands of Lemnos, Scyros and Imbros; all other Greek states, great and small, were to enjoy autonomy, and whichever of the two sides refused to accept the terms was to face the prospect of war with the King and those participants in the Peace who were willing by land and by sea, with ships and with money. The last clause was in all probability suggested by Antalcidas on behalf of Sparta. The Peace was shrewdly compounded of ideology and self-interest and if it lasted it seemed likely to induce contentment with a state of peace and to hinder effective combinations of cities which might make war upon their neighbours, whether Sparta or Persia. Early in 386 the Peace was accepted upon terms which had been discussed intermittently for some years, and the Greek world passed from war to peace.[111]

The settlement could be condemned insofar as it enabled the King of Persia to impose his will upon the Greeks by the exercise of diplomacy and the distribution of *largesse* and to succeed by such means in doing what his armies had failed to do at Marathon and Thermopylae. It offended the patriotism of many Greeks, including the Athenian orator Isocrates, but it had the merit of realism granted that the prime interest of Persia and of Sparta was nothing more than to live and let live. According to where the critics, both ancient and modern, have supposed that the blame or the credit for the treaty reposes they have called it the Peace of Antalcidas or the King's Peace. But whatever the immediate quarrels were the treaty enshrined the principle of autonomy, which was universally accepted if not implemented, and came to have a profound effect upon all forms of bilateral and multilateral treaties. In that respect it has been handed down to posterity by those who were more sensitive to diplomatic niceties under the title of the Common Peace.

CHAPTER VIII

THE PRINCIPLE OF AUTONOMY AND THE ATHENIAN NAVAL CONFEDERACY

OMINOUSLY THE THEBANS ALONE of the Greeks who assembled at Sardis declined to accept the Peace and its implications, for they claimed the right to ratify on behalf of all the Boeotians, whereas the Spartan King Agesilaus, who scarcely forgave the Thebans for their insult in interrupting the sacrifice at Aulis and was to exert a great influence over the next few years, refused to allow them to be included in the treaty in that case. Thebes was isolated and so, as Agesilaus mobilized with relish, she agreed to concede the independence of the Boeotian cities and the dissolution of the Boeotian League. Agesilaus too forced the Argives to sever their union with Corinth in the cause of autonomy.[112]

Thereafter 'armies and fleets were demobilized and peace ensued. In the war the Spartans had just about managed to hold their own but immediately afterwards in the Peace which followed they emerged as the victors. There was never any serious risk that Athens would be deprived of the gains which she had made up to 392/1 although some treaties were effectively nullified and her aspirations were sharply curtailed. The Peace was a skilfully contrived document in which only Athens and Persia were specifically named as receiving benefits, action was proposed against no specific state, and autonomy was guaranteed to all who were not subjects of the Persian King. In the Peace of Antalcidas the Spartans could bask in the reflected glory of their traditional stand for liberty, but they in particular could afford to back the terms for they secured Corinth as an ally, neutralized Argos and weakened Thebes as a military rival. As Sparta had the clear support of Persia the responsibility for interpreting the Peace fell upon her, for although the Persian King threatened to make war on transgressors by land and by sea, with ships and with money, he carefully avoided repeating the errors of Marathon and Thermopylae in committing his armies to Greece.

As Keeper of the Peace and Protector of Greek Independence Sparta committed many errors and so alienated the Greeks at large that by

378/7 Athens was able to emerge from almost total isolation to a position as defender of the independence of the Greeks against their protector. For the decade or so after the King's Peace King Agesilaus dominated Spartan foreign policy and he lost no time in attempting to improve Sparta's strategic position. The Peloponnesian League was reorganized to provide more troops, and deficiencies in contingents of citizens were made up by the hire of mercenary soldiers. Then, after the Spartans had fulfilled their aims in securing the terms of peace which they desired, they turned their attention to reviewing the recent conduct of states which were nominally their allies.[113] Mantinea was the first of Sparta's neighbours to bear investigation, for Mantinea had a core of influential leaders who were inclined to democracy and to alliance with Argos. Consequently Sparta sought to weaken Mantinea by demanding the destruction of its city walls and the dissolution of the city into its five constituent villages, thus setting the political clock back by a century or so. The city was forced into surrender and the sixty democratic leaders found that their worst fears were not realized for they were ushered into exile in a disciplined way, whilst the wealthy landowners were pleased at being able to concentrate their energies on their estates rather than upon combating troublesome demagogues. It is plain that the Spartans were concerned to act in a disciplined manner, for King Agesilaus asked to be excused from the command of the forces against Mantinea since that city had given help to his father in war against the Messenians. Then when Agesilaus' junior colleague, Agesipolis, took over the command the latter adopted a considerate attitude to the democratic leaders of Mantinea since they had been on friendly terms with Agesilaus. As the Spartans were reviewing the conduct of their allies in the war their attention was drawn next to Phlius by exiles from that city. The exiles thought that the moment was opportune for them to point out to the Spartans that so long as they had participated in its affairs, Phlius had remained loyal in fulfilling its commitments to Sparta, but after they had gone into exile Phlius had failed to follow Spartan leadership. Accordingly the Spartan ephors found it convenient to take up the case of the exiles and sent a message to Phlius declaring that these exiles, who were friends of Sparta, had been unjustly expelled. Again the Spartans moved with some discretion by declaring that the exiles should be recalled, not by compulsion but with the consent of the people of Phlius. Within the city there were friends and relatives of the exiles and there were many others who were not averse to a change in the political order. In addition the

Spartan interest caused fear and apprehension among the Phliasians, who were led to restore the exiles and their property with provision for compensation and judicial arbitration.

In so far as the Spartans had been dealing with delinquent allies in Mantinea and Phlius their conduct, even if it cannot be praised, can be appreciated, but the Spartans were led to attempt to make dispositions elsewhere where their writ was neither accepted nor acceptable. In 382 they were led to intervene in the affairs of Olynthus and the Chalcidic League, for envoys came from Acanthus and Apollonia, the biggest cities in the area around Olynthus, to ask for Spartan help in resisting attempts to draw them into the federal Chalcidic League. It was perhaps appropriate to make an appeal to Sparta who stood as the champion of autonomy and had dissolved the Boeotian League in its pursuit, but the most powerful argument which was brought to bear upon the Spartans was that Thebes and Athens were active in their diplomacy in the region of Olynthus, an area of considerable wealth and resources.[114] Without a doubt there was scope not merely for force of arms but also for diplomacy since the Spartans sent out a modest mixed force under Eudamidas, who supplied garrisons upon request to Thracian cities and encouraged Potidaea, an ally of Olynthus, to come over to him voluntarily. What Sparta was not justified in doing, except for her own self-interest, was to follow this up by mounting a campaign to force the dissolution of the entire Chalcidic League by 379 in the same way as the Boeotian League had been dissolved.

But perhaps the Spartans were encouraged to deal with Olynthus by the prospect of achieving a positive settlement in Thebes by diverting forces on their way to Olynthus for activity in Thebes. For ever since the end of the Peloponnesian War there had been rival political factions in Thebes looking respectively towards Athens and Sparta in their external policy and by 383 neither faction had decisive control, for both Leontiades, who favoured Sparta, and Ismenias, who favoured Athens, were among the chief elected officials. Leontiades lost little time in approaching Phoebidas, the brother of the Spartan commander Eudamidas, to ask for his help in organizing a *coup d'état*.[115] Leontiades pointed out that whereas the Thebans had begun to negotiate an alliance with Olynthus and had decided not to participate in the Spartan expedition there, if Ismenias' group were driven out then Sparta would find plenty of help from Thebes. This proposition had an intoxicating effect upon the inexperienced Phoebidas, a man who had a passion for performing a famous exploit but who was not noted for any great mental insight or application. The *coup* was successfully and efficiently engineered, but when Leontiades went to Sparta he found little apparent enthusiasm and considerable displeasure there, though King Agesilaus stated that what the Spartans had to weigh up was whether or not a particular move was beneficial to Sparta. Thereafter the Spartans gave more help than was asked of them and they participated in a mockery of a trial of Ismenias, who was charged, among other things, with befriending a Persian satrap and accepting money from the Persian King.

Whether or not the Spartans had out of forethought or by accident become involved in the Theban *coup*, they initially derived from it considerable benefit. Xenophon sums up their position by noting that the problem of Thebes and Boeotia had been brought under control, Corinth had become a reliable ally of Sparta, Argos was of little consequence and Athens was isolated. Thus it appeared that now at last Spartan supremacy had been well and truly established.[116]

But the King's Peace had not been explicitly designed to ensure the supremacy of Sparta. Its terms did not necessarily empower Sparta to act as she had done since 386 and such allowances as could be made for most of what she had done could scarcely be extended to cover her intervention in Thebes and her later intervention in Attica in 378. And it was to be events in Thebes and Athens which were to weaken, quickly and decisively, the prospect of Spartan security as it had appeared to Xenophon.

Three years after the coup of Leontiades and Phoebidas in Thebes their work was undone. For, writes Xenophon,[117] many examples can be given from the history of nations to show that the gods are not indifferent to perpetrators of evil, and now divine wrath was to chastise the Spartans, who had sworn to leave the cities independent but had nevertheless seized the Theban Acropolis. In 379 it took reputedly only seven men to put an end to the puppet régime of the Spartans in Thebes. The Spartans, who were taken by surprise, mobilized in an attempt to make good this reverse but a year later the activities of their commander Sphodrias, who was stationed at Thespiae, caused alarm in Athens. Without the prior approval of his domestic authorities he launched a raid on the Piraeus at a time when Spartan envoys were in Athens. The Spartan envoys immediately fell under suspicion and were placed under arrest, but when it was plain that the attack was not authorized they were released. At that point the Spartans could have made some useful diplomatic attempt to undo the harm which had been done, for the Athenians were by no means quick to restore their former alliance with Thebes, which had by then lapsed. The Spartans, however, not only failed to punish Sphodrias but publicly praised him. Consequently Athens strengthened the defences of the Piraeus and before long made an alliance with Thebes.[118] That combination of power was a decisive event, for once again Sparta was left in the minority of the three traditional Great Powers of Greece and her capacity to reassert herself might depend on her ability to persuade the Persian King to reassert himself. Athens was immediately able to harness the widespread fear of Spartan encroachment in Greece to rebuild her naval power and eventually Thebes was destined to depose Sparta from the greatness which she had misused.

In Athens since the King's Peace the old energy and optimism had given place to resignation tempered with a faint nostalgia of greatness. Athens had in 384 signed an alliance with Chios on terms of strict equality and conformity with the King's Peace,[119] but the Spartans had managed to forestall her flirtations with Thebes and Olynthus in 383/2 and little further happened until 379/8. Then the alliance of Athens and Thebes, precipitated by Spartan clumsiness, removed the intellectual isolation of Boeotia, and in Athens there came back into prominence Callistratus, an eminent practitioner of statecraft. He was a brilliant orator whom ancient critics ranked with Pericles, and with his vision and resourcefulness went a strong admixture of that useful ingredient of diplomacy, a sure sense of what was possible and what was not.

One of the most momentous documents of Greek diplomacy is the stone set up in Athens in early spring 377 to record a decree passed on the proposal of the statesman Aristoteles, amounting to what is often loosely called the Foundation Charter of the Second Athenian Naval Confederacy.[120] Aristoteles proposed that 'in order that the Lacedaemonians may allow the Greeks to enjoy peace and quiet in freedom and autonomy possessing all their land in security, and in order that the Common Peace which the Greeks and the King swore may be valid and in force for ever it shall be decreed by the Assembly as follows: if anyone of the Greeks or of the barbarians that live on the mainland or of the islanders, as many as are not subjects of the Persian King, wishes to be an ally of Athens and her allies, he shall be able to do so, in freedom and autonomy, practising whatever form of constitution he wishes, neither admitting a garrison nor being subject to a governor nor paying tribute, but on the same conditions as are the Chians, Thebans and the remainder of the allies.'

The general invitation to join the alliance on clear terms was
followed by a clause containing elaborate precautions against the
Athenian acquisition as private or public property of any lands in
the territory of members of the alliance. A short clause then committed the Athenians and their allies to give the utmost possible
assistance to any member of the alliance who might be attacked by
land or sea. Then followed sanctions against any legislation contrary
to the decree. Finally, the Secretary of the Athenian council was to
erect a marble pillar containing the decree beside the statue of Zeus,
the Defender of Freedom, at the expense of the Treasurers of the
Goddess Athena. On the stone were to be inscribed the names of
current and future allies. Three envoys were also to be chosen forthwith to visit Thebes to secure any benefit which they could. After
the names of the three envoys so elected, all distinguished men known
from other inscriptions to have been diplomatically active, appeared
a general heading 'The following cities are allies of the Athenians'
with the names of states in the order of their accession to the alliance,
as may be seen from the different hands or style of the masons who
inscribed the names.

The virtually unprecedented attention to detail in drawing up the
document shows that care had been lavished upon the proposals.
Athens was not on this occasion being propelled into the leadership
of an existing alliance but was taking the lead in creating it. She had
her own past from the fifth century and even the period before the
King's Peace to live down and so her chances of success depended
upon the extent to which both her sincerity and her guarantees could
be accepted at a time when most states were convinced that Spartan
rule was in any case harsher than that of Athens. The motives of the
Athenians were complex; there was altruism and there was a readiness
to restore to the city its former prestige and power. The architect of
the alliance certainly hoped by extending a general benevolence and
consideration towards the allies to augment the influence of Athens
at the expense of that of Sparta. As has been seen, care was taken to
disown any intention of challenging the validity of the Common
Peace or of the rights of Persia as defined in it. The terms also carefully precluded any recourse to those practices which had generated
ill-will towards the late unlamented Athenian Empire of the fifth
century. That Empire had grown up partly as a natural consequence
of the inequality between the power of Athens and that of the members
of her alliance. It has often been said that justice and good faith between
states are most durable when the parties are of comparable strength.

From 377 it was hoped that such a balance could be achieved by promoting a synedrion, or council, of allies stationed in Athens to keep in touch with the Athenian assembly, dividing between them the responsibility for the actions of the alliance as a whole.[121] In the previous century Sparta had accepted obligations towards her Peloponnesian allies so far as these could be reconciled with her hegemony, but since the fall of Athens Sparta had asserted this hegemony as against the rights of her allies. Athens now made an attempt to avoid that, just as Brasidas had done on his early enterprises for Sparta in Chalcidice.

For a time the new Confederacy was successful and so far as its aim was to prevent Spartan encroachment it completely succeeded by 371. While Thebes and Sparta engaged each other in inconclusive operations by land the Athenians were enabled to concentrate on naval affairs especially in areas where they had once had diplomatic links. Before long most of the smaller states outside the Peloponnese who were subject to Spartan control threw off their shackles to join Athens, who gave appropriate political and military assistance where necessary, for often a change of alliance accompanied a change of political régime. The initial tide of enthusiasm was such that within a few years some seventy states, many of them once members of the Delian League, joined the new alliance, which also had its religious centre at Delos.

It was not easy for the new Confederacy to maintain its initial momentum, for Thebes had her own preoccupations with Sparta in respect of which a naval offensive could count for little and the Confederacy was always in danger of demanding more from its members than they were willing or able to give. That was not necessarily because the Athenian assembly was too consciously sovereign to go in step with the synedrion of the allies, but there was no initial accumulation of funds or equipment. Although the Athenian admiral Timotheus might have seemed like a second Pericles to some allies he was unable to command the Periclean ingredients of victory in war, a reserve of money and a shrewd policy. Of course he had his naval and diplomatic successes but the margin of reserve was unduly slender, and it is instructive to read the account of Xenophon at the point where he records the Athenian naval victory at Alyzeia in 375.[122] Timotheus sailed straight for Corcyra after rounding the Peloponnese and took over the island. There he engendered a favourable attitude towards Athens among the states in the area, for he refrained from enslaving inhabitants, banishing citizens or subverting constitutions. With his sixty ships he defeated the fifty-five Peloponnesian vessels but did not prevent them from erecting a trophy of victory near by. Thereafter, although he maintained a superior position, he repeatedly sent to Athens for money, of which he had a great need for he had many ships. Before too long indeed he was reduced to spending his own private fortune on his forces.

In 374 the Athenians saw that they had achieved as great a success as was possible commensurate with barely tolerable expenditure and decided to make overtures to Sparta. For Thebes was less intent on helping to develop the Naval Confederacy than on restoring her position in Boeotia and that seemed to be a suitable moment for the Athenians to think of reaching an accommodation with Sparta which would recognize the Athenian naval interest and the Spartan position in the Peloponnese. Such an accommodation would perhaps lead to the degree of stability which had existed in the middle years of the previous century and could yet be consistent with the King's Peace. Accordingly amid great hopes peace was concluded and the Athenians decreed an annual sacrifice on its anniversary.[123]

The Peace, however, broke down almost immediately. For Timotheus, having set out for home, on the way restored some exiles to Zacynthus, which immediately appealed to Sparta. Fighting was resumed but it was inconclusive. The Athenian commander Iphicrates was reduced to such a state that Callistratus, his colleague, undertook to return to Athens with the resolve to secure either more money or peace. The factors which had induced peace in 374 were just as, if not more, compelling in 371, especially the conduct of Thebes. The Athenians sent a large delegation to Sparta and in accordance with the King's Peace it was agreed that all states should be independent and free from the imposition of garrisons.[124] Thereafter there was to be a general demobilization. On those terms the Spartans, Athenians and Thebans swore their oaths, but then, as in 387/6, the Thebans returned to claim the right to ratify on behalf of all Boeotia. Naturally the Spartans were strongly opposed to that, but their opposition in 371 was to bring consequences which shocked the rest of Greece and showed that no longer were the Greeks to be subject to a supremacy which either oscillated between, or was shared by, Athens and Sparta.

CHAPTER IX

THE RISE OF THEBES

THE APOGEE OF THEBAN INFLUENCE was reached in the years between 371 and 362, the so-called decade of Theban supremacy in Greek affairs. Thebes had been very slow to reach the status of a recognized Greek power, for traditionally in the mists of Boeotia her principal aim had been to dominate her immediate neighbours and to incorporate them in a federal combination of Boeotia. Beyond that natural wish to obtain local security within a local federation the main preoccupation of the Thebans was with powerful neighbours in Thessaly and Attica. Occasionally Theban interest was drawn farther afield, to Macedon or the Peloponnese, according to whether it was desirable to check or encourage Thessaly or Athens, but it was not until 366 that Thebes seriously contemplated the acquisition of naval power and maritime contacts. Consequently even when Thebes was propelled into a role of supremacy by the relative weakness of Athens and Sparta her institutions and political horizons were not quite adequate to enable her to grasp her opportunity. Certainly Epaminondas and Pelopidas, unusually far-sighted and competent statesmen as Thebans went, were unable to persuade their countrymen to accept their advice at crucial diplomatic moments, and when these two statesmen had been removed by death the poverty of Theban institutions was revealed by the lack of any men of stature to take their place in Thebes, to say nothing of the arena of Greece.

For most of the sixth century, when the power of Thessaly was considerable, relations between Thebes and her northern neighbour had been cordial, but towards the end of that century the Thebans had become aware that Thessaly might extend her power into the northern area of central Greece. And when Thebes consequently attempted to strengthen her hold over Boeotia this brought her into conflict with the town of Plataea which lay in Boeotia astride the road from Athens. As has been seen, Plataea had appealed c. 519 first to Sparta for protection against Thebes, and then upon Spartan advice to Athens, whose rulers took the field both to confirm Plataean independence of Thebes and to provide themselves with a strategic outpost. Thus Plataea, which was for long to hold a position of its own in the conscience of Athens, became an outpost of Athenian power, and in the dangerous moment of Marathon Plataeans fought by the side of the Athenians to share the glory of that famous day.

Ten years after the first Persian invasion came that of Xerxes, in which Thebes deserted the cause of Greece, as did Thessaly, when by contrast Plataea gave her name to the battle which turned back the tide of invasion. The role played by Thebes at that time, however much forced on her by her defenceless position, became a lasting reproach to her. In the middle years of the fifth century when the Athenians extended their influence by land in the Peloponnese and in central Greece they developed contacts with democrats in Thebes and managed to dominate Boeotia for a decade after their victory at Oenophyta in 457, until their fortuitous defeat at Coronea in 447 ended their power in that region.

The Thirty Years' Peace confirmed the acquiescence of Athens in her abandonment of Boeotia apart from her durable alliance with Plataea. Thereafter the opponents of Athens in Boeotia were the oligarchs who had been in exile and from then onwards for many years most of the Boeotian cities had oligarchic governments. In these circumstances it was natural for Thebes herself to favour the interests of Sparta, with whom she preserved a connexion even if she did so only out of fear of Athenian retaliation. Early in 431 it appeared to be to Thebes' advantage if war were to break out between Athens and Sparta and she took steps to that end. There were at that time in Plataea those who wished to break with Athens and to bring the city into alliance with Thebes. One night they admitted a small Theban force to prepare the way for a reinforcement strong enough to hold the city against help from Athens.[125] Such a move was likely to precipitate the outbreak of a general war which might otherwise have been averted or postponed by diplomacy, the more so as the Spartan king Archidamus was inclined to see the peace preserved, at least for a time. There was one other consideration – that Thebes might profit, as she did, from the plundering of Attica by an invading army.

The plot failed and the Plataeans massacred the Theban force after tricking it into surrender. Two years later with the help of an Athenian garrison Plataea was strong enough to resist a siege by a Peloponnesian army, but the Athenians were unwilling to risk a battle to raise the siege and so in 428/7 the garrison made good its escape. Within a short time the Plataeans were reduced by famine to surrender on terms which seemed to offer fair treatment,[126] but the Thebans were set upon revenge and after a mockery of a trial one massacre avenged another. The city was destroyed and the land was annexed by Thebes. If Thucydides may be trusted, the advocates of Plataea at the trial had recalled the help given to Persia by the Thebans. The defence of the latter was that they had resorted to treason towards Greece owing to coercion by a close cabal to suit its own purposes, and the execution of the Theban leaders soon after the Battle of Plataea (479) suggests that the statement was not far from the truth.

The military value of Boeotian cavalry and infantry was high when under the over-all command of Thebes, as was apparent when they defeated the Athenians at Delium in 424. If the Boeotians were almost proverbially boorish, they had minds of their own when it came to war. They profited by the ten years of war from 431 and stood aloof from acceptance of the Peace of Nicias, contenting themselves instead with a cessation of hostilities renewed for successive periods of ten days.[127] After the Peace, in failing to give up the Athenian prisoners who were in their hands and the frontier post of Panactum, which had been betrayed to them in the previous year, they continued to be guided by opportunist self-interest and a shrewd observance of the changing constellations of the diplomatic sky during the ensuing five years.

In the latter years of the fifth century the nearest approach to a sustained motive of policy was a neighbourly suspicion of Athens, which after the final defeat of the Athenians prompted the Thebans to side with those who demanded the destruction of Athens. After that had been denied to them the Athenian democratic exiles under Thrasybulus found refuge in Thebes, which provided them with the opportunity to regroup and force their return to Athens.[128] Whoever may have been the architects of Theban policy, they must have enjoyed a notable versatility and power of forgetting today the passions or principles of yesterday. Before a decade had passed Thebes joined the coalition of Greek states which challenged the Spartan hegemony in Greece.

By that time, if not earlier, the organization of the Boeotian federal state had so developed as to secure the domination of Thebes over the other cities, and any state which needed the voluntary co-operation of Thebes during the fourth century, whether Athens or Macedon, had first to recognize Theban aspirations. In 386 the declaration of the Persian King in favour of the autonomy of the Greek cities was a diplomatic defeat for Thebes in so far as it ran counter to the subordination of the Boeotian cities to her hegemony. In the years immediately after the King's Peace the area in Boeotia under Theban control diminished and what may have been especially resented was the restoration of Plataea and its protection by a Spartan garrison. It certainly cannot have given much satisfaction to many Thebans when in 385/4 the Spartans required the help of a Theban contingent to coerce Mantinea in the name of autonomy. If such humiliation were not enough the Spartans caused intense resentment by staging the *coup* which brought to power in Thebes a faction which took its orders from Sparta. After the overthrow of that régime in 379[129] there was a determination to rebuild Theban power, a determination which was not to be as easily diverted in 371 as it had been fifteen years earlier.

After the peace conference at Sparta in 371 King Cleombrotus of Sparta was instructed not to dismiss his army until the Thebans agreed to ratify the peace merely for themselves and not on behalf of all the Boeotian communities. The Thebans realized that if they did not stand up to fight, their federal allies might desert and they themselves might be besieged. Furthermore many of the Theban leaders had suffered exile before and could not bear to repeat that experience. Accordingly they resolved to do battle with Cleombrotus who had already marched into Boeotia and taken up position at Leuctra. The result was that nearly one thousand men of the Spartan army were killed, including four hundred out of the seven hundred officer class.[130] That loss and defeat was a far more shattering experience than the capture of so many Spartans by the Athenians a little over fifty years before at Pylos.

In their elation the Thebans sent a garlanded messenger to Athens bearing news of the victory and inviting the Athenians to join in making the Spartans pay for what they had done to them. The Athenians, however, felt little reassurance at the victory of Thebes, who had been a selfish ally and was now an uncomfortably powerful neighbour with no adequate countervailing force. Consequently the Athenians declined the invitation to participate with Thebes and before long tried diplomatic initiatives to strengthen their own position.

The Battle of Leuctra was no ordinary victory, for its effect was lasting. For Sparta it was her heaviest defeat, and an irreversible one, for it broke her grip upon the Peloponnese, which had been for so long the foundation of her power and influence. By destroying a legend Leuctra created a vacuum of power, and foreign policy, as does Nature, abhors a vacuum. Leuctra did to Sparta what Pydna was to do to Macedon (168 BC), Rocroi to Spain (AD 1643) and Valmy to Frederician Prussia (AD 1792).

Immediately after the battle Thebes turned her attention to central Greece and Thessaly, where there had arisen in Pherae a ruler, Jason, whose military power was a match at least for her own. For he could add to the aristocratic cavalry of the Thessalian plains a very considerable mercenary army of his own making. When he arrived in Boeotia he avoided committing himself to a campaign in which he had no vital interest, for although Xenophon described him as the greatest man of his time,[131] he could not afford to entertain with equanimity the prospect of a Theban supremacy replacing that of Athens or Sparta. Therefore he advised the Thebans to avoid driving Sparta into such a tight corner as to arouse fanatical resistance and as *proxenos* of Sparta in Thessaly he advised the Spartans to make their peace. There was at the time a very real prospect of Jason becoming a major diplomatic influence, since his forces were so strong that few could afford to leave him out of their calculations. He announced his intention of appearing at the Pythian Games in September 370 with an army at his back. He was expected to seize the treasures at Delphi and there was no sign that anyone could, or would, stop him. But he was assassinated at a military review. That left central Greece from Aetolia to Attica to fall under Theban control.

Meanwhile as the Thebans were preoccupied in the wake of Leuctra the Athenians made a bid for the diplomatic leadership to fill the vacuum left by Sparta's fall. It was not so much an attempt to incorporate Sparta's allies in the Naval Confederacy as to inherit the hegemony of the Peloponnese, something which she had not managed even in her heyday in the fifth century. Envoys were sent out to summon representatives to a conference at which all states pledged themselves to abide by the terms of the King's Peace and by the decrees of the Athenians and their allies.[132] There was universal satisfaction at the move, except in Elis, and Mantinea was enabled to restore political unity to her autonomy in spite of Sparta's opposition. Athens had executed a brilliant diplomatic move, but what was needed at that time was not envoys, but an army such as Epaminondas had led for Thebes down the Eurotas valley as far as Sparta.

The federation in Boeotia was now beyond challenge and the Thebans found it convenient to encourage federalism elsewhere.

Whereas previously the enemies of Sparta had placed their reliance upon Argos within the Peloponnese the Thebans now encouraged the federation of Arcadia in the hope that the Arcadian League would form a suitable diplomatic and strategic implement; in this they were successful, for the League continued to exist in spite of Spartan wishes and indeed it proved to be rather too independent in spirit for Thebes to manage to her own liking. The other favourite manoeuvre of Sparta's enemies was the subversion of the subordinate classes of Laconia and not only were the Messenians encouraged to bid for their autonomy but also *perioeci* were to be found fighting in the ranks of Theban allies.[133]

The establishment of Theban military supremacy was a source of fear to both Athens and Sparta, and so to some it seemed the logical move for the two states to combine in their opposition to Thebes. Before long therefore envoys arrived in Athens from Sparta in search of such an accommodation, but in the early stages of the debate in the assembly the Athenians were not receptive. A Corinthian delegate however rose to remind them of their recent oaths by which they had guaranteed assistance to victims of aggression, and it was impressed upon them that an alliance with Sparta would be especially beneficial to Athens who could scarcely afford to tolerate the Thebans as the first power in Greece just across her border. By 369 the Athenians and Spartans were in the field as allies, not dividing up their respective spheres by land and sea but each holding supreme command in turn.[134]

Within the Peloponnese Thebes encouraged the establishment of democratic régimes, which were likely to transfer their loyalty away from Sparta, but Epaminondas realized that civil war and the perpetration of excesses committed in the cause of political rivalry, such as occurred at Argos, were debilitating. Consequently he favoured alliances with other federations which were founded on the Boeotian model, such as those in Arcadia, Aetolia, Western Locris, Thessaly and Achaea, and left them to manage their own affairs. In Achaea, for example, an oligarchic régime was allowed to prevail for a time;[135] in the case of the Boeotian recalcitrant, Orchomenos, in 366 Epaminondas deplored the violence used by the federal authorities.[136] Although such federations were encouraged the Thebans protested their loyalty to the cause of autonomy as loudly as ever Athens and Sparta had done and exploited the principle to devastating effect in Messenia and Laconia to destroy Sparta's wealth and security.

The tolerant diplomacy and shrewd propaganda of the Thebans was supported by considerable military backing, for Epaminondas had demonstrated his ability to march into the Peloponnese with forty thousand men. Consequently if Sparta was placed in a weak position Athens was placed in an embarrassing one in her search for allies. For her Confederacy had been directed against Sparta; now the two were in alliance, and as if that was not enough, Athens was drawn not only into active support of Sparta in the Peloponnese but also into co-operation with Dionysius, tyrant of Syracuse,[137] and the pro-Spartan oligarchs of Corinth. Athens, therefore, clutched gratefully at the chance offered by the Persian King, whose agent Philiscus summoned a conference of the opposing states at Delphi in 368.[138]

The conference foundered on the issue of autonomy, for Sparta refused to acknowledge the independence of Messenia, but negotiations were resumed before long – in Persia. Athens was nervous of the loyalty of her maritime allies and so in order to ensure the co-operation of Persia she followed the Spartan initiative in sending envoys to Susa, but that initiative back-fired. For the Boeotians also decided to send envoys and Pelopidas made a great impression on the Persians, who had hitherto derived little satisfaction from supporting Athens and Sparta in turn. Pelopidas managed to obtain a rescript which was favourable to Thebes and which was designed to put Thebes in a position comparable to that which Sparta had held in relation to the Greek states and Persia after the King's Peace in 386.[139] Peace was to be concluded on the basis of autonomy for all, as before, but then there were specific provisions to weaken both Athens and Sparta, for the independence of Messenia was to be recognized and the Athenians were both to withdraw their fleet from the seas and to abandon their claim to Amphipolis, a place which gave them access to resources for maintaining a fleet.

The terms were not accepted by the Greek states and Persia showed herself unwilling or unable to intervene on behalf of Thebes. Epaminondas realized that the best way to weaken Athens was to destroy the basis of her power, the Confederacy. To do that it was necessary to construct a fleet both to challenge that of Athens and to convey help to dissident factions within the communities of the Confederacy. No doubt with Persian encouragement and help from Carthage,[140] which was opposed to the interests of Dionysius in Sicily, a Theban fleet was organized and by 363 one hundred ships were able to operate against Athenian interests in the Bosporus, where the loyalty of Byzantium and Chalcedon turned from Athens. An inscription records too how Thebes encouraged the anti-Athenian faction in Ceos,[141] while nearer home the cities of Euboea deserted Athens for Thebes.

The year 366 marks the beginning of a sequence of events which
virtually drove the contemporary Athenian historian Xenophon
to despair in 362. For no state could either by itself or with its alliance
decisively influence the direction of affairs and the stalemate was
broken by no outside intervention. Sparta had little power for major
campaigns and the Athenians, worn out by financial expenditure
since 378, found no single ally to help them in their dispute with
Thebes over Oropus. To keep their men paid Athens and Sparta
were both reduced to offering mercenary service to the satrap Ario-
barzanes, in revolt from the Persian King, while at the same time
trying not to offend the King. If that action appeared incongruent
there were other contradictions in their policies, for while Athens
decided that to reduce Theban influence she would accept the Arcadian
plea for a defensive alliance,[142] yet Sparta though an ally of Athens
campaigned against Arcadia. Meanwhile there was a war of pamphlets;
Alcidamas of Elaea in Aeolis echoed the ancient aspirations of the
Messenians in the famous phrase 'God has set all men free; Nature
has created no man a slave.' The Athenian orator Isocrates replied
in his brochure the *Archidamus*, in the form of a speech by the young
Spartan prince, the son of Agesilaus, 'For my part I would rather die
at once than live a thousand years at the command of Thebans. . . .
If we cannot live with honour, let us die with honour.' In such a
mood peace was not possible.

In 362 the Thebans had a formidable list of allies in central Greece.
In Thessaly they had few worries, although Pelopidas had died there
on campaign in 364, and in Macedon they had found a defensive
ally whose good faith was ensured by the presence in Thebes of the
future King Philip as hostage. Then they were drawn into conflict
once more in the Peloponnese in a complicated dispute involving the
Arcadian League. The presence of Epaminondas in the Peloponnese
resulted in the coalition of Sparta, Arcadia, Achaea, Elis, Phlius and
Athens.[143] According to Xenophon, almost all of Greece was involved
in the crisis on one side or another and it was widely expected that
in the battle there would be a clear decision as to who would be
master of Greece. Epaminondas failed in his attempt to surprise
Sparta, but at the gates of Mantinea his generalship reached its zenith
and there was a prospect that Boeotia would emerge triumphant in
the confirmation of the process which she had begun in 371. But in
the hour of victory Epaminondas followed Pelopidas to his death,
and with his last breath he bade his countrymen make peace. With
his death the dominance of Thebes vanished save for her hold on

central Greece. In the closing words of his History Xenophon wrote:
'From this time onwards a mounting confusion and discord prevailed
more than ever before in Greece. Here shall end my work, and what
follows will perhaps fall to another's care.'[144]

There was a conference of the Greek states who met on their own
initiative to agree on a Common Peace,[145] but it was a Peace of the
exhausted with no one to guide it or guarantee it. All possible permuta-
tions of alliance and coalition had been tried and found wanting by
the traditional powers, but while they had been exhausting each other
by their efforts there had been developing quietly and unseen in the
wings an outsider who was to change the whole perspective of Greek
history.

CHAPTER X

PHILIP OF MACEDON
AND DEMOSTHENES

AFTER THE END OF THE Peloponnesian War the three traditionally
powerful states, Sparta, Athens and Thebes, had all enjoyed moments
of supremacy, but none managed to assume the role played by the
Great Powers of the fifth century. Stability was lacking and the intervention of Persia merely aggravated the situation as her support
switched from one party to another in the furtherance of her own
objectives. Sparta no longer possessed adequate reserves of man-
power, Athens did not manage to accumulate the resources such as
she inherited after the Persian Wars and Theban aspirations could
flourish only by virtue of the weakness of the other powers.

The peace of 362/1 showed the determination of the Greeks to
avoid needless strife with one another and to steer clear of involvement in Persian affairs. That determination, however, was manifested
too late in the day even if the intention was sufficiently resolute. The
whole perspective of Greek diplomacy was to be radically changed
from 359 by the entry of a new power, a comparative outsider, to the
scene. From that time on the power of the formerly dominant city-
states was never again to have the opportunity to exert itself and none
of the city-states, although they continued to exist, was able to enjoy
the same freedom as hitherto in the exercise of sovereignty and the
direction of its own external affairs.

The weakness of the old powers provided the occasion for both
a man and a state to assume a dominant role. Hegemony had been
assumed by states in turn, but in the fourth century there had been
much thought given to the nature of political leadership in the belief
that appropriate training and education were prerequisites for the
political leadership which the Greeks needed. Plato, in disillusion
with the instability of Athenian politics, devoted a lifetime of academic
study to the subject and sought to conduct practical experiments
with Dionysius II, tyrant of Syracuse. At the Panhellenic level
Xenophon viewed with approval the policies and aspirations of King

Agesilaus of Sparta in his role as a champion uniting the Greeks against Persia, an aspiration briefly rekindled by Jason of Pherae. Isocrates at Athens took up the theme of Panhellenic leadership and to head the crusade against Persia he suggested Philip of Macedon. By 338 Philip was without any serious rival in the Greek world and he created a power which could not be surpassed in military or economic resources by any other Greek community. Most of the Greeks were drawn into alliance with him under the umbrella of the League of Corinth from 338 and by the time of his death in 336 he stood poised to invade the Persian domains at the head of the League's forces. His death, however, scarcely postponed the invasion, for his successor Alexander the Great rapidly exerted his authority and subsequently brought the Persian Empire under Macedonian control.

Philip of Macedon was undoubtedly one of the greatest military and diplomatic practitioners of all time. As his career developed he was increasingly impelled to seek co-operation or confrontation with Athens and that brought into conflict with him Demosthenes, a skilled Athenian diplomat and the supreme orator in all Greece. Each represents clearly in retrospect one of the two polar influences evident in Greece, the need to combine more effectively and the deeply rooted traditions of local independence; the course of their rivalry was one of the most dramatic and piquant episodes of all history.

The course of Greek affairs can be represented as a battle of the two giants in the years after Philip's accession in 359, for Philip had contemporary admirers, such as Ephorus[146] and Theopompus,[147] who wrote historical accounts while the speeches of Demosthenes survive in abundance; yet in the early years Philip's position in Macedon was precarious and Demosthenes was but a mere stripling. Geographically and politically Macedon was divided. It had considerable resources of minerals and timber which had made it the object of the military and diplomatic attention of other communities such as Corinth and more especially Athens, who had at frequent intervals staked her claim to Amphipolis. More recently, since the Athenian naval revival, the Macedonian coastline saw the establishment of Athenian naval bases at Methone and Pydna. Macedon's size and topography were such that other states did not so much desire to conquer it entirely as to gain access to its resources and prevent others from doing so. Consequently it was traditionally a theatre of considerable diplomatic activity and it was by the exercise of devious and opportunistic diplomacy that its rulers, always beset with rivals and pretenders, managed to survive. In the Peloponnesian War the Athenians had attempted to dictate terms to Macedon but Perdiccas continued to oscillate between alliance with Athens and Sparta. Relations too with Balkan neighbours in Illyria and Thrace needed careful manipulation as did those with neighbouring Thessaly and the Chalcidic League, which was based on Olynthus.

The management of internal problems and of external relations with so many neighbours absorbed the energy and attention of Macedonian rulers sufficiently to prevent them from impinging too far upon the Greek world before Philip's accession, and in any case Macedonians, on the fringes of Greece, were scarcely considered even to be Greeks, apart from their rulers who were at least admitted to the Olympic Games, for which Greek nationality was an essential prerequisite. From the end of the fifth century, however, there had been a long but undramatic process of internal consolidation in Macedon, and more recently as a deliberate policy the Macedonian court had encouraged exposure to Greek cultural influences. Furthermore those influences were not confined to spheres of drama and literature, for Callistratus, in exile from Athens, was called in to reorganize the finances of Macedon by Perdiccas II.[148]

Upon his accession Philip inherited a strong army. It was powerful in cavalry led by the tribal nobles, who saw in the king their natural leader, and the cavalry had been reinforced by a robust peasantry whose loyalty was attested by the title of Foot Companions conferred upon them by Philip's predecessor. The army, however, could not be used initially for external adventures, for its resources needed to be conserved and consolidated. To that end Philip withdrew the Macedonian garrison which had been stationed to guard the independence of Amphipolis from Athenian attention. The first care of the new king was to make his frontiers secure and to eliminate his rivals, some of whom received external support. A discreet combination of financial inducement and military activity was used to ward off the threats posed on his frontiers by Paeonians, Illyrians and Lyncestians; Berisades of Thrace was bought off and so withdrew his support of a rival pretender, while Argaeus, whose claim to the throne was backed by Athens, mustered insufficient local support. Other rivals were assassinated or found refuge in neighbouring territory such as Chalcidice, which was Philip's only ally at the time in the area.

Philip owed nothing to any other state, except the experience of his observations as a hostage in the Thebes of Epaminondas when he was a young man.[149] In dire straits he had stood the test as a man who was willing to deploy any strategic or tactical move, including bribery and marriage, to protect his interests. After a year or so Philip had secured his position and preserved Macedon from risk of disintegration. In that process he had overcome enemies but created no new or powerful ones; he even attempted to allay the fears of Athens, whose vital interests lay somewhat to the east in Amphipolis and in the Chersonese, by offering an alliance and renouncing any claim to Amphipolis.[150] As yet there was no reason to suppose that Philip had any aspiration to be anything other than King of Macedon, certainly no reason to suppose that his actions would be directed against the interest of any other particular state, nor that his impact upon the Greek world would exceed that of his predecessors. Consequently those outside Macedon were slow to take his measure, but when after the initial period of internal consolidation he sought to secure the position of Macedon in the vicinity he could scarcely avoid trespassing on the traditional spheres of those outsiders who had been in the habit of exploiting the area. Crisis came but he shrank from total war with states such as Athens and was often ready to make a conciliatory gesture while he bided his time, either to take advantage of diversions such as the war of Athens with her allies (the Social War 357–5) and the so-called Sacred War or to create diversions where none existed.

The year 357 was one in which Philip made remarkable headway, for then Athens was preoccupied elsewhere. Several allied communities had broken away from the Naval Confederacy. Theban diplomacy had caused disaffection in Euboea and Mausolus of Caria encouraged oligarchic movements at strategic points such as Chios, Cos, Rhodes and Byzantium, which naturally broke away from the predominantly democratic League. Athens' resources were strained in fighting what by 355 turned out to be a losing campaign against her delinquent allies and so she could do little but observe Philip assert his sovereignty over her bases at Pydna (357[151]) and Methone (355[152]). Athens' interests too were damaged when he took a force to establish the independence of Amphipolis, whose democrats promptly expelled Athenian sympathizers.[153] Moreover Philip was able to present himself in a favourable light in Thessaly, an important area to the south of Macedon whose wide plains produced excellent cavalry and whose aristocratic landowners found in Macedon invaluable support in their campaign of liberation against the tyrannies which had been established in several of its cities, including Pherae.[154] In that area too Philip's move could hardly be welcome to the Athenians who had gained influence there and signed a perpetual alliance with Thessaly in 361/0.[155] Then not only did Philip seal his alliance with Epirus after the defeat of the Illyrians by marrying Olympias, who was to have a great influence in Macedonian affairs, but he also sealed his new relationship with Thessaly by marriage with Philinna of Larissa. Athenian diplomacy was thwarted in two more areas at a time when Athens was preoccupied with the Social War. The Chalcidic League came to the decision that its interests were complementary to those of Philip rather than to those of Athens, especially when he offered it Anthemus and promised to give Potidaea after removing the town from Athenian control. Consequently in 356 the League signed a defensive treaty with Philip.[156] In an attempt to divert Philip Athens attempted to create an alliance with his Illyrian and Thracian neighbours,[157] but he proceeded to extend his influence beyond Amphipolis in Thrace, where he took over Crenides, renamed Philippi, and used it as a base to exploit the mineral resources of Mt Pangaeus which was to provide him with a steady source of income. It amounted to one thousand talents a year, an income such as no other state had enjoyed since the collapse of the Athenian Empire.

By 355 Athens was obliged to recognize the independence of her dissident allies[158] whilst Macedonian power had been consolidated largely at her expense, if not to her detriment. The growth of Philip's territory was observed at Athens with a natural suspicion, especially on account of what had happened at Amphipolis, and Athens regarded any new power within reach of the Dardanelles as a potential threat to the passage of corn from the Black Sea. But there were those at Athens, including Isocrates, who were willing to recognize that the presence of a large number of bases on the northern littoral constituted not only an over-insurance, but also a liability and a provocation, though it required a brave man to say so in public.[159] As if to try to convince Athens that his plans were directed to secure Macedon and not to injure, Philip allowed the Athenian garrison to depart freely from Potidaea in 356[160] although the Athenians had declared war.

Over the next few years the past connexions and sympathies of Athens turned her attention to affairs in many parts of Greece. She was for example the object of appeals from within the Peloponnese and from the democrats of Rhodes, but Eubulus, who played a strong role in advocating retrenchment from 355, ensured that funds and resources were conserved for action in more vital areas. The initiative, however, lay with Philip who was not only head of a powerful army of citizens and allies but also his own Foreign Minister and there were many states other than Athens which provided him with an opportunity for action. In central Greece he not only took advantage of the Sacred War as he had done of Athens' war with her allies, but actually intervened in it, for he was eager to cultivate the religious authorities at Delphi and by acting as their protector to reveal himself to be as obviously Greek as the rest of the Greeks. The war, which lingered on until 346, began in late 355 when the Delphic Amphictyony at Theban insistence declared war against Phocian elements for infringements against the sacred plain. Thebes was supported by Thessaly, which in turn brought in Philip whose presence in central Greece was a new factor. His presence in Thessaly astride the traditional routes of invasion from the north at Tempe and Thermopylae caused widespread fear and alarm that he was bent on conquest. The Sacred War, therefore, became for Athens and others not so much a test of support for Delphi but a crusade to confine Philip within his former sphere in the north. Philip failed to carry all before him, but he managed to consolidate his hold over Thessaly, including the former coastal stronghold of the Athenians at Pagasae, before being turned back by powerful opposition at Thermopylae in 352.

Philip's withdrawal from Thermopylae allowed only temporary respite to Athens for he was left free to pursue his interests elsewhere to the detriment of others. He made progress in such sensitive areas as Cardia and found common cause against his troublesome eastern neighbour, Cersebleptes in Thrace, with Byzantium,[161] Chalcedon and Perinthus, which controlled the Black Sea route. Not only was Athens alarmed but also the Chalcidic League, which in the years since her alliance with Philip had become so convinced that he was now the greater menace that it opened negotiations for an alliance with Athens.[162] He regarded that action as perfidious and unleashed his anger with such a fury that Athens could not help to avert it. At the time in 348 Athens was militarily involved in the strategic area of Euboea, but her failure was not so much due to a lack of resources as to political incompetence and a lack of concerted military leadership. Those were years of great frustration for the young orator Demosthenes, for his vehemence in attacking Philip was almost matched by his impatience with his fellow citizens.

In 350 Demosthenes delivered his first speech on the subject of Philip, a speech referred to as the first of a series of *Philippics*, which gave the name 'philippic' to denote in general a piece of political invective. In it he painted a black picture of the character of Philip and contrasted his nobility and decisive attitude to the hesitancy and procrastination which prevailed in Athenian democratic institutions at a time of crisis. He advocated the stationing of a mobile Athenian force, composed of infantry, cavalry, warships and transport, to divert Philip in the northern Aegean, and the commissioning of a large force which could be despatched from Athens at short notice. Demosthenes' three speeches on Olynthus, the *Olynthiacs*, contained further proposals, especially to improve financial resources, as well as abuse of his political opponents and Philip; but Philip exploited his political friends and the political divisions which existed within and between the states of the Chalcidic League, which he managed to deal with one by one.

The collapse of Olynthus as a centre for resistance to Philip and the loss of Euboea to Athens so weakened the Athenian position that there was little prospect of keeping Philip at bay should he take advantage of the continuing Sacred War to make his way down the old invasion route through Thermopylae. The Athenians took a test of the diplomatic temperature around Greece but their envoys reported that there was no prospect of finding further help against Macedon.

Philip, however, was careful to keep his options open and to provide some opportunity for Athenian opinion to come round. Athens' action might so far have seemed ineffective, but it was one thing for Philip to operate on internal lines and eliminate Athenian naval bases in operations by land, quite another to contemplate direct action against Athens and against the Athenian fleet, which had no serious rival. Consequently he made overtures to Athens through many emissaries. Athenian captives were released from Olynthus bearing friendly messages and Euboean emissaries also bore messages of Philip's friendly intentions towards Athens. By the year 346, after a decade of military activity, there was a bright prospect for Macedon to capitalize its gains by a peaceful settlement which offered a general security. Accordingly the Macedonian proposals were presented at Athens and there the statesman Philocrates proposed acceptance of the peace which subsequently bore his name. Demosthenes did not oppose the proposal at that time, for it was manifestly in the interest of Athens to secure a respite from fruitless war.

There were those who hoped for a Common Peace, open to all who wished to participate, but in the end a simple bilateral treaty was concluded between Athens and Philip and their respective allies.[163] There was no complicated exchange of territory, such as bedevilled the Peace of Nicias, but the treaty contained no specific inclusions or exclusions and omitted certain important but unresolved matters, such as the status of Phocis. The major powers could not possibly satisfy all of their allies yet they felt an overriding need to conclude terms, thus leaving the seeds of future dissension.

Envoys were sent out from Athens to Philip in order to confirm and ratify the terms of peace. Demosthenes and a rival orator, Aeschines, were among the envoys.[164] They were received politely by Philip but failed to achieve all that they had hoped about the timing of the ratification so as to suit Athens. On the mission Demosthenes held aloof from his colleagues and attacked their conduct on his return. Precisely what happened on the mission is obscured by a thick veil of mendacity in the legal proceedings which followed over the next fifteen years or so. Hostility between Demosthenes and Aeschines developed into what was to become a fundamental issue in foreign policy. Demosthenes brought charges of treachery and diplomatic misconduct against Aeschines, who replied with attacks in court against the former's political allies, and Demosthenes was by no means alone in developing opposition to those who were associated with the policy of peace with Macedon, for others pressed home capital charges against Philocrates. In the wake of the Peace of Philocrates, as hopes were dashed and the atmosphere soured, Athens and Macedon began to drift once more to war. Philip sent a letter with complaints[165] – and not unreasonable ones – of the behaviour of Athens, and was repaid in kind.

At Athens there were those who after the lapse of two or three years were ready to challenge the whole basis upon which peace had been concluded, and Philip's offer of arbitration was spurned. He was prepared to go to some lengths by gesture and negotiation, offering to give to Athens Halonnesus, a recently cleared pirates' outpost, but the Athenians were prepared only for him to give it *back* and thereby recognize their prior right.[166] Halonnesus was of little account in itself but the dispute was symptomatic of the Athenian reluctance to recognize the permanence of Philip's position any more than that of Sparta or Thebes earlier in the century. Amphipolis might not be restored by negotiation but there was always the prospect that sufficient force could be mustered. Demosthenes and his generation had grown up at a time when many social and political divisions had been evident in Macedon and, as Demosthenes argued, there was no reason to believe in Philip's immortality. Furthermore as Philip's power grew so too did his diplomatic commitments, and the lesson which the Athenians drew from history was that there would be a reaction *against* him as dramatic as that which there had been *for* him. His involvement in Aetolia, Acarnania, Achaea, Arcadia, Argos and

Messenia stood every chance of producing such a reaction, of which there were signs in Ambracia, Corinth and the Peloponnese.[167] Boeotia had changed sides many times before and late in the 340's there were those in Boeotia who considered that Philip's presence and alliance constituted more of a hindrance than a help. For the moment, however, the Athenians rejected overtures from Persia.

In Athens the prevalent assessment of Philip was that outlined in Demosthenes' *Third Philippic* – a tyrant who was bent on the elimination of Athens and the extinction of Greek liberty. Both sides prepared to resume war and there were numerous clashes and provocations as each attempted to consolidate its position in the north-east Aegean. The incipient reaction against Philip which had been evident in the Peloponnese then gathered momentum. For as he made the strategic move to exert a stranglehold on Athenian supplies from the Black Sea, many Greek communities, some formerly dissident allies and enemies of Athens, became equally alarmed. Their support and the apprehension of Persia at the approach of another power to Asia Minor encouraged the Athenians to abrogate their treaty of 346. The crunch came at the Battle of Chaeronea in 338, a watershed in the history of Greek affairs.

Philip found that his attempts to deploy the classical strategy against Athens of securing the Dardanelles worked too slowly. He tried first to take Perinthus and then Byzantium, but they were within reach of Persia and their neighbours, he was ill-equipped for besieging such coastal locations, and luck ran against him. Therefore he changed his strategy, and one evening there came news that his army was at Elatea within striking distance of Athens. The one chance left to Athens was to enlist the help of Thebes. Now Thebes had been hostile to Athens, but Demosthenes, the *proxenos* of Thebes, had worked for good relations between the two states and persuaded the Athenians to seek Theban help. He hastened as envoy to Thebes and by exercising skilful diplomacy and making concessions which flattered Theban pride he won his way.[168] The Athenian hoplites and a force of mercenaries, stiffened by the famous Sacred Band of Thebes, could hope to face the Macedonians in the field. In the end by brilliant strategy Philip brought his enemies to battle at Chaeronea, where his tactics completed what his strategy made possible, and his opponents were routed. That the battle happened was due to the diplomacy of Demosthenes, but the results refuted this diplomacy, as eighty years before the Spartan victory at Mantinea had refuted the diplomacy of Alcibiades. Demosthenes was committed to oppose Macedon but

Aeschines was inclined to a more flexible and opportunist policy and found credit as envoy to Philip on the morrow of his victory. On a calculation of present material interest it is hard to deny that Aeschines was justified, and there is no need to suppose that he was bribed by Philip any more than that Demosthenes was bribed by Persia. It must, however, be borne in mind that within two years after his victory Philip was assassinated in a domestic feud and succeeded by a youth aged only nineteen, and in 336 there were vain but nevertheless reasonable hopes that the clock of history could be turned back by a quarter of a century. Both Aeschines and Demosthenes wanted what they believed to be best for Athens, but the one looked at the Athens of his day, the other to the Athens of her glorious past.

The initiative in diplomacy and policy now passed to Macedon and the king made good use of it. Philip in a typical exercise of generous statesmanship and shrewd self-interest founded the League of Corinth,[169] comprising most of the Greek communities. They had no option about joining but the terms laid down incorporated all that was best in the practices of treaty-making in the fourth century, guaranteeing independence and assistance against attack. The practical effect of the foundation of the League suited the current needs and purposes of Philip to secure contingents of troops both to strengthen his army for the invasion of Asia Minor and to act as hostages for the behaviour of the cities which supplied them. After Chaeronea Thebes was eliminated for her treachery from the military map of Greece, whilst Athens was spared the imposition of a garrison and Philip the expense of a siege of her strong walled defences. The fleet of the Athenians was now at Philip's disposal and they could comfort themselves with the thought that alliance with Macedon[170] was likely to serve their interests at the expense of Persia. Sparta remained sulkily aloof but there was little point in directing a campaign against her to complete the façade of Panhellenic unity for that could be done only at the expense of another hard-fought battle.

When Philip conceived the enterprise of crossing over into Persia's domains in Asia Minor is not known but the measure can hardly have caused much surprise when it was put into effect. For in the year which saw the conclusion of the Peace of Philocrates the orator and publicist Isocrates had preached the virtues of such an enterprise and pointed to Philip as its leader in the cause of Greek unity.[171] Artaxerxes III of Persia had concluded a non-aggression pact with Philip,[172] an act of diplomacy which might in itself suggest a latent conflict of interest between the two powers whose spheres met at the Dardanelles. There the interests of the parties clashed and in the years leading up to Chaeronea the Persian satraps in northern Asia Minor worked against him. Then in the year of Philip's great victory in Greece Persia was left paralysed by the assassination of Artaxerxes. The opportunity was too good to be missed, but even though Philip himself did not live to execute his plans the result was that no longer could Greek history be written solely with reference to what happened within the old geographical limits and confines.

CHAPTER XI

ALEXANDER THE GREAT AND THE EXTENSION OF GREEK HORIZONS

THE DEATH OF PHILIP and the dynastic crisis in Macedon was taken by many as an opportunity for revolt from the League of Corinth, for, although the League incorporated enlightened federal institutions and was based upon the diplomatic practices which had evolved in the fourth century, membership had not been voluntary. The young Alexander, only nineteen years of age, rapidly assumed authority at home and made it plain that the League was to continue as before and that he was to replace Philip as its military leader.[173] During the next few years until the death of Alexander at the age of thirty-two in 323 there was to take place the first major territorial expansion of Greek influence for two centuries. It was an expansion over an area much larger than that of Greece itself and through the extent of the Persian Empire. Furthermore the result was that the centre of gravity of Greek affairs shifted eastward, for although Athens, for example, could retain its cultural importance, the major diplomatic movements revolved around the activities of the successor kings who inherited the parts of the empire which Alexander created. The Macedonian dynasties of the Seleucids at Antioch in Syria and of the Lagid Ptolemies in Egypt assumed such strength that they at times overshadowed the kingdom of Macedon in Greece. Consequently it can be readily appreciated that although states such as Athens and Sparta might assume a diplomatic role in Greek affairs in the third century, that role was likely to be as pawns in wider diplomatic struggles. Even within what constituted the old bounds of Greece federal institutions such as the Aetolian League and the Achaean League eclipsed the old powers.

The achievements of Alexander can be ascribed to the military resources that were at his disposal and to the tactical and strategic insight with which he deployed them, but the speed with which he achieved success was maintained partly by his keen political insight in handling relations with other communities. Now it cannot be pretended that over the short time and the vast area of his exploits any particular goal or unified policy can be discerned, for Alexander had to assume many guises both at different times and at the same time, but it is instructive to follow in outline the successive campaigns of his diplomacy.

Alexander immediately revealed himself as a successor who was intent on resuming the activities of Philip as leader of the Hellenic campaign against Persia. The decision was perfectly natural, for the general Parmenio had remained with a force east of the Dardanelles and the acquisition of resources in Asia Minor was the most obvious way to repair the financial straits in which Alexander found himself. Alexander's intention to take up the campaign begun by Philip involved the rapid settlement of affairs both with the Greeks and with Celtic elements in eastern Europe which were a source of danger to the north. There had been no concerted move towards revolt among the Greeks and so Alexander immediately requested that the League of Corinth appoint him as its leader. Naturally his opponents were slow to reveal themselves in their isolation. Resistance collapsed in Athens and Thebes, and Sparta alone held out, maintaining that her traditions prevented her from acting under the military command of another. There Alexander quietly let the position rest and was content not to exact retribution. On the other front with the Celts he swallowed his pride and concluded a treaty of friendship and alliance though heartily disliking them.[174] Military activity in the area diverted his attention and his preoccupation with the Taulantians diverted the attention of elements in Greece. For just as the absence of Philip encouraged the circulation of rumours, so too it was now believed that Alexander was dead and that the moment for revolt and freedom had arrived.

Alexander moved rapidly to contain the revolt and with such ease wrecked the powerful city of Thebes that the rest of the Greek world was stunned.[175] The other Greeks who had participated in the movement were quick to send their apologies to Alexander and he was content to let them as members of the League of Corinth seek their own revenge upon Thebes for all the errors and sins which they could attribute to her since the Persian Wars of the preceding century. To Athens he was lenient, for she was quick to fall in line and he needed her fleet to help in the invasion of Persia.

Alexander began his Panhellenic crusade in impressive style. After making a pilgrimage to Troy, where he was reputed to have placed wreaths on the tombs of the Homeric heroes Achilles and Patroclus, he proceeded to his first battle at the River Granicus. There he won a clear victory over the Persians and the Greek mercenaries who were employed by them. Then in order to emphasize the theme of his diplomatic propaganda, a crusade of liberation from Persian tyranny and retribution for Persian encroachments, he made two gestures. First the Greek mercenary prisoners were sent to Macedonia for penal servitude as a punishment for their treachery to Greece, and then he sent back as a dedication from himself and the Greeks three hundred suits of Persian armour for the Temple of Athena at Athens, the scene of Xerxes' outrage committed some one hundred and fifty years before. Thereafter he continued his liberation of Greek communities such as Ephesus,[176] which were, of course, obliged to accept liberation from Persia willingly or unwillingly. Alexander swept on with his campaign of releasing the Greeks of Asia Minor from Persian control, but there were many non-Greek communities, and for them too liberation was offered. At Sardis, for example, Alexander took over the Persian treasury and granted to the Lydians liberty and freedom to maintain their ancestral customs. At the same time he was careful to leave Macedonians in charge of their administration. In Caria the local ruler Ada was left as satrap and she adopted Alexander.

Alexander proceeded eastwards along Asia Minor and secured control of the ports, for he wished both to deny bases to the Phoenician fleet and to reduce his own dependence upon the doubtful loyalty of the Athenian fleet. But before he turned south along the Levantine coast to attend to Tyre and Sidon he fought a victorious battle at Issus, which gave him the entry to Asia proper. The battle was followed reputedly by a diplomatic exchange between Alexander and King Darius.[177] The latter despatched a letter asking for the return of his wife, mother and children and requesting that a treaty of friendship and alliance be concluded as had existed between their predecessors, Philip and Artaxerxes. Alexander for his part maintained that he had been drawn to attack Persia since the Persians had attempted both to subvert Macedon and to cause disaffection in Greece. Furthermore Darius had merely usurped the throne of Persia and by his defeat at Issus and subsequent flight had forfeited his rights to the throne. In future therefore communications between the two parties were not to be conducted as between equals but on the basis of recognition of Alexander as master of Asia. A little later, when Alexander was conducting the siege of Tyre, Darius again resumed the diplomatic initiative, for his forces proved no match for the

Greeks and Macedonians, and Alexander's interception of envoys to Darius from Greek cities, including Athens, Thebes and Sparta, at Issus removed all hope of diverting Alexander's forces. Darius made three offers, to give ten thousand talents in exchange for his captive relatives, to renounce all his domains to the west of the Euphrates in favour of Alexander, and to conclude friendship and alliance by the marriage of Alexander with Darius' daughter. Alexander truculently retorted that he had no reason to accept a part of Asia rather than the whole.[178] With that Darius gave up hope of making terms.

Alexander had every reason for confidence, since after Issus the capture of further treasure at Damascus put an end to his financial worries, the Phoenicians in general welcomed him although Tyre had stubbornly held out for neutrality, and Egypt remained, as ever, ready for liberation from Persia.

With the liberation of Egypt in 332 Alexander greatly strengthened his strategic grip on the eastern Mediterranean, bringing the coastline from the southern Balkans round to Egypt and Cyrene under unified control for the first time. Thereupon he returned to Asia to seek out Darius, whom he soundly defeated and put to flight once more at Gaugamela. Then at Babylon Alexander made a favourable impression once more upon Persian subjects, the Chaldaeans. He encouraged them to resume their traditional religious practices and ordered the reconstruction of the temple of Bel (Baal), which had been destroyed by the Persian King Xerxes. Twenty days' further march brought Alexander to the Achaemenid capital at Susa where, in addition to fifty thousand talents of silver, there were found all the treasures which Xerxes had removed from Greece. Among them were the statues of Harmodius and Aristogeiton; these were reputedly tyrant-slayers in the folk-memory of Athens, and so Alexander returned them to Athens, where they were erected in the Cerameicus on the road up to the Acropolis. Thus far Alexander had worn many guises but in the following year (330) he brought to a formal end his Pan-hellenic crusade. For then he arrived at Persepolis and burnt there the palace of the Persian kings, an act which he defended as retribution for the Persian destruction of Athens in 480 and for all the wrongs committed by Persia against Greeks.[179] After the capture of the summer capital at Ecbatana Alexander paid off the Greek forces of the League of Corinth and continued his campaign with a force of Macedonians and volunteers.

Thereafter Alexander continued to hunt down first Darius and then the pretender Bessus until he established himself as undisputed successor to Darius. His policy and his plans for the succession were not determined before his death, but he established many Greek and Macedonian communities in the vast tracts of Asia and sought ultimately some fusion of the Macedonian and Persian kingdoms. After the death of Alexander in 323 there was dynastic confusion of the sort which Demosthenes and others had long assumed to be endemic in Macedonian affairs, but even though Alexander's empire split into the three components of Macedon, Egypt and the Seleucid Empire the split was of little comfort to Demosthenes and his political heirs. For whereas Macedon, with a population estimated at about four millions, had established such a superior position in Greece, Egypt had a population about twice as great as that of Macedon and the Seleucid Empire could support a population of some thirty millions. In such company the old city-states, even when they could exercise their independence, were but as minnows. Lycurgus, the Athenian statesman who died in 325/4, instituted financial reforms to bring in revenues which exceeded those of the fifth century and enabled the accumulation of reserves greater than had existed in 431. The money was carefully spent on many projects including dockyards and the provision of a fleet of a size that had been customary in the fifth century, but such effort availed the Athenians little.

Indeed the final flourish of the naval power of Athens was observed in 322. For upon the death of Alexander the Athenians took the lead in organizing a coalition to obtain Greek independence from Macedon. Among the communities which joined the revolt were Boeotia, Thessaly, Illyria and most of the Peloponnese. In the so-called Lamian War the Greeks made some headway but in the naval engagement near Amorgus the Athenians were unable to gain control of the seas and so they sued for terms. The terms which the Macedonians dictated involved the suppression of the democracy at Athens, the installation of a Macedonian garrison and the surrender of the leaders of the revolt.[180] Demosthenes evaded capture by committing suicide. With the defeat of Athens the rest of Greece except Aetolia abandoned its resistance, but Antipater in reimposing Macedonian domination made little concession to Greek sentiment and made no pretence of reviving the League of Corinth, which had provided some minimal safeguards for the independence of the Greeks.

Macedonian control over the Greeks, however, was not as secure as it might have been, for quarrels between the leading factions and generals absorbed Macedonian energies and the position of the Kingdom of Macedon in European Greece became relatively much weaker

PAEONIA

LYNCESTIS

MACEDONIA

Crenides •

Pella •

Amphipolis •
Eion

Methone •
Pydna •

CHALCIDICE

• Olynthus

Potidaea •

Mende •
Scione

EPIRUS

THESSALY

Pherae •
Pharsalus •

Corcyra

Ambracia

Artemisium

ACARNANIA

Leucas

AETOLIA

Naupactus •

Thermopylae

LOCRIS

EUBOEA

Delphi
PHOCIS

BOEOTIA

Chalcis

LOCRIS

Chaeronea

Thebes

Eretria

Cephallenia

Coronea
Plataea

Tanagra

Delium

Oenophyta

Oropus

ACHAEA

Sicyon

ATTICA

Marath

Elis •

ARCADIA

Phlius •

MEGARA

Athens
Piraeus

Zacynthus

• Olympia

Mantinea •

Corinth

ARGOLIS

Salamis

Carys

Argos •

Aegina

Megalopolis •

Epidaurus

Ceo

Tegea •

Troezen •

Messene •

MESSENIA

• Sparta

LACONIA

Sicily

Rhegium •

Messana

Segesta •

Gythium •

Melos

Catana

Acragas •

Leontini

Gela •

Syracuse

Camarina

Cythera

miles   0   100 200
Scale   km 0   200 400

0   50   100 miles

0   100 200 km

Scale

Map II   Italy, Greece and the Near East

THRACE

bdera

asos

Samothrace

Imbros

Lemnos

alonnesus

cyros

Bosporus

Selymbria

Perinthos

Byzantium

Chalcedon

CHERSONESE

Proconnesus

Lampsacus

Sestos

Abydos

PHRYGIA

Methymna

Lesbos

Mytilene

Pergamum

LYDIA

Sardis

Chios

Erythrae

Colophon

Notium

Ephesus

Samos

Andros

Tenos

Priene

Delos

Miletus

CARIA

nos

Paros

Halicarnassus

Naxos

Amorgos

Cos

Cnidos

Thera

Rhodes

than that of the other constituent parts of Alexander's empire. Indeed its weakness was apparent when after Antipater's death his successor proclaimed the re-establishment of the freedom which the Greek states had enjoyed in the time of Philip and Alexander and the recall of those who had been banished. The weakness of Macedon was to endure until 276 when Antigonus virtually refounded the Macedonian monarchy. Even so Greek freedom remained a commodity which could be granted and revoked at will according as it suited the various Macedonian military barons, for there was no stability infused into the chaotic problems of the succession to Alexander until 281 when the Battle of Corupedium fixed the political boundaries of the successor kingdoms for some time. Meanwhile there were those who made attempts at re-unification, a policy which naturally affected the Greeks. Athens, for example, after the proclamation of Greek freedom in 319 re-established her democracy only to have it superseded in 318/17 for a decade at the dictate of Cassander, the son of Antipater.[181] During that decade, although the Athenians enjoyed efficient and sensible government under Demetrius of Phalerum, his position as 'epistates' or 'president' was akin to that of the former Peisistratid tyrants and he survived the next proclamation of Greek freedom and autonomy issued at the conference which the Macedonian military leaders called in 311 to share out power among themselves. None of the signatories of the agreement reached at the conference in 311[182] had any greater attachment to its terms than they had to the cause of Greek liberty. But in their renewed rivalry first Ptolemy and then Demetrius Poliorcetes made a bid for Greek support.[183] In 308 Ptolemy attempted to revive the League of Corinth for his own benefit, then in 307 Demetrius Poliorcetes restored to Athens not only her democracy but also those former outposts of empire, Lemnos and Imbros, and he went on to promise a Panhellenic assembly at which states would be able to discuss their problems. The year 302 saw the revival of the League of Corinth and the election of Demetrius Poliorcetes as its *hegemon*.[184]

There was little to unify the League in a common purpose and so it failed to find a role, while Demetrius similarly failed to find a role. For in 301 the Macedonian military leaders again staged a battle, at Ipsus in Phrygia. The battle left Cassander with his domain in Macedon and Greece, Lysimachus in Thrace and Asia Minor, Seleucus in the eastern provinces and Ptolemy in Egypt. Antigonus, who had come nearest to re-establishing Alexander's empire in Asia, was dead and his son Demetrius Poliorcetes, who had garrisons and bases in

Corinth, Chalcis, Demetrias and in the Piraeus, next to free Athens, failed to stake an effective claim and after a brief period as King of Macedon (294–288) drank himself to death while a guest of Seleucus.

From 281, however, there was some respite for the Greeks in their relations with the Macedonians, for the conflicts between the generals showed some signs of resolution and events even conspired to enable Athenians and other Greeks to find a common cause with Macedon as they had done under Philip and Alexander. At Corupedium in Asia Minor Lysimachus, who controlled much of that region and Thrace was killed in defeat at the hands of Seleucus, who himself was assassinated on his entry into Macedonia. Thereafter there was a satisfactory division of the successor kingdoms of Macedon, Asia and Egypt. There were however other pressures and movements of population which had their impact on the Greeks, for in 279, just over a century after a Gallic leader, Brennus, had descended with his horde upon Rome, another Brennus led a similar invasion into Greece. Just as in 480 the Greeks had united to resist the Persian invasions, so too there was now a measure of co-operation with Macedon to resist the invasion.[185] The day was not saved by the Macedonians and, as in 480, the invaders outflanked their opponents, who stood again at Thermopylae. Significantly the credit for the defeat of the Gauls went to the Aetolian League, but for the time being Antigonus Gonatas established himself in 276 as king to revitalize Macedon and basked in the acquiescence both of Athens, in spite of the Macedonian garrison in the Piraeus, and of Sparta.

Macedonian power in Greece was nevertheless far from absolute. For although the Seleucid monarchy was weakened by natural centrifugal forces, the emergence of an autonomous dynasty at the key point of Pergamum and the rivalry of Ptolemaic Egypt, there were at work two other influences besides the natural sentiments of Greek independence. First, and ominously for Greece, was Pyrrhus, King of Epirus, who challenged his Macedonian neighbour. Just as Alexander the Great had brought the Greeks into wider contacts in the eastern Mediterranean and beyond, so Pyrrhus by his activities in Italy and Sicily as well as Greece demonstrated that Greek affairs could become inextricably bound up with those of powerful states in the central and western Mediterranean, including emergent Rome. The second influence which worked against Macedon was that of the Ptolemies who not only occupied Greek cities in the Seleucid domains but also extended their naval influence to the Cyclades and by their diplomacy encouraged those in states such as Athens and Sparta who preferred the old ways of Greek independence.

Initially Antigonus Gonatas found the attitude of Sparta to be helpful for it was the failure of Pyrrhus in his attempt to win over the Peloponnese and to storm Sparta which led to the Epirote withdrawal. But the establishment of Macedonian garrisons at Demetrias, Chalcis, Corinth and the Piraeus, the 'fetters' of Greece, served as a reminder to the 'independent' Greeks of the true extent of their 'freedom'. Shrewdly Ptolemy was able to exploit the situation, for in Sparta there were those who, in the light of recent events, contemplated a revival of the old Peloponnesian League and in Athens Chremonides and his political associates looked back on the past with longing. Consequently c. 267–5 the two former leading states were once more drawn into alliance. The inscription which records the alliance survives almost complete, and it is ironic that whilst the document is one of the fullest and most effusive records in the diplomacy of the two states, making reference among other things to the solicitude of Ptolemy for the common freedom of the Greeks, it was one of the least effective treaties they ever concluded.[186]

Politically and diplomatically, however, all was not as bleak as might be imagined. The old states could not find a new role but formerly insignificant institutions took on a new lease of life, initially with Macedonian consent. The Aetolian League which earned credit for its role in repelling the invading Celts in 278 continued to grow in influence in the Delphic Amphictyony until it became the principal power in central Greece. After 280 the Achaean League developed from a local confederacy into a federation which incorporated most of the Peloponnese. In both leagues the principle of federalism was applied in such a way that no single state could be regarded as the dominant member and foreign policy and military organization were matters to be resolved by federal decision. It was of great significance when in 243 the Macedonian garrison was expelled from Corinth and in 241 Aratus, the general of the Achaean League, concluded an alliance with the Aetolian League.[187] With the Ptolemies confined to Egypt, the Seleucids preoccupied in Asia, and Macedon reduced to what it had been in the early years of Philip, it was still too much to expect that the movement which had begun with the League of Corinth would be consummated by a spontaneous union of the Aetolian and Achaean Leagues into a Panhellenic federation, but the two leagues in spite of the separatist tendencies of the Greek cities remained institutions with which eventually the Romans had to deal, and in the meantime they could command the respect of Macedon.

CHAPTER XII

ROME UNDERWRITES GREEK FREEDOM

EVENTS WITHIN THE PELOPONNESE saw a divergence of the interests of the two great leagues in Greece. Their quarrel was ended by the general peace which was concluded in 217,[188] but by that time the affairs of the Greeks and the Successor Kingdoms could no longer be settled in isolation. For already the Romans had come to control the Italian peninsula and Sicily. On that account they had an interest in promoting security in the Adriatic Sea and its coastal regions, which were the traditional resort of pirates. The Roman interest in that direction was plainly demonstrated in diplomatic form by the conclusion of a treaty in 228 between Rome and Teuta, the Illyrian queen.[189]

The policy of Rome at the time seems to have been devised with no ulterior motive in view, but by 146 the Romans were drawn into exercising their military might in Greece and bringing it fully under the control of their provincial administrators. In the fifth and fourth centuries the Persians had managed to secure an equilibrium at times by lending their support first to one Greek state and then to another. The Romans, however, found such manipulation more difficult; for they did not have the financial reserves such as were at the disposal of the Persian kings, whereas they did have by the late third century good reserves of well-trained military and naval manpower. Furthermore Persia had been accustomed to dealing with relatively few and small communities, whereas Rome could not manipulate the situation in Greece by remote control. For not only was there a multiplicity of interests as represented by the Macedonian monarchy, the great leagues and strong independent communities such as Rhodes, but there were too the monarchies in Egypt and Asia, of which Rome was nervous, and the links which her inveterate north-African enemy, Hannibal of Carthage, established first in Macedon and then in Asia.

The demonstration of Roman concern in Illyria was not directed against any Greek or Macedonian interest, but it constituted a new factor which was at least potentially a complication and at worst something which Macedon could not control. Furthermore the development was particularly unwelcome to the Macedonians at a time when their influence was being restored in Greece. For in 224 Aratus led the Achaean League into alliance with Antigonus Doson,[190] who turned out to be an effective occupant of the Macedonian throne when the Spartans had again attempted to restore their former position in the Peloponnese at the expense of the Achaeans. Antigonus used that alliance as a springboard to revive the Hellenic League,[191] which comprised most of the local federations and important states, except Athens, which previously had participated. According to precedent he was elected as hegemon, and led its forces to victory at Sellasia, a battle which in 222[192] concluded for Sparta the process which Leuctra had begun in 371. The position of Macedon was further strengthened by Antigonus' successor, Philip V. For the Aetolian League too had intervened in the Peloponnese, but after realizing that further campaigning against Philip and the Achaeans would be fruitless it was persuaded by Aratus and Philip to accept the situation and to conclude a treaty of peace.[193]

In 217 Agelaus, a statesman of Naupactus, had emphasized the need for peace and a consolidation of the ranks in Greece, in a famous speech which conjured up the spectre of what may be called a 'Roman peril'.[194] In fact his eloquence seems to have foreshadowed a Roman control of Greek lands, of which no Roman statesman could have dreamt at that time. In the year of the Peace at Naupactus, the Carthaginians under Hannibal carried all before them in their invasion of northern Italy at Lake Trasimene. Then in the following year came Hannibal's great victory in the south at Cannae, an event which seemed likely to lead to a Roman surrender. That prospect, however, receded owing to the strength of the Roman alliance and its hold upon central Italy. Hannibal, therefore, turned to build up a coalition which would distract Rome and strain her resources, and as Philip had clashed with a Roman fleet in 216 the obvious move was for the two of them to join in an alliance, which they did in the spring of 215.[195] Philip sent Xenophanes of Athens to Italy in order to conclude an agreement with Hannibal. The text of the treaty, as it has been set down by the historian Polybius, seems to have been drawn up on the assumption that Rome would continue to be a formidable power and in the hope that she could be brought to make peace short of victory. Macedon was committed not so much to send an army into Italy as to co-operate generally in the light of such military conditions as might prevail.

It further prescribed that in any treaty of peace the Romans were to be bound not to attack Macedon. It was natural that if Philip consorted with enemies of Rome, Rome should consort with Philip's enemies or potential enemies. After the interception of the Macedonian envoy who carried with him the text of the treaty, the Roman Senate set itself to guard against its effects. Marcus Valerius Laevinus for the Romans spent time in confidential discussions which led to an alliance with the Aetolian League c. 211.[196] Its terms, recorded by the Roman historian Livy, provided that the Aetolians should retain the land and buildings in any places captured in allied operations and that the Romans should seize any other kind of booty. Each of the contracting powers thus could obtain what it wanted most. Rome needed slaves to serve the landowners who were members of the Senate, and the Aetolian League wished to expand its membership or add to its subject towns. The agreement implied that Rome was not at that time anxious to acquire cities or territories in Greece, which would in any case have required protection. It may be asked why the Aetolians allowed Rome to enslave the inhabitants of Greek towns; the answer to that may be that if the Aetolians had any scruples they were scruples against themselves enslaving fellow-Greeks. In any case the main object of Laevinus' commission was to render Philip less likely to commit his troops to operations in Italy.

The alliances between Philip and Carthage and between Rome and the Aetolians brought with them the prospect of a massive extension of each of the areas of conflict, between Rome and Carthage and between Philip and the Aetolians, who had also made common cause with the Attalids of Pergamum in Asia Minor. The prospect of such a 'global' conflict receded before long. The Romans campaigned with increasing success against the Carthaginians in Italy and by the capture of the port of Tarentum they virtually secured themselves against any intervention by Philip. The Aetolians therefore found the Romans less inclined to provide help for their cause in Greece, help of which they were in greater need than had been anticipated before the alliance had been concluded between the Aetolians and Rome. There were two reasons for the changing situation in Greece; Pergamum had more immediate problems with her neighbours in Asia Minor, and the Achaean League, which had been led by the able diplomat Aratus, chose as his successor Philopoemen, a more able soldier, who had shown his mettle in the defeat of Sparta at Sellasia in 222. The cause of peace was therefore urged by many, not least by the Rhodians, whose trade stood to gain much from an end to conflict. The oppor-

tunity was seized by the Epirots who summoned a conference at
Phoenice, at which, as the Aetolians had already made their peace,
the Romans and Philip concluded peace for themselves and their
respective allies.[197]

The Peace of Phoenice might have seemed to symbolize the end
of Roman involvement and interest in Greece, the more so as Roman
security seemed assured by the subsequent surrender of Carthage.[198]
Disengagement, however, was easier to will than to practise, for just
as the Greeks had once been ready, despite their protestations, to
appeal to Persia, so too they now directed their appeals to Rome for
intervention. Just as the Persians had exploited political divisions both
between and within states so too did the Romans learn to do this,
but the impatience of Rome and her sense of honour, as well as the
ambition of her generals, led to different conclusions.

Philip used his position in Greece to join with Antiochus in Asia
against their common enemies in Pergamum and Egypt.[199] Pergamum,
Egypt and, as might be expected, Rhodes concerted their diplomatic
efforts and made an appeal to Rome for intervention. At Rome the
request was something of a political embarrassment, coming after a
period of prolonged war against Carthage, but excessive fear of the
combined power of Philip and Antiochus turned the issue in favour
of such a move. Initially there was no general enthusiasm in Greece
for Roman intervention in spite of Philip's transgressions. The Aetolians
had good reason not to place reliance upon Roman support and the
Achaeans were slow to break their alliance with Macedon concluded
in 224. The situation needed careful management but the Romans
had in Flamininus a man who was more than equal to the task. Not
only was he eager to succeed but also he was skilled in war and allied
to his diplomatic sense was a sound acquaintance of Greek ways gained
from his experience at Tarentum, a Greek city in Italy. His initial
military successes conciliated the Aetolians and Achaeans and culminated in Philip's defeat in Thessaly at the Battle of Cynoscephalae in
197.[200]

At the ensuing peace conference held at Tempe in the following
year Flamininus handled the situation well and Philip rose to the
occasion.[201] To those Greeks who wished to compound the defeat
of Philip with the elimination of his monarchy the Roman impatiently
replied that such a measure would merely open the gates to the
barbarian hordes in the north. The terms imposed by the Romans
demanded that Philip was to evacuate the cities in Greece and Asia
Minor and confine his authority to the area which constituted Macedon

in the mid-fourth century. Furthermore the evacuation was to be completed before the Isthmian Games of that year. The timing had been carefully managed by the Romans, for the Greeks assembled for the Isthmian Festival in a state of great excitement awaiting the expected Roman proclamation. For although Philip had been obliged to leave the 'fetters of Greece', Demetrias, Chalcis and Corinth, there were few who really believed that the Romans would relinquish all their positions in Greece whatever Philip had been obliged to promise regarding Greek liberty and institutions. At the meeting the herald announced that the states which had been subject to Philip were thenceforth to be free, exempt from tribute and subject only to their own laws.[202] At that the spectators could scarcely believe their ears. Freedom and independence are easier to proclaim than to implement but within two years Flamininus was in a position to withdraw.[203] States which had been for long in subjection and deprived of their institutions could scarcely be spontaneous recipients of freedom, but, somewhat ominously, Flamininus was equal to the task of dealing with the chaotic state of Greek politics and appointed councils and officials from the ranks of responsible propertied classes.

Once again an outsider had proclaimed Greek freedom and displayed an unwillingness to be continuously involved in Greek affairs by maintaining a physical presence. But whereas Persia had left the practical supervision to a leading Greek power the Romans themselves became responsible for detailed administration and adjudication, a task for which they were temperamentally suited and in which they were becoming well practised after taking over Carthaginian territory in North Africa, Sicily, Sardinia, Corsica and Spain. While Flamininus was involved in making his settlement in Greece there were signs of yet another crisis looming, for experience in the third century had shown that the affairs of Macedon, Aetolians and Achaeans were also the concern of Pergamum, Syria, Egypt and Rhodes. The weakness of Macedon led Antiochus to attempt the reoccupation of former Seleucid territory in Europe and Asia Minor while there were rumblings of discontent in the Aetolian League at the revival of the Thessalian and Euboean federations, which received Demetrias and Chalcis, and at the apportionment of Corinth to the Achaean League. Roman fears at the way in which the situation was developing were heightened by the flight of Hannibal, now in political exile from Carthage, to Antiochus in 195. It needed little encouragement from Eumenes of Pergamum and Rhodes to prompt Roman intervention by 191.

For some time the Romans had kept an eye on Antiochus. In the winter of 198/7 he had transferred his attention from Egypt to western Asia Minor, where his Seleucid ancestors had owned possessions. So long as their war with Philip had remained undecided the Romans had not taken any notice of his movements, but later they may well have thought that he was moving westward to help Philip, when in fact he was coming to help himself. After Philip's defeat the Roman commissioners, sent to Greece to settle terms with Philip, then tried to check Antiochus' progress by diplomatic protests, which ended in 196 with a visit to the king, who had just crossed into Thrace where too the Seleucids had held possessions. From this point it is instructive to relate in more detail the interaction of the Hellenistic diplomacy of King Antiochus with the new Roman influence.

Two cities in Asia Minor, Lampsacus and Smyrna, to which Antiochus had an ancestral claim, had applied to the Roman commissioners for inclusion in the peace which they were then drawing up with Philip. The reason for their request was that if it was granted then they might claim to be covered by the Roman declaration of freedom which was announced at the Isthmian Games by Flamininus. In this way Rome would be committed to protect them against annexation by an alien power.

Antiochus according to Hellenistic practice had an indefeasible claim to cities which had belonged to his ancestors. The Roman commissioners for their part had recently told Antiochus' envoys that their master must not attack those cities in Asia Minor which were independent nor make war on any of them. To that Antiochus, who was by then at Lysimacheia in Thrace, answered that the Romans had no right to dispute with him the status of cities in Asia Minor which had passed into the possession of one of his ancestors by right of conquest nearly a century before. The leader of the Roman commissioners demanded that the envoys from Lampsacus and Smyrna should be heard, but Antiochus silenced them: he refused to leave a decision to Rome, but prepared to submit the matter to arbitration by the Rhodians, who had a reputation as fair-minded judges and could not but rule that the cities had been subject to Seleucid Syria. The Romans could not deny the competence of the Rhodians to judge what was a matter of historical fact. It was beyond doubt that in those diplomatic interchanges between Roman envoys and a Hellenistic monarch the Romans were outmanoeuvred and all they could do was to report to the Roman Senate the line adopted by Antiochus as being unfriendly to Rome. For the time being the matter rested there since the Senate was preoccupied with complications in Spain and northern Italy.

In the next year (195) Antiochus, who had settled things to his liking in Asia Minor, including the annexation of the two cities in dispute, proceeded to overplay his hand. He sent an embassy to Rome to propose a treaty of friendship and alliance between his kingdom and the Republic. His envoys were referred to Flamininus and the Roman commissioners, who made an astute reply which widened the controversy: if Antiochus was prepared to withdraw entirely from Europe, Rome would not interest herself in Asia Minor, but if he remained in Europe, then Rome would claim the right both to protect her friends in Asia Minor and to add to them. The king had to accept one or the other of those alternatives. The envoys, not knowing what to reply, departed, asking the Senate only to take no action for the time being.

What was Antiochus to make of the Roman reply? He had declared his intention of restoring to the Syrian kingdom what it had lost whether in Thrace or Asia Minor. If this could be done without going to war with Rome, then that was so much to his benefit; if a treaty of alliance and friendship could remove Roman suspicions, then that was a small price to pay. His request was not politically opportune in Rome. It was to be expected that Flamininus at least was reluctant to forget the declaration at the Isthmian Games which had earned him so much praise. That declaration had been made in the name of the Senate, and the Senate was not likely to disown him. Furthermore Scipio Africanus, conqueror of Carthage and consul in 194, will have regarded Antiochus as dangerous if only because Hannibal was at his court. Where Rome had feared before she was apt to fear again. The upshot of the impasse was that Antiochus looked to find an ally among the enemies of Rome, and he found one in the Aetolian League which had felt cheated by Flamininus in view of its role in the defeat of Philip at Cynoscephalae in 197.

Encouraged by the attitude of the Aetolians, Antiochus landed an expeditionary force in Greece in 192. The Romans sent a force down through Macedon, outflanked at Thermopylae the forces which Antiochus had brought through Demetrias and Chalcis and proceeded to Asia Minor, where naval forces had been prepared by Rhodes and Pergamum. The Aetolians could achieve little after Antiochus' failure to hold Thermopylae, and all of his seventy-two thousand men and his elephants availed him little at the Battle of Magnesia in 190.[204] The architect of the victory on that day was Eumenes, King of Pergamum, the last in the line of the great Macedonian generals. Philip had wisely hurried to the help of the stronger cause and assisted in the Roman invasion of Asia Minor.

In 189 Rome reduced the Aetolian League to a second-class power by imposing terms which were designed to end its independent initiative in foreign policy and to destroy its leading position in the Delphic Amphictyony without leaving a power vacuum on the fringes of Macedon.[205] In the following year the conclusion of the Treaty of Apamea[206] with Antiochus presented the Romans with more difficulty, for both Pergamum and Rhodes expected to be rewarded at Antiochus' expense. The impatience of Rome at the insistence of the Rhodians led her to favour Eumenes of Pergamum, but, what was more important, in making her dispositions she was led into dispensing with the principle of autonomy for all Greek states in the area.

So far as the events concerning Antiochus' encounter with Rome can be interpreted in terms of diplomacy, they register a triumph of superior force, shrewdly applied by Rome, over the niceties of Hellenistic practice. The Roman Senate that had learned both to survive defeats at the hands of Carthage and to organize victory had not so much outwitted as outlasted the malice of her enemies and exploited the goodwill of her friends. Her own friendship had been of that specialized kind which does not forget that friendship may one day turn into enmity. Her word had in many respects been as good as her bond, but there was a suspicion that her bond had been written in evanescent ink.

CHAPTER XIII

GREECE PASSES INTO ROMAN DOMINION

IN THE LAST YEARS of the fourth century Antigonus Monophthalmos had a declared policy of maintaining the independence of the Greek communities. He was surprisingly scrupulous in observing Greek independence and, even where it would have been to his immediate interest to maintain garrisons or to exercise direct supervision, he refrained from doing so. The cities maintained and exercised that independence, but the bounds of prudence had to be carefully observed if the precarious balance was not to be upset. The real difficulty came not when a state wished either to be co-operative or to be hostile, but when it wished to be ostensibly independent or neutral, as in the case of Rhodes, which by its geographical situation and through its economic and naval power was able to stand aloof.

Rome too in the early second century had found her interests coincided with the maintenance of Greek independence, but the balance between principle and self-interest was even more difficult. Furthermore the delicate codes of conduct and expression which had been evolved in the diplomacy of the cities and kings could not be maintained so easily in dealings with a hard-headed and republican Senate at Rome. The Romans had dictated a settlement of Greek affairs and had a continuing interest in observing them. As a Mediterranean naval power Rome had interests beyond the Adriatic: it was to her interest to prevent large combinations of power by, for example, ensuring the separate existence of Syria and Egypt. Such a policy meant that in some communities certain elements or classes became clients of Rome and in other instances whole communities, such as Pergamum and Egypt, became virtually so.

The Romans were, therefore, caught in a cleft stick. They wished to have the benefits of controlling the Greeks without the necessity for intervention, yet intervention proved necessary to support their own interest or that of their friends. Brute force had been displayed at times but a sense of impatience brought with it the exercise of force on such a scale that all diplomatic dissembling and pretence was abandoned.

No sooner had Rome arranged a settlement of the affairs of King Antiochus and the Aetolian League than the seeds of trouble with yet another king and yet another league became apparent. The Romans looked on with apprehension at the dispute between Sparta and the Achaean League, but more concern was caused by Perseus, who succeeded Philip V of Macedon in 179. He set about strengthening his truncated monarchy and enhancing his prestige among the lower classes both within Macedon and outside.[207] Furthermore his marriage into the Seleucid family could do little other than alarm Eumenes of Pergamum, who was quick to denounce him to the Romans. They, in 172, made a concerted diplomatic move to unite his enemies by the despatch of envoys. A letter specifying fifteen complaints against Perseus was sent to the Amphictyons, who set up an inscribed copy at Delphi in the following year.[208] In that year the Senate voted to undertake war against him unless he gave satisfaction in respect of these complaints.

By 169 the Romans under Aemilius Paullus emerged victorious at the Battle of Pydna. Each decisive campaign provides the prelude to a settlement, but the Macedonian and other monarchies had been brought to terms before. A different kind of settlement was needed if a more permanent solution was to be found, especially as Perseus' initial success and the protracted campaign had caused the Greeks to hedge their bets by maintaining open or secret contact with both sides. Once more the Romans prepared to make a public announcement of their settlement, but it was no such occasion as Flamininus had organized at the Isthmian Games of 196. For at Amphipolis in 167 Aemilius Paullus announced on the one hand that the Macedonians were to be free, their monarchy was to be abolished and that Macedon was to be divided into four republics.[209] As for the other Greek communities, those elements which had supported Perseus were summoned to Rome to explain their conduct if they could. In Epirus one hundred and fifty thousand men were enslaved. The Romans also displayed their impatience with Antiochus Epiphanes, the Syrian king, and with Rhodes. In 169 Antiochus, who was conducting operations against Ptolemy in Egypt, was confronted with a demand to desist by the Roman Popillius Laenas on behalf of the Senate. The king asked for time to consider the demand with his friends, whereupon Popillius described a circle on the ground with a stick and forbade Antiochus to leave it before replying. Upon his compliance the king was greeted warmly and shaken by the hand.[210] Rhodes fared less well in 166. Economic recession had caused the lower economic groups to supplant those who had cultivated Rome and, although there had been a timely counter-revolution staged after the defeat of Perseus, the Romans were not inclined to treat Rhodes as an ally. She was deprived both of her territories in Asia Minor and of the basis of her economic strength by the Roman establishment of Delos as a free port.[211]

By 166 it was plain that Rome was prepared to assert her own interests in such a way that whereas her enemies could anticipate her wrath, her friends did not know what to expect. In Rhodes there had been room for doubt in a confused political situation, but Eumenes saw his loyalty to Rome rewarded by Roman recognition of the dissident Galatae. Nevertheless there had been no territorial annexation by Rome, and, although slaves had been carried off to Italy, neither Romans nor others were permitted to exploit the gold and silver mines of Macedon. Within the next twenty years it became plain that Roman terms needed more direct supervision. For in 148 there appeared in Macedon a pretender to the defunct monarchy at the head of a dissident movement, which required the presence of Roman arms to suppress it. This presence then acted as a reminder to others who were involved in local disputes that there was always a possibility of intervention, mediation or at least arbitration from an outside source. The recrudescence of the old dispute between Sparta and the Achaean League produced an appeal from Sparta to Rome. The Romans then sent to the League a demand not only that Sparta should be left independent but also that Argos and Corinth should be forced to secede. Needless to say the demand was unacceptable both to the League and to the prevailing popular elements in Argos and Corinth, where Roman envoys were treated with public contempt.

The year 146 saw drastic solutions applied by the Romans to their problems in Greece and elsewhere. Their political settlement of 167, which had involved dissecting Macedon and taking political hostages from the Achaean League and others, had failed. Therefore in the same year both Carthage and Corinth were ruthlessly destroyed. All other city defences in Greece were destroyed, and the great political leagues and, even if only temporarily, the ethnic leagues were dissolved.[212] Macedon, however, was reunited, placed under direct Roman rule and added to the list of Roman provinces. Elsewhere democracies were suppressed in favour of constitutions which were more amenable to Roman interests and which operated under the

eye of the Roman provincial governor of Macedonia. The durability
of Roman power in the eastern Mediterranean was confirmed in 133
when Attalus of Pergamum bequeathed his kingdom to the Romans,
as also Bithynia came to be bequeathed by its king Nicomedes to
Rome in 75/4. The formal extension of the Roman provincial apparatus
in the creation of the province of Achaea out of the rest of Greece
was merely an administrative measure taken by the first Roman
emperor, Augustus, in 27.

From 146 the Greeks were no longer free to quarrel with themselves or with their neighbours. There were, however, some compen-
sations, for the sack of Corinth and the dispersal of Corinthian works
of art in that year did not usher in an age of barbarism. This event
ushered in for the Greeks a period of one century and a half of
unparalleled peace and prosperity, during which the military victor
was taken culturally captive by the vanquished.

CHAPTER XIV

THE RECORDS AND PRACTICES
OF DIPLOMACY

SO FAR WE HAVE DEALT WITH the general political environment in which the Greeks conducted their inter-state relations. We have also traced in broad outline the external policy of states and the way in which various groupings and alliances were effected. In this the second part of the book it is the aim to examine in a more analytical manner the development of various institutions and means of diplomacy, and the expectations which the Greeks entertained in respect of this. Diplomacy, however, is a term which can embrace much or little. Here it is proposed to discuss the topic in those respects in which it is a means of achieving declared aims of public policy. Consequently we will not devote detailed attention to what might be described as International Law and those aspects of inter-state provisions which affect arrangements concerning individual persons, such as the rights of strangers, prisoners and property in time of war, which are of significance and for which there is evidence available for discussion. Furthermore, as in the world of medieval cities and states, there was some developed sense of religious ideals and moral scruples, but there was not an accepted body of International Law to which appeal could be made or which defied disobedience or misrepresentation.

Diplomacy was not viewed as a function of government to be set apart from other affairs such as those of war or finance. It was an aspect of political activity which in common with others required the deployment of knowledge, the art of persuasion and political *savoir-faire*. Therefore it did not become the subject of treatises in its own right. Handbooks appeared, for example, in the fourth century BC on military and financial management and skills but not on diplomacy. Even in those comprehensive works of political theory, Plato's *Republic* and Aristotle's *Politics*, there is little that touches specifically upon diplomacy or the political regulation of matters of peace and war. Plato is concerned that political leaders should realize the consequences of their action and that they should not be affected by motives of greed or ambition. Aristotle has an accurate understanding of Athenian naval power and strategy of the fifth century but in the regulation of state affairs he gives little advice on how to avoid war except to suggest that a state would find its citizens reluctant to vote for war if they were compelled to own property in border territories, where it would be exposed to enemy incursions.²¹³

As in the field of law so too in diplomacy there was comparatively little development of peculiar and specialized terminology. None of the Greek words used to describe types of envoy, *angelos* (messenger), *presbeis* (envoys or elders), or *keryx* (herald), specifically or principally denotes a role in inter-state affairs. Only the *proxenos* (consul) had a title which denoted such a role, and even that gave him no consequent official standing in his own state of residence. Many concepts of diplomacy that are current in modern times found no place in Greek language or practice. No theory of diplomatic immunity prevailed until the emergence of Roman power; until then envoys relied on the traditional codes of religion and hospitality in their movements. Concepts such as 'imperialism' or 'balance of power', with which the Greeks were familiar in their practical manifestations, could not be expressed conveniently in any common word or phrase. There was a rich variety of words to denote various kinds of treaties and alliances, but there was a disinclination even in official documents to use them all in their own peculiar sense. *Spondai*, basically libations, then by extension the agreement solemnized by the libation, was used extensively first to denote a truce, then as a synonym for an agreement or treaty in general. Even where there were separate words to describe a defensive alliance (*epimachia*) and an offensive/ defensive alliance (*symmachia*) the latter was used almost exclusively to denote alliance of either kind.

There are then limits upon the kinds of question which we can ask concerning Greek diplomacy and upon the extent to which we can pursue them. But although the historian traditionally goes through the motions of pleading the lack, if not the unsatisfactory nature, of the evidence, there is, as can be deduced from the narrative of the first part of this book, a wealth of material available, sparse though it may be in some particular respects. The information available is basically of two types, that which is recorded in publicly inscribed documents and that which survives in literature of various kinds.

Inscriptions survive in considerable quantity, for increasingly in the fifth century it became the habit to inscribe public decrees and documents on durable material such as stone. Many stones which record treaties or parts of treaties have come to light. In one of the riders of the Peace of Nicias in 421 Athens and Sparta agreed to inscribe the terms on stone not only in their own territory, but also at Olympia, Delphi and the Isthmus.[214] The fact that none of those inscriptions is known serves to underline the hazards of survival and discovery of archaeological evidence. The distribution of such evidence is by no means uniform, for the wealth and habits of the ancient Athenians and modern archaeological effort have ensured that a disproportionate amount of known material concerns Athens. Nor is it a question merely of modern archaeological emphasis, for in Sparta one will search in vain for appropriate inscriptions of the Classical era. Other centres have, of course, produced significant material. Epidaurus, for example, was the site of the discovery of an inscription which contains much of the text of the agreement of Antigonus and Demetrius with the Greeks for the revival of the League of Corinth in 302.[215] Delphi was the site of the inscription set up by the Amphictyons in 171 recording a copy of the complaints which had been transmitted by the Romans against Perseus of Macedon.[216]

Such documents may give the appearance of objectivity since they tend to be a record of diplomatic appointments, the award of honours, the terms of treaties and bare official resolutions which have but brief preambles. It must, however, be remembered that they are political documents in origin and set down official resolutions in a certain light. Invariably they do not record much of the background to transactions and even less are they likely to record two sides of an episode, by, for example, recording Perseus' reply to the charges made against him. One example of an inscribed decree which arouses our curiosity but fails to satisfy it is that which the Athenians set up on the Acropolis in 367.[217] In that year the Athenians appointed Coroebus of Sparta as their *proxenos* in the light of a report by Athenian envoys of his goodwill. The document survives almost entire and can be completely restored with certainty, yet it tells us nothing further about Coroebus' activity or the transactions between Athens and Sparta.

Often, of course, the inscriptions corroborate literary evidence and literary evidence provides a context for the material contained in the inscription. The inscription set up by the Amphictyons at Delphi in 171 corresponds with the account given by the Roman historian Livy of Roman complaints against Perseus.[218] Thucydides gives an account of the terms of the treaty agreed between Athens, Argos, Mantinea and Elis in 420 and adds details of the subsequent formalities, including the inscription of copies in the contracting cities.[219] A fragment of marble was discovered in 1876 near the Theatre of Dionysus at Athens and sufficient of the inscribed text remained to show conclusively that Thucydides' version corresponded with the wording of the officially inscribed text of the treaty.[220] In some cases a sufficiently good sequence of inscriptions survives to form the basis of an account which could not otherwise be set down. Thucydides, for example, gives but a thumbnail sketch of developments in the Athenian empire of the fifth century, with references to some of the major crises. Inscriptions enable historians to trace in some detail the centralized financial administration and the central political control established at that time over communities whose loyalty or institutions were in doubt. Similarly in the following century inscriptions provide the essential information on Athenian diplomacy both at the time when the Athenian Confederacy was established and in the preceding and subsequent episodes.

The literary material varies in form and content. The work of no historian survives in its entirety for the whole of the period under examination. Diodorus of Sicily, the Greek writer whose work dates from the period 60–30, was influenced by the notion of the unity of world history at a time when Rome had extended her control over the whole of the Mediterranean world and Greece. Most of his books survive in fragmentary form and those which substantially survive show that even then it was beyond the ability of one man to cope with the whole of known history. He had perforce to place an undue reliance upon the work of other writers rather than upon original research, but occasionally his 'scissors and paste methods' of compilation have preserved useful authorities. It is, for example, through his exploitation of the fourth-century historian Ephorus that much of our knowledge of the Common Peace survives. The majority of historians were content to write about the main wars, alliances and constitutions but had little reason to report all the diplomatic nuances. Herodotus, for example, a good historian of catholic interest, set down much about the Persian Wars and their aftermath, but showed a marked disinclination for the details of diplomacy, as did the Greek biographer Plutarch (c. AD 60–120), who wrote essays on the lives of the principal Greek and Roman statesmen. The Athenian historian Xenophon who wrote on contemporary Greek affairs from 411 to 362 was particularly interested in the education of leaders and in the interaction of leaders and events in certain situations. On occasions he gives us valuable insight such as in his report of the speeches of the three Athenian envoys, Callias, Callistratus and Autocles, who went to Sparta in 371.[221] He did not care for the documentary detail and so records little of what was actually concluded in 371 and completely omits from his work all reference to the Common Peace and even to the foundation of the Second Athenian Confederacy.

Historians of both Greece and Rome were keenly aware that the writing of history was essentially a literary exercise and so we cannot expect constant attention to minor detail or detailed digressions into undramatic technicalities. One method which they did employ to heighten the dramatic effect was to insert into their narrative speeches which were purported to have been given by participants in the events. These speeches may well not have been based on any documentary evidence in most cases, but in the case of Thucydides, who completed as a contemporary of the events a history of the great Peloponnesian Wars to 411, they did represent factors and arguments of which he and the participants were aware. Consequently it is salutary to read his account, for example, of the great debate in Athens in 433 when envoys from Corcyra sought Athenian help against Corinth.[222] In that debate there is argument over fundamental attitudes in diplomacy and, for the first time, a clear exposition of the notion of a balance of power. The fifth book of Thucydides is one of the most revealing discourses on the subject of diplomacy ever written. The drama lies both in Thucydides' account and in the events which surrounded the Peace of Nicias and its subsequent erosion. There are few periods of history in which diplomatic manoeuvring has been so complex and so futile, and Thucydides has preserved a very full account of it. The account contains an unusually high proportion of documentary reportage, either because the historian had insufficient time to edit it in purely literary form or because he thought it instructive to leave it as it was in the circumstances.

Of those historians who wrote of events after the horizons of Greek history were extended Diodorus continues to provide some continuity but Arrian (second century AD), who presents an excellent account of the activities of Alexander the Great, has little eye for diplomatic detail, except perhaps for some record of correspondence exchanged between Alexander and Darius. In the second century BC we are well served by the critical historian Polybius. He was a man of affairs in the Achaean League and was in the company of those who were taken hostage by the Romans after they had beaten Perseus of Macedon at Pydna in 168. His work dwells on the factors which led to the decline in importance of the Greek world and to the rise of Rome. Consequently not all of what he writes is of interest to the exclusively Greek historian, but his analyses are penetrating and as a conscientious historian he had regard for the documentary detail. From him, for example, we have the full details of the alliance signed between Carthage and Philip V of Macedon in 215.[223] Polybius, too, gives a fairly full account of the peace treaty concluded between Rome and the Aetolian League in 189.[224]

Polybius, however, was a literary historian as well as a political analyst and we cannot place the same reliance on his accounts of documentary material as we can in the case of the fifth book of Thucydides. Of that we do have some check. For the Roman historian Livy, who wrote at the turn of the first centuries BC and AD an account of Roman History from the beginnings, provides an alternative source at some points. Livy too had a conception of history as a decidedly literary, as well as moral, exercise, but at times his account of treaties seems to betray a closer relationship to the original document. In the case of the Roman treaty with the Aetolian League in 189 Polybius' account is generally fuller but Livy's version of the treaty is more specific and less of a literary paraphrase.[225] In dealing with the treaty of peace between Rome and Antiochus of Syria in 188 Polybius gives a fuller version of the details, but neither his version nor that of Livy survives in its entirety; nevertheless by a careful conflation of both versions what seems to be a full record of the terms can be established.[226] Such compilation and conflation of accounts is found necessary not only in modern analyses but also in ancient writings. Livy, for example, set down a generally received and agreed version of the treaty between Rome and Philip V in 196,[227] but then at the end recorded variant accounts of details set down by two early annalists, Valerius Antias and Claudius Quadrigarius, whom he used for his sources.

For full information on the practices of diplomacy there are few works of ancient literature which could be excluded from examination. For ceremonies regarding heralds and oaths we need to consult works of tragedy and comedy, for current public opinion on events comedies offer insights, for other details we need to consult the geographical accounts of Strabo and the travel guides of Pausanias. And so the list could go on. But it is the orators who should perhaps have the last word, for they were either the practising politicians or the men who taught the politicians how to practise. In particular the speeches of three men are especially relevant. Andocides, an Athenian orator and diplomat who went on a mission to Sparta in 392/1, was arraigned on his return. His brief speech in defence of his policy and mission survives under the title 'On the Peace' as the third in his collection. That work tends to be overshadowed by the speeches of two other Athenian orators and diplomats who became inveterate enemies after their embassy to Macedon in 346. They were Aeschines and Demosthenes. The evolution of Demosthenes' policy can be seen in many speeches, especially in the three concerning Olynthus (*Olynthiacs*) and the four tirades against Philip II of Macedon (*Philippics*). But far more instructive both for the formulation of policy and the methods and responsibility of the envoys for its execution are the three speeches of Aeschines which attack Demosthenes and his friends, and two speeches of Demosthenes (*On the Crown* and *On the Misconducted Embassy*) which attack Aeschines. Tantalizingly the speeches, though concerned with similar events, coincide in almost no detail. Nevertheless they serve to remind us that diplomacy is not so much a recondite activity for skilled practitioners as a manifestation of political will.

CHAPTER XV

THE AIMS OF DIPLOMACY

IN THE WORLD OF CLASSICAL GREECE the aims of diplomacy were conceived normally on quite a modest scale compared with later ages of maritime and imperial achievements. Diplomacy was directed mainly to the regulation of relations between small states or groups of states and their immediate neighbours.

The most common source of conflicts of interest was territorial ownership and rights of access. The result was that frequently the bitterest relations existed between neighbouring rather than distant states. Until the intervention of the Persians in Greece and the consequent changes caused by the establishment of substantial naval forces in the fifth century the main preoccupations of the Athenians were likely to be with the surrounding islands Euboea, Aegina and Salamis, which gave access to her shores, with Boeotia, which had a long land boundary with Attica, or with Megara, which had a common boundary with Attica and lay astride land routes to and from the Peloponnese. Spartan preoccupations were similarly local, especially with her Peloponnesian rival, Argos. Disputes were referred to arbitration, sometimes arbitration was offered and refused, and sometimes by agreement issues were left to be decided by a single military contest. But many settlements did not have an air of finality about them, for in view of the scale and conditions of ancient warfare it was difficult for a state to follow up its victory with territorial extension and military occupation on any large scale. Few states could either afford or provide the manpower, whether of citizens or of mercenaries, to maintain standing armies or sufficient forces to be stationed outside their own territory. Sparta, which until the early fourth century had the most powerful army, organized on a standing basis, needed its forces for internal security as much as for external campaigns. Such factors made the establishment of empire, as it has been known in subsequent ages, fairly difficult.

Forces and garrisons, both military and civilian, were sent out to maintain influence in other communities. The Athenians, for example, sent out settlers (*cleruchs*) to reside on land forming part of the territory of allied communities, especially those with which some difficulty had been encountered. Such an alien presence was a civilian settlement but it obviously had political and strategic implications, which led to resentment. Consequently in founding the Second Athenian Confederacy the Athenians promised not to establish such *cleruchies* or garrisons in allied territory, for they were offensive to local pride and sovereignty. Governors or official agents were occasionally sent out and welcomed by the recipient community. Potidaea, for example, in the fourth century welcomed an Athenian *cleruchy* for political reasons;[228] so too did Arcesine, on Amorgus, appreciate the presence of the Athenian governor Androtion, who supplied from his own resources a loan without interest, for which the community gave public thanks.[229]

Just as unusual economic growth and the remarkable development of Athenian naval power in the wake of the Persian Wars enabled Athens to devote her resources to an unprecedented extent to affairs outside Attica, so too Sparta, harnessing the resources of the Peloponnesian League and receiving Persian subsidies, was drawn into activity beyond her immediate neighbourhood. As Sparta fought Athens and took over her subjects and allies so too she was obliged to stretch her resources of manpower in order to install garrisons and governors (*harmosts*) in other communities in the late fifth and early fourth centuries. The *harmosts* were appointed to work with a local committee of politically reliable men who were drawn from the ranks of oligarchs. Invariably the committee consisted of ten men (*decarchs*) and was supported in appropriate cases by a small Spartan garrison. Of the *harmosts* appointed one of the best known is Clearchus, the Byzantine *proxenos* or representative in Sparta, who was sent to Byzantium in the final period of the Peloponnesian War after its oligarchic revolution and secession from Athens.[230] The appointment of these officials by Sparta was associated with the repressive policies of Lysander, and since they were dependent upon the support of only a minority in a community their position was precarious and unpopular. Typical of the men appointed was Callibius, whose brutality and high-handed conduct led to his early recall from Athens to Sparta in 404/3.[231] Even with such reliance upon local sympathisers Sparta had insufficient citizens or even non-citizens under arms to give them adequate support. In addition Spartan men were rendered socially and politically unreliable by such service abroad and so the system of *harmosts* gradually broke down by the time of the King's Peace in 387/6. Sparta's last such intervention was in Thebes in 382 in an attempt to install a governor, Phoebidas, with a garrison to support a minority régime, but the Thebans successfully staged a counter-revolution in 379.[232] The Spartan diplomacy of those years, which sought to extend her influence beyond the capacity of her resources, was so counter-productive that it led to the end of Athens' diplomatic isolation and the re-emergence of Athens as a major power at the head of a new confederacy whose purpose was to protect the freedom of the Greek cities from Spartan oppression.

If in the fifth and fourth centuries neither Athens nor Sparta had the resources to protect or control far-flung points, with the support of either popular democrats or oligarchic minorities, it was not likely that any other city-state could entertain such notions. The extension of the power of Macedon after Philip's victory at Chaeronea in 338 brought in a new factor, for the Macedonians had as great reserves of military manpower as the rest of the Greeks together could muster, but even so the Macedonians were not inclined to spread their power by detailed military occupation and were cautious even in their demands for political hostages. It served their purpose to ignore certain dissidents such as Sparta and to make their presence felt merely by the installation of garrisons at key points such as Corinth, Chalcis, Demetrias and the Piraeus. Such control enabled them to forestall combinations against them, though even then they did intervene in internal politics of other states from time to time, to install, for example, the puppet régime of the surprisingly efficient and competent Demetrius of Phalerum in Athens (317–307).[233]

The establishment of independent colonial settlements was a method of extending strategic influence or confirming a position already held. It was, for example, symptomatic of Megara's commercial and strategic interest that she founded Byzantium and Chalcedon on opposite sides of the southern end of the Bosporus; but such links were of little direct benefit to the immediate and local interests of a state and they did not have the significance of modern colonial outposts, for they were constitutionally independent and sovereign units. Colonists were invariably despatched far afield, not to support distant commercial interest, but in the search for vacant land in which to settle surplus population. That involved movement from Balkan Greece to the far east and west of the Greek world, that is to such regions as Italy, Sicily, Provence and Asia Minor. Naturally strong cultural and religious bonds existed between colony and mother-city (*metropolis*) and the latter could expect to be regarded with deference and respect in a way which did not need to be described in contractual form. Nevertheless as such communities were politically sovereign, bonds tended to weaken, and as the great movements of colonization were over by the late seventh century they did not significantly affect the patterns of diplomacy from the fifth century onwards. The passage of time and the interposition of distance weakened ties, but even socially the colonial population initially might not represent a cross-section of the founding city; for certain social or political elements might be drawn to emigrate and so predominate in a foundation. Sometimes a foundation had more than one sponsoring mother-city, thus finding its loyalties divided, as was the case with Epidamnus founded jointly by Corinth and Corcyra.[234] For all those reasons it caused no surprise when Byzantium, the foundation of Megara, was in alliance with Athens, the enemy of Megara. Similarly there was nothing contradictory in a situation whereby Potidaea was in the Athenian alliance, yet as a colony of Corinth, the enemy of Athens, it received Corinthian governors.[235] Nevertheless that was a situation which the Athenians set about changing for their own security.

A conspicuous example of a colony which retained links with the mother-city was Tarentum, founded in southern Italy by Sparta at the end of the eighth century. Those links persisted even after democracy was established in Tarentum c. 475 and the colony proved to be a useful strategic outpost for the enemies of Athens at the time of the Sicilian expedition. Then when the Spartans and Corinthians despaired of their cause in Sicily and in Syracuse, the Spartan commander Gylippus was able to find a haven in Tarentum,[236] which had previously closed its gates to the Athenians. The ties persisted during the following century, for even a generation after the Spartan débâcle at Leuctra Spartan forces were sent out to assist Tarentum in dealing with pressures from the tribes of the interior of Italy.[237]

In the search for security a state could further its aims either by the acquisition of allies or by pursuing the ideal of self-sufficiency, thereby at the same time avoiding the need for friends and reducing the risk of incurring enemies. Self-sufficiency was not always easy to achieve, even in a primitive agricultural community which lived for the most part at or a little above subsistence level, as did most Greeks, and isolation could be attained rather by geographical environment than by political will. Corcyra provides the classic example of a community which sought to avoid involvement in alliances and being drawn into disputes by the activities of other parties. The envoys of Corcyra

acknowledged the folly of their former policy when they arrived in
Athens to seek alliance in 433.[238] That policy had not been altogether
without its benefits, for Corcyra had sought to achieve status as an
open port of call in a geographically isolated position; the policy
became a folly only in the circumstances which brought her into
dispute with a stronger naval power, Corinth.

It was possible for states to adopt a position of neutrality, either
by formal declaration or by treaty. Argos provides the most obvious
example of a state which adopted a neutral stance. It was not capable
of serious resistance to Sparta and it did not wish to follow Sparta,
its jealous neighbour. In the period of the Persian invasions and in
the first ten years of the Peloponnesian War to 421 it maintained a
neutral position.[239] Neutrality, however, was rather a sign of weakness than of military strength and offered no effective protection, and
in 446/5 Athens and Sparta made specific provision in their treaty
for the voluntary recruitment of neutral states to their respective
alliances.[240]

It was usually a reaction to a danger rather than an abstract anticipation of some situation that led states to seek allies. Unnecessary
alliances always involved some commitment and often there were
too many possibilities for intelligent prevision. The search for allies,
even in a local dispute, tended to lead communities away from their
immediate neighbourhood, and a dispute between minor communities
could soon involve the major states. A typically obvious move for
Athens to make in the course of a dispute with Sparta was to encourage
Argive pretensions in the Peloponnese, and we find Athens in alliance
with Argos when Athens was countering Spartan activities in 459,
420 and 395. An obvious move for Sparta to make under such circumstances was to involve Athens on a second front, for example in
Boeotia. Athens would then have the possibility of continuing the
game of diplomatic chess by finding friends on the other side of
Boeotia in Thessaly. Disputes between Athens and Boeotia invariably
involved competition for the support of communities in Euboea,
which as an island stretching along the coastline of both Attica and
Boeotia was a regular diplomatic battleground.

The larger states foresaw most of the obvious possibilities and came
to see situations repeat themselves. They were all acutely aware of
their individual and separate needs and consequently even when they
were in alliance they were wary allies. They easily slipped from
friendship to enmity. The smaller states were aware of the way in
which they could turn such situations to their advantage and so

involve the larger powers. A good illustration of that is the dispute which arose in 435 between Epidamnus and Corcyra. Athens and Sparta had no immediate interest in the dispute, but by a chain reaction in the search of the antagonists for allies they and their respective alliances became involved. Consequently a minor issue became the immediate cause of the Peloponnesian War. Phocis and Locris were two other lesser communities whose disputes had wider ramifications. In the early years of the fourth century they were in conflict, and as Locris had the backing of Thebes Phocis appealed to Sparta, which was eventually drawn into the war.[241] If it was easy for the smaller powers to play upon the susceptibilities and suspicions of the larger powers, who were ever concerned to watch the balance of power in the Greek world, the latter too exercised considerable caution at times, knowing that they might be drawn into an unexpected sequence of events over which they had little or no control. When Corcyra appealed to Athens for help in 433 her envoys were careful to explain how there were three naval powers of any consequence in Greece and to point out that the adhesion of Corcyra's navy to Athens would guarantee Athenian naval supremacy, whereas if her navy joined that of Corinth then Athens would be in a weak position. Envoys of Corinth came to Athens to point out that their state in 439 had recognized the impropriety of intervening in a dispute between two allies by arguing against Peloponnesian inclinations to help Samos in her revolt from alliance with Athens.[242] They stated that Corinth expected Athens to display similar consideration in return by refraining from intervention in the argument between Corinth and Corcyra over Epidamnus. The Athenians listened carefully and acknowledged the force of the Corinthian arguments, but after weighing up the risks decided to make a defensive alliance with Corcyra,[243] hoping that Corcyra's navy would thus be secured in friendly hands but calculating that war would not automatically stem from such a move. Sparta for her part was not quick to declare war upon Athens; Corinth, Megara and Aegina had to bring considerable pressure to bear on her before she decided to move against Athens in 432/1. Similarly in 395 when Phocis appealed to Sparta against Locris and Thebes the Spartans were slow to intervene and suggested first that Phocis take the matter to arbitration. Eventually Sparta was obliged to intervene to prevent the erosion of her position and authority. Athens too in 395 was slow to make any formal and decisive move to achieve independence from subservience to Sparta and acquiescence in her policy, which had characterized their relationship since Sparta's victory in 405/4. In spite of growing signs of independence in Athens and in spite of Theban assurances that Athens and Thebes together could outmatch a Sparta bereft of allies the Athenians moved cautiously, if unanimously, by signing only a defensive treaty with Thebes.[244]

The Persian invasions of Greece in the early fifth century changed the diplomatic map of Greece and hastened the day of the great hegemonial alliances. Athens would in any event have developed her naval strength, but the speed and unprecedented scale of that development was determined by the need for effective and co-ordinated naval resistance to Persia. Athens was not instrumental in creating a naval alliance; she was put at the head of an existing and far-flung alliance which incorporated many communities[245] scattered in the Aegean and Ionian seas and on the coast of European Greece and Asia Minor. Before that time Athens had given support to the attempted revolt of the Ionian Greeks from Persia in the 490s, but was not heavily committed, and Sparta despite her alliance of c. 550 with Lydia[246] had been reluctant to be drawn into distant adventures. Thucydides was fascinated by the phenomenon of naval power and explained how in the second millennium King Minos of Crete had been enabled by wielding it to extend his influence over widely spread communities of the Aegean. Thucydides argued too that the alliance led by Agamemnon, welded by fear as much as by friendship, would have been ineffective but for the existence of naval power, which enabled common action to be taken against distant Troy.[247] In the fifth century in the wake of the Persian Wars, when Athenian naval influence straddled the seas from Asia Minor to Italy, appeals to her for intervention became more common; and similarly Athens' principal rivals or opponents such as Sparta, Corinth and Thebes tended to become involved. The extension of the naval activities of European Greeks and their involvement in Asia Minor brought them into more frequent contact with Persia – and not always as foes.

Naval armaments were costly; they could not be levied and disbanded as lightly as could land forces to meet the needs of brief campaigns. The burden of expense meant that supporting alliances of a naval power had to be held together more closely and thoroughly. Persia realized these factors and instead of despatching large expeditionary forces tried to keep the major Greek powers at bay by playing off one against the other. Persian support was instrumental in helping Sparta to match Athens' efforts by sea in the last stage of the Peloponnesian War, and for a substantial period in the late fifth and early fourth centuries the relative successes and failures of Athens and Sparta were a measure of Persia's role in redressing the balance of forces in Greece. In that period Sparta did extend her influence outside the Peloponnese, for she took former allies of Athens under her wing; in 399 she answered the appeal of Miletus for help against the Persian menace[248] and in 382 she set up a garrison in Thebes while organizing a force in answer to the appeal of Acanthus for the dissolution of the Chalcidic League.[249] Essentially however Sparta's social and political organization rendered her unsuitable for such distant activities and she was basically a Peloponnesian power. Athens on the other hand headed the largest alliances, based on the adhesion of many small maritime communities; the Delian League consisted of over two hundred member-states and in the fourth century the Second Athenian Confederacy had more than seventy members.

The economic resources of a state were of course a factor in war and diplomacy, for the reserves of men and material determined the kinds of campaign which could be sustained and the goals of policy which could be entertained. Sparta, for example, had few commercial interests and no silver mines such as Athens was able to exploit at Laurium. Consequently the acquisition of naval power by Sparta required far more than the mere passing of a resolution in the Spartan assembly.[250] One of the strongest incentives which Philip and Alexander of Macedon had for invading Persia was not so much to take upon themselves a Panhellenic crusade as to gain access to the Persian treasuries, whose eventual capture solved their problem of shortage of money. Athens, too, was influenced by what we would term economic and strategic goals. She was dependent upon sea power and free navigation to maintain essential supplies of cereals, especially from the area of the Black Sea. Accordingly her diplomacy was geared to maintaining friendly relations with rulers in that area and to controlling naval bases. In the latter respect she felt unable to contemplate any diplomatic settlements which did not recognize her claim to Lemnos, Scyros and Imbros, staging posts on the naval route from Athens to the Black Sea. Similarly, for many decades she tried to ensure recognition of her claim to Amphipolis,[251] a strategic point which provided access to supplies of timber and the mineral wealth of Pangaeus. Andocides, in pleading for his return to Athens from exile in 399, stressed the benefits of supplies of timber and cereals he had secured for Athens through the relations which he had maintained during his absence with the rulers of Macedon and Cyprus.[252] The Thebans benefited from the Peloponnesian War by appropriating

Athenian livestock and chattels, and in war generally the victor stood to profit by booty, in cash and in kind, and by the sale or ransom of captives.

The strategy of war at times dictated the direction of economic measures. One of the clearest forms of economic offensive was the imposition of sanctions by Athens against Megara before the Peloponnesian War broke out.[253] Then a blockade was declared in order to cripple Megara's trade, either locally or in the Aegean and the Black Sea. The Athenian ability to survive in war depended partly upon her capacity to withstand a direct siege but even more upon her ability to maintain imports of essential cereals. It was Spartan success in interrupting those supplies which brought Athens to terms in 405/4 and 387/6. It was likewise a threat to do this by Philip of Macedon which stung Athens into the diplomatic and military initiative in 340/39.[254]

In spite of the importance of economic considerations, war and diplomacy were not ultimately directed by motives of economic imperialism or mercantilist enterprise, although some would argue that Athenian intervention in Sicily in 416/5 was affected by such motivation. The state in the ancient world had the responsibility of supervising' supplies and controlling internal markets in a few basic commodities such as cereals and olive oil, but it had no vital interest or responsibility in producing, promoting and marketing goods. Even basic commodities were handled by private contractors and entrepreneurs. Sectional interests did make themselves felt in the political assemblies when proposals were made and voted, but electorates for the most part consisted of men who lived on the fruits of a low-level agricultural economy.

Xenophon tells of one campaign which did attract participants by the expectations of gain which it aroused. At the beginning of the fourth century King Agis of Sparta marched out with a force, firing Elean crops, felling trees and capturing an abundance of slaves and cattle. News of the scale of the plunder attracted many volunteers from Achaea and Arcadia, and, as Xenophon puts it, the expedition turned into an exercise for providing provender for the Peloponnese. That, however, was not the motive for the expedition, for which there were clear political reasons which had given rise to many previous acts of hostility from the time of the alliance between Elis and Athens in 420.[255]

Treaties and alliances were normally concluded for immediate and pressing reasons, not for remote contingencies; once those immediate

reasons ceased to be an active consideration the diplomatic arrangements which had been made to satisfy them tended to lapse. Some
treaties did endure for long periods. The treaties of peace concluded
by Sparta and Argos in 451/0[256] and between Sparta and Mantinea
in 418/7[257] lasted for their full term of thirty years. Other agreements were less specific and were superseded by events; the defensive
treaties which were signed by Athens and Corcyra in 433 and by
Athens and Boeotia in 395, whilst they mentioned no specific enemy,
were conceived specifically to counter the activities of Corinth and
Sparta respectively and so could not be expected to persist. The great
Athenian naval alliances of the fifth and fourth centuries were, in
origin, specifically directed against Persia and Sparta respectively; they
were not conceived between friends as alliances which were to cover
a variety of contingencies, although Athens sought in practice to take
advantage of the alliances for other purposes. The nature of the
administration of states, which lacked bureaucracies and depended
upon the ascendancy of politicians and régimes of the moment, makes
it more likely that short- rather than long-term aims would be upper-
most in political and diplomatic operations. Of course in purely local
or regional affairs certain strategic requirements and considerations
persisted, such as those of Sparta within the Peloponnese; also in
some states, such as Sparta, the conduct of politics was less volatile
than in others, such as Corcyra. Athens in the two decades before the
Peloponnesian War was enabled by the peculiar political ascendancy
of Pericles to pursue a fairly consistent and restrained policy designed
to secure strategic position in the longer term. The aim then was to
avoid too great an extension of activities and to build up military,
naval and financial reserves. In the period after the alliance of Athens
with Thebes in 395, however, no such firm hand was at the helm
in Athens, and short-term considerations prevailed against Andocides'
advice to conclude a peace with Sparta in 392/1 on relatively favourable terms, terms which in the event had to be accepted within five
years.

In view of the multiplicity of states and the nature of their government it is surprising that many alliances were as durable as they
turned out to be. In some respects diplomacy appeared to be a negative
and defensive reaction rather than either a positively constructive or
altruistic activity, but even small communities did not adopt fatalistic
or pessimistic attitudes. For although a few large states such as Athens,
Sparta, Thebes, sometimes Persia, and, later, Macedon could have a
decisive influence on affairs they never all stood together. Their

suspicions and their several strategic requirements led some of them now into alliance or even into professions of friendship, now into conflict. Such a situation always engendered hopes and fears in smaller states and the factions within them of a reversal of fortune once it became the habit for the larger states to intervene far beyond their own borders. Early in the fourth century Elis fully realized that she faced overwhelming odds in refusing to accept Spartan demands. But recent history had shown that Argos, Elis and Mantinea managed to stand in alliance with Athens in 420,[258] and even if that alliance had been ineffective and was not in immediate prospect of revival after the Athenian defeat of 405/4 there were other communities in the neighbourhood of Elis whose influence Sparta was likely to view with even less favour near Olympia. Consequently Elis and Sparta in 400 concluded peace and alliance on terms which were not too unpalatable to the Elean democrats.[259]

As can be seen in the case of Elis war did not necessarily, as is so often stated, signify the failure of diplomacy. It is true that before wars were declared civilized diplomatic preliminaries were observed. Diplomatic positions were adopted, demands and offers were made, and challenges to arbitration were issued. Indeed there was a feeling that a state was obliged to put itself, at least in the eyes of its own army, in a morally just position. After the shocks received in the first period of the Peloponnesian War from 431 there were many Spartans who feared that their state had failed to establish such a position and consequently was suffering divine retribution in the reverse suffered at Pylos.[260] Among diplomats themselves there was always the notion of achieving feats comparable with those which generals could achieve only by war. For all that, war was usually but a preliminary to further diplomacy. Enemies became friends, but if that did not always happen, only rarely was a community or a town totally erased or removed by war. The destruction of Olynthus in 348[261] and that of Thebes in 335[262] by Philip and Alexander of Macedon respectively were acts of unusual severity, and even then there was a reconstruction of Thebes within twenty years[263] and an incorporation of the defunct Olynthus in a new town in 316[264] under Macedonian auspices. It was normal for an unconditional surrender, such as that of Athens in 404 and that of Olynthus in 379 to Sparta, to precede the imposition of terms in the form of an agreed treaty. If conquest and occupation of hostile territory brought with them practical problems at least political friends could be installed in power and a position of diplomatic influence or leverage could be established.

After Athens' defeat in the Peloponnesian War there were parties who called for the complete destruction of the city, and there is little doubt that the victors had the capacity to accomplish that, for the only friends whom Athens had anywhere among either Greeks or barbarians were in Samos. The Spartans, however, declined to adopt such a policy,[265] for they realized that their axis with Thebes was one of convenience and not necessarily durable. Thebes was, after Sparta, the second strongest power on land, and Sparta preferred to have as many viable communities as possible between Laconia and Bocotia.

War could be economically disruptive, though less so in ancient agriculturally based communities, and socially and psychologically destructive, as it was in the generation of the Peloponnesian War;[266] but it could also be productive of positive attitudes. If we look back once more at the war between Sparta and Elis, we find that it did not result merely in peace, but in peace and alliance. The Peace of Nicias, concluded in the spring of 421 between Athens and Sparta, was followed in the summer by an alliance between them,[267] and there can have been few less auspicious occasions or signatories than in 346 when Athens and Philip of Macedon contracted both peace and alliance.[268] Sometimes alliance between former enemies was necessary to enable them to join in coercing reluctant allies; Sparta certainly hoped in 421 that her alliance with Athens would bring recalcitrant Peloponnesian allies to heel. Argos and Sparta had fundamentally opposing interests within the Peloponnese; it was not possible for both of them to live in harmony without dispute, yet both recognized that a state of permanent war was ruinous. Accordingly in their diplomacy they were inventive enough, not to eradicate a cause of war but to limit by diplomatic contract the scale of a dispute. In 420 the Argives were anxious to conclude a peace for fifty years without surrendering their title to the disputed territory of Cynuria and so they successfully asked for the following concession: that in the absence of plague or war in Lacedaemon or Argos it should be permissible to issue a formal challenge to settle the dispute over the territory by a battle; if the challenge was taken up the battle should be limited to the disputed area and there was to be no right of pursuit across the frontier of Argos or Lacedaemon.[269]

Ideological considerations were apparent in the aims and practice of Greek diplomacy, but they were largely evident as pretexts and material for propaganda. No state had such a deeply ingrained faith in its own political system as to lead it to attempt to convert with a missionary zeal others to its ways. A certain polarization of democratic and oligarchic communities around Athens and Sparta respectively was apparent in the fifth century, but both of those states were prepared to work with régimes of differing complexions. In any case democracy and oligarchy were not regarded as opposite terms and there were many varieties of each form of constitution, as can be seen readily from even a brief glance at Aristotle's *Politics*.

In most communities there was acute rivalry at some stage between political factions. Sometimes political antipathy took the form of a struggle between oligarchs and democrats, at other times it did not. Invariably, however, protestations of patriotism did not prevent factions from seeking external support for their position. The result was that frequently at a time of crisis a state was unable to present a united front to its opponents, who before engaging in full-scale war would employ political means, subversion or diplomacy, to achieve their aims. The possibilities of diplomatic and political intervention were enhanced by the constant presence of a potential 'fifth column' either resident within a state or in exile from it. Indeed many disputes arose from the appeals of exiles seeking assistance for their restoration as well as from appeals of factions still present in cities. In return for assistance from another state a faction would be expected, and indeed would find it beneficial, to follow a policy of co-operation with that state.

One of the clearest indications of a change of policy associated with a change in the political leadership in a state is evident in the policy of Thebes after the Peloponnesian War. The political group built around Leontiades concentrated on co-operation with the Spartans in defeating and suppressing the Athenians. The opposing faction, led by Ismenias, found itself able to exploit the situation when Sparta's allies were disenchanted with the Spartan propensity to disregard them and their interests once victory was secured.[270] Then when support was offered from outside Ismenias gained the upper hand and subsequently requested an alliance with Athens. The Persians realized that much could be achieved at that level and they too exploited the situation after the Peloponnesian War. For they sent round as their agent Timocrates of Rhodes to distribute fifty talents wherever it might be most effective in helping the political opponents of Sparta in the Greek states.[271] Ismenias and his group were among the Persian beneficiaries in Thebes. In such cases the borderline between personal greed and political motivation was a precarious one. At the onset of the Persian Wars of the fifth century the Thebans were reputed to have told the Persians that invasion was unnecessary since they could achieve all their aims by the appropriate distribution of money.[272] Philip of Macedon too was alleged to have achieved his ends through bribery on a grand scale. At the outbreak of the Peloponnesian War in the preliminary diplomatic manoeuvring the two sides presented one another with various diplomatic demands. Sparta demanded that the Athenians should expel the Alcmaeonids in accordance with the ancient curse upon their family.[273] The Spartans could not hope that their demand would actually result in the expulsion of Athens' democratic leader, the Alcmaeonid Pericles, but at least it gave them a moral stance and helped to expose the position of Pericles, who was not without his political opponents in Athens. At other times the surrender or extradition of politicians was demanded and granted when one state was in a greatly superior position. Thus the surrender of Demosthenes and other leading Athenians of the anti-Macedonian cause was demanded by the Macedonians on more than one occasion.

As Athens and Sparta were the leading examples of democracy and oligarchy political factions in other states tended to set their sights accordingly in the fifth century. Whereas Athens had been prepared to work with non-democrats in her allied communities, when intervention proved necessary to her aims she stepped in to install democratic régimes in the expectation that they would have a greater inclination, by sympathy and dependence, to work with her. At some time before 453/2 Erythrae was in the hands of a small faction which looked towards Persia for support. That was incompatible with membership of the Delian League, whose activities were directed supposedly against Persia, and so the faction was driven out and a democratic régime was installed under Athenian protection.[274] Such an Athenian policy was not entirely devoid of embarrassment for allied democratic factions, but it was effective, for the Delian League did not disintegrate until the widespread adoption of oligarchy in member states. The democratic régime at Samos, supported by the Athenians after the Samian revolt of c. 439,[275] remained loyal until the end of the Peloponnesian War[276] and played a valuable role in the re-establishment of democracy in Athens after the oligarchic coup there in 411.[277] So difficult was it for the Peloponnesians in that war to obtain diplomatic leverage by promising liberty to Athens' allies and subjects or subversive encouragement to revolt, that it was Athens rather than Sparta which caused the defection of Athenian allies on a considerable scale. For when the oligarchs, following their coup, sought to obtain wider support from outside Athens they thought that they could enhance their influence in the empire by supplanting the democracies by oligarchies.[278] Their plan proved to be a miscalculation, for the newly created oligarchies immediately turned to Sparta.

When links between régimes in two states had been established, any treaty or alliance often depended upon the maintenance in power of the leading factions in those states. In the Delian League the Athenians secured protection throughout their alliance for their *proxenoi*. Similar measures were adopted by the Athenians in the fourth century for the protection of their political representatives after the murder of Athenian *proxenoi* in Ceos at a time when Thebes was fostering political revolts in the Second Athenian Confederacy.[279] When revolts from the Confederacy occurred in such cities as Chios, Cos, Rhodes and Byzantium outside influence could be seen at work in the form of Mausolus of Caria, resulting in democracies being supplanted by oligarchies. Newly established régimes were quite sensitive about their external contacts. The Athenian oligarchs, for example, who took over in the anti-democratic revolution of 404 cancelled the appointments of *proxenoi* in several states, but after the democratic restoration of the following year it seems that such appointments were renewed.[280]

It was more difficult for régimes of opposite complexion to co-exist in neighbouring states, for the risk of appeals and of subversion across the border was greater. One of the manifestations of the acute and inveterate rivalry between Argos and Sparta was the existence of democracy in Argos for long periods in the fifth century, but the possibility of political revolution spreading from such a focal point was evident, especially early in the fourth century. For by then Corinth had long been established as an oligarchy, though as a result of demographic changes and casualties in war there was a change in the social balance of the community. The democrats saw their opportunity and concerted their plans with the Argives; the upshot was a political union between the two states, which helped to maintain democracy in Corinth. Sparta, however, interpreted the events as an exercise in Argive imperialism and soon had the union dissolved in the King's Peace of 387/6.[281]

The existence of a democratic constitution in a Peloponnesian community was not automatically a cause of annoyance to Sparta. Two Spartan kings indeed had connexions with democratic leaders in Mantinea. In 384 when relations between Sparta and Mantinea had deteriorated after the expiry of the Thirty Years' Truce, concluded in 418, King Agesilaus requested that he be excused from command of an invading force on the ground that his father had received assistance from Mantinea. King Agesipolis took over the command although friendly relations existed between his father and Mantinea. There the anti-democratic faction did benefit from Spartan intervention, as did the opponents of democracy in Phlius at about the same time, for political exiles appealed successfully to Sparta for help in their restoration and the democrats were frightened into acquiescence.[282]

The Spartans, however, did not intervene to impose oligarchic rule upon Phlius any more than they did at Elis *c.* 400. For, when Sparta sent out an expedition to break Elean control over surrounding districts, Xenias, the wealthy leader of the Elean oligarchs, saw his opportunity to arrange a coup and gain Spartan support. But in spite of the presence of the Spartans with a force under King Agis, Thrasydaeus and the democrats prevailed and came to reach an agreement with Sparta.[283]

The greater the distance which separated states the greater was the equanimity with which they could tolerate régimes of different complexions. A prime example of a case in which the necessity of seeking alliance outweighed any sense of political solidarity between corresponding groups in two states is to be seen in the complicated relations between Corinth and Corcyra and their joint colony of Epidamnus. The noble and oligarchic group in Epidamnus was expelled by the democratic faction. Thereupon, when the exiles joined forces with barbarians to exert pressure on Epidamnus, the Epidamnian democrats appealed first, in vain, to Corcyra and then, after consulting the Delphic Oracle, to Corinth with more success. Thus Corinth, under an oligarchic régime, came to assist Epidamnian democrats against Epidamnian oligarchs, contrary to the wishes of Corcyra, at that time a democracy. Eventually at Anactorium Corinth took many prisoners from the Corcyraeans, of whom two hundred and fifty men of prominent position were retained in captivity. They were well-treated and held until an opportune moment for their release. That came in 427 when revolution was fomented in Corcyra: then the captives were released nominally on security of a ransom but in reality to foster an oligarchic coup which was designed to detach Corcyra from alliance with Athens and bring her over to the side of Corinth.[284] Thus Corinth had assisted on the one hand democrats in Epidamnus and on the other oligarchs in Corcyra.

A common expectation of historians is that community of language and other institutions, such as religion, will lead by some inevitable process to political unification. A look at the patterns of events in the history of all periods shows that such development is by no means to be expected. A brief examination of the history of the English- and German-speaking peoples should be sufficient to illustrate the point. Conversely political unions of some permanence have been formed out of diverse linguistic and ethnic groups. The attitudes of the ancient Greeks become that much more intelligible if the student can rid himself of customarily imbibed notions of what ought to happen or what ought to have happened.

The Greek-speaking peoples of antiquity did in general set themselves apart from others and ethnic considerations were a factor in inter-state affairs, but we should be hesitant about attempting to attribute to the ancient Greeks the characteristics of a nation or a nation-state. According to Herodotus the Greeks did think of themselves as enjoying an identity of language, religion and customs,[285] but the force for political unity was lacking, and even most of Herodotus' contemporaries had little conception, if any, of the extent to which non-Greek communities had institutions and customs that were not unlike those of the Greeks.

It is identity of interest between communities or the military capacity of a conqueror which leads to political unity. Neither of those forces was at work to any great extent in the formative years of ancient Greece. No Persian force was powerful or persistent enough either to conquer the Greeks and incorporate them into satrapies or to compel them to unite for long periods in self-defence. If the force of Persia was insufficient to achieve such changes certainly no other Mediterranean power before the rise of Alexander the Great or the advent of Rome could achieve such effects; and even the Romans attempted to achieve their ends by diplomacy and by preserving a balance of power between conflicting elements before dividing the area into Roman administrative provinces.

The absence of any continuous external challenge or pressure meant that there could be no response. The capacity to respond was there, as the existence of numerous alliances, federations and political unions shows. The greatest response to pressure from outside in historical times was the concerted resistance to the westward progress of Persian power. First Asia Minor and the Ionians were engulfed then invasions of European Greece were mounted in 490 and 480. The result was a common effort by the principal Greek states to defend themselves and later the formation of the Delian League, a long-lasting alliance of more than two hundred states and one of the most significant alliances in political history. Even so, some states, such as Thessaly and Thebes, doubted the capacity of their fellow-Greeks to protect them and were induced to make their own accommodation with the Persians; as for the rest such unity as did result from the Persian challenge was a temporary and desperate alliance, effective for the short term but ill-secured for the long term.

On the fringes of the Greek-speaking world relationships with non-Greeks were generally not of confrontation but of a search for common interests and co-operation. Ample evidence for that can be found in Egypt, Asia Minor and Italy: if a confrontation occurred it could produce a degree of local solidarity, as in Sicily, where Syracuse was involved with other Greeks against Carthaginian interests. Even in Asia Minor there were long periods of amicable relationships between Greeks, Persians and other non-Greeks, as is shown by the alliances concluded between Miletus and Alyattes (c. 600[286]) and between Miletus and Cyrus (c. 546[287]). Even Lydia and the Spartans concluded an alliance (c. 546) at the request of Lydia and on the advice of the Delphic Oracle.[288] In the fifth century the leaders of minority factions in Greek communities such as Miletus in Asia Minor derived much support and comfort from the Persians. In other areas Greek fought Greek, and non-Greek elements, such as Sicans and Sicels in Sicily, made useful allies for one side or another.

The Greeks made a good deal of propaganda concerning their assumed natural physical, intellectual and moral superiority over non-Greeks, and it is true that in times of war they did observe certain civilized conventions. It was thus quite unusual for Greeks to sell into slavery other Greek prisoners of war, who were generally retained as a bargaining counter or a pawn for ransom in negotiations for settlement of war: truces were obtained in warfare to enable the great Panhellenic festivals and religious ceremonies to function. But in the fifth and fourth centuries Sparta, Athens and Thebes in turn all competed for Persian support to redress the balance of power in their own favour against their fellow-Greeks. Even at a time when the Athenians sought to achieve the maximum propaganda against Sparta for infringing the autonomy of the Greeks and for co-operating with Persia to that end they invited in 378/7 all Greeks and barbarians who were not subject to Persian sovereignty[289] to join in the cause of freedom against Spartan encroachment.

If between Greeks and non-Greeks there were certain evident characteristic differences, so were there between Greeks of different

ethnic and dialect groups. At the time of the outbreak of the Peloponnesian War in 432/1 much play was made of the idea of a confrontation between the Ionians and Dorians under Athens and Sparta
respectively. The idea had its value for some in creating an impression
of a certain solidarity or the existence of a natural bond between allies,
but there was little practical substance to the notion.[290] Indeed ethnic
considerations as such did not act as a major factor in Greek diplomacy.
That can be seen quite plainly in the events preceding the Peloponnesian War. For the dispute between Corinth and Corcyra was one
between two Dorian communities. Corcyra as a Dorian community
had no hesitation in turning to an Ionian community, Athens, which
was glad to have one of the principal naval powers removed from
the grasp of her actual or potential enemies. Other Dorian communities such as Argos and the islands of Melos and Thera were
neutral at the onset of the war, although Argos and Thera later
inclined to Athens and Melos displayed an obstinate neutrality which
provoked Athenian intervention. In 415, after the Athenians had
sent out their first expedition to the west against Syracuse, which
had been traditionally hostile to Chalcidian communities in the area,
they called upon Rhegium to help its kinsmen in Leontini. Rhegium,
however, declared that it would observe neutrality until the Italiots
had determined what their policy was to be.[291]

The Athenians gave help to their fellow-Ionian Greeks of Asia
Minor, who found common cause in revolt from Persian domination
in the Ionian Revolt, but those Ionians also sought help from Sparta.
Spartan help was not forthcoming and subsequently the Athenians
found that the assistance they gave had a value out of all proportion
to what might have been expected. For after the Persian invasions
the Ionians were most apprehensive of Persia and managed to secure
Athenian leadership of their cause in the Delian League. The League
had its headquarters at the Ionian religious centre on the island of
Delos, and so one can see that initially common cult and ethnic
considerations were to some extent a factor in the diplomacy of the
time, but regional interest as much as anything else initially welded
the League together. The Delian League was to extend its membership
far beyond the bounds of the Ionian communities which formed an
initial nucleus. Rhodes and Cos, Dorian communities, joined the
Delian League, as did the Aeolian communities of Lesbos. Later,
revolts from Athens and the League occurred as readily in Ionian
communities such as Samos, as in Aeolian communities such as
Mytilene and in Dorian communities such as Byzantium.

In 457 Dorian Sparta was glad to intervene in order to help the communities of Doris in central Greece. Sparta found a ready argument to justify her action, for Doris was regarded as the motherland, or metropolis, of the Dorians.[292] Sentiment no doubt played its part in the motives of the Spartans but the overwhelming arguments for Spartan intervention were based on strategic considerations. For the cities of Doris were under pressure from the Phocians, who at the time were sympathetic to the Athenians. Therefore if Sparta wished to weaken Athens' position, then it made sense to help Doris against Phocis. In that case the needs of policy and of propaganda could be met suitably at the same time by assisting the Dorian metropolis.

From the fourth century ethnic considerations found even less place in the patterns of policy and propaganda. Dorian Byzantium was among the earliest members of the Second Athenian Confederacy, whose efforts were directed principally against Dorian Sparta. The Athenians, whose strategic interests involved building up a substantial naval alliance, managed once more to secure the allegiance of many of the Aegean islands, which happened to be Ionian, but she also secured north-western Greeks such as Cephallenians and Arcarnanians. Ionian Euboea oscillated between alliance with Athens and sympathy with Aeolian Thebes.

Several communities which enjoyed ethnic and close linguistic links developed also close political relations. In particular several leagues or political federations spring to mind. The Arcadians, for example, were in isolation in the interior of the Peloponnese and formed a federation in the fourth century. Aetolia, Boeotia and the Chalcidice each formed their own federal units, as did Thessaly. In those cases, however, it was a regional interest which was the chief factor in determining political events; the historical patterns of migration into those areas were no longer part of the conscious consideration in the political issues. The original Achaean League was somewhat unusual, for non-Achaeans could be members. Calydon, for example, in Aetolia was a member.[293]

Panhellenic considerations played little part in the practice of Greek diplomacy. In common parlance it was possible to speak of the Greeks on the one hand as opposed to non-Greek-speaking peoples, the barbarians. But it was not easy to argue on political grounds or to maintain on intellectual grounds that such a division had any real meaning, and neither politicians nor philosophers were able to construct anything positive out of popular notions and prejudices in that respect.

It was not until the last third of the fifth century, during the Peloponnesian War, that much was written or spoken about Panhellenism.
Then it was the comic playwright of conservative tendencies,
Aristophanes, who broached the topic in public at Athens. He was
concerned at the waste of men and resources in the long and fruitless
war between Athens and Sparta and their respective allies, which
involved most of the states of European Greece and many beyond.
It was the severest war of the Greek experience up to that time and
in Athens its social and economic consequences were unprecedentedly
severe. In his play *The Acharnians*, produced in 425, Aristophanes portrayed the effects of the embargo which Athens imposed on Megarian
trade and depicted the penury to which men were reduced. His
concern with war was shown further in 411 in the *Lysistrata*, in which
Greek women of all states were represented as seeking to ensure peace
by withdrawing conjugal rights from their menfolk. The source of
Aristophanes' Panhellenism was the suffering which the Greeks
inflicted upon themselves by waging endemic war. To the horror
of war was added the disgrace incurred by the combatants in seeking
the help of the Persians, the barbarians whose encroachments had
only comparatively recently been the cause of almost universal alarm
to the Greeks. Local interest, however, prevailed in political considerations. Each community was prepared to extract whatever benefit
of propaganda it could manage from the dealings of another with
non-Greeks. Political opponents in Athens could make accusations
of Laconism, politicians in Thebes were accused of Atticism, but
Medism, or siding with Persia, was a sin in the eyes of all those who
at a given time were not enjoying its advantages.

In 388 the orator Lysias chose the Olympic Festival as the occasion
for his famous oration on the theme of peace and war in Greece.
He took up the theme expounded by the orator and philosopher
Gorgias in his Olympic oration late in the fifth century. Both urged
the Greeks to lay aside their conflicts with one another and to conserve
their energies for fighting against their common enemy the 'barbarians', that is, the Persians. Lysias took his theme one step further
and urged an end to inter-Greek wars in order that unity might be
achieved to deal with the two tyrants, Dionysius, tyrant of Syracuse,
and the King of Persia. There is in Gorgias and Lysias, but not in
Aristophanes, a recognition that some external factor was needed in
order to achieve the unity of Greece, and in their experience only
one series of events had gone some way to arousing such a co-operative
spirit, namely, the Persian Wars. For then Athens and Sparta had

eventually worked together, after which the Greeks experienced nearly two whole decades of relative peace between themselves. In fact there were acute rivalries between the Greek states during the Persian Wars, but those were largely forgotten in the recollection that in 481/0 the Greeks, or at least many of them, formally agreed to put aside their differences in order to concentrate on the common cause.[294] Isocrates took his arguments further still in the middle years of the fourth century. He realized that two external factors were needed: a common cause before which to stand the banner of unity and the leadership necessary to guide united efforts. Before the Persian Wars Sparta had stood pre-eminent as a military power in Greece, but from 446/5 she was obliged to recognize Athens as a military and diplomatic equal. Accordingly from Cimon's day to Isocrates men had argued for the division of the leadership of Greece between Athens and Sparta, but the rivalry of the two powers and the interplay and influence of other communities both within Greece, such as Thebes and Corinth, and outside Greece, such as Persia, caused men to look elsewhere for leadership. Education for leadership and the character of the ideal leader were topics which fascinated philosophers of the fourth century and led to the consideration of contemporary individuals as possible champions of Hellenism. Hiero and Dionysius of Syracuse, and Evagoras of Salamis in Cyprus were the subjects of study, but most practical of all was Isocrates' open invitation to Philip of Macedon to command the Greeks. There were certainly men who had the capacity to undertake successful military command. King Agesilaus of Sparta, in the wake of the march of the Ten Thousand, had taken upon himself the mantle of King Agamemnon by proceeding to Asia Minor in 399[295] in the cause of Greek independence from Asiatic encroachment. Agesilaus had consciously gone to make sacrifice at Aulis in imitation of his hero. Jason of Pherae cast himself in a similar mould[296] but premature death cut short his ambition while preserving the ambition intact. Philip and Alexander of Macedon were not influenced in their aims of policy by intangible ideas; they had grievances to pursue against Persia and the hope of material gain. In subduing their opponents in Greece they were able to offer an honourable programme based on the traditions created by the sentiment and propaganda of others during the preceding century.

A part of the tradition of which Philip and Alexander were able to make use was the idea of the Common Peace, a multilateral institution which in theory could cover all Greek communities without exception to guarantee their individual sovereignty and freedom from oppression. The idea originally developed within a fairly narrow framework and was a tactical device to deal with a specific situation; later it assumed a much greater significance. At the outset of the Peloponnesian War the Spartans mounted a propaganda offensive against the alleged tyranny exercised by the Athenians over their allies. Sparta claimed to be fighting for the freedom and independence of the Greeks,[297] but when she was faced with the embarrassing situation of emerging victorious and dissolving the remains of Athens' empire she assumed the mantle of Athens. Then it was the turn of the Athenians and others to judge Sparta by her words on the one hand and her deeds on the other. Sparta had won her victory with Persian support, but by 399 Persia transgressed against Greeks in Asia Minor and so Sparta could hardly ignore the plight and the appeal of Miletus if she was to act consistently with the propaganda which she had poured out for a generation or more.

In the period which ensued Persia was able to play her favourite game of not intervening directly in Greek affairs but of supporting first one side, then the other, switching sides with equanimity when self-interest so dictated. Accordingly in the first decade of the fourth century Sparta was cast in the role of an imperialist power and an enemy of Persia, who consequently leaned over to support Athens, Thebes and other Greeks who wanted to achieve or defend their liberty from Spartan control. By 392/1 Athens appeared to the Persian satrap Tiribazus as the main threat to Persian power and so the Spartan diplomat Antalcidas was able to exploit the situation by proposing a peace which guaranteed the autonomy of all Greek states except those over whom Persia claimed sovereignty.[298] It was suspected that Antalcidas' proposals were, in spite of their bland appearance, specifically designed to weaken the principal opponents of Sparta, for he hoped to weaken the position of Thebes, which controlled the federated communities of Boeotia, to break up the political union of Argos and Corinth, whose existence weakened Sparta's strategic position in the Peloponnese, and to prevent the resurgence of Athens' naval power and the recrudescence of her old network of alliances. In return for Persia's recognition of Sparta as her most suitable ally and of Athens as a dangerous threat, Sparta was prepared to see Persia act as the overlord of the Greek cities of Asia Minor.

Sparta's diplomacy failed to convince the Persian King at first, but by 387 he came round to accepting Sparta's idea. For immediate tactical and practical purposes the most powerful combination of forces, Sparta and Persia, was thus able to harness the propaganda that had permeated the atmosphere for so long, to procure an almost all-embracing declaration of autonomy for all states.[299] Sparta incurred the odium of causing the Persian King, as arbiter, to issue an edict which instructed the Greeks how they were to arrange their affairs, but the settlement was the most comprehensive to date, and on it were based for a long time thereafter most major settlements and alliances. The terms of the Peace which guaranteed autonomy were used as the model for subsequent general settlements of Greek affairs in 375, 371, 362/1 and 338/7, and they formed the basis of proposals made at other conferences for general settlements, such as the abortive conference proposed by Thebes in 366. On them were also based many other treaties and alliances of more limited scope; most importantly, they acted as an inhibiting factor in the conduct of the Athenians in the organization and management of their Naval Confederacy from 378/7, for its terms of membership were quite clearly designed to prevent the accretion, and abuse, of imperialist power which many had endured in the previous century.

The idea of the Common Peace transcended local and regional considerations and continued long after the threat of Persian intervention had disappeared. In 362/1 the Greek communities were invited by rebellious satraps to join their cause against the Persian King. The Greeks refused, not so much for fear of Persia as out of weariness with interminable conflicts, and we can detect a note of pride in their reply, which stated that they had no quarrel with Persia and that they had themselves settled all their differences with one another according to the terms of the Common Peace in order that they might enjoy peace and prosperity.[300]

There was, however, no sufficiently influential international forum or sufficiently effective guarantee. The Common Peace needed a protector, if not an arbiter, and so the need for a Panhellenic champion was not obviated by the Common Peace. In fact Philip of Macedon was able not only to adopt the best diplomatic practices of the fourth century but also to improve upon them in forming the League of Corinth, thereby making his position diplomatically more acceptable to the Hellenic community.

CHAPTER XVI

THE METHODS OF DIPLOMACY

THE CONDUCT OF DIPLOMACY depended upon direct oral exchange and contact between men and constitutional organs of the various states. It did not depend upon indirect methods of communication either by means of formal letters, at least until the Hellenistic era, or by means of third parties. Direct communication was maintained between states both in war and in peace as occasion demanded, and in the absence of permanently established diplomatic missions the affairs of diplomacy were a constantly recurring item on the agenda of councils and assemblies. For not only were decisions of policy to be made, as might be expected, but also even more frequently men had to be appointed to expedite those decisions in the absence of an established bureaucracy.

A variety of words was used by the Greeks to describe those who were despatched on diplomatic missions. Heralds (*kerykes*), envoys (*presbeis*) and messengers (*angeloi*) are all found, and the main distinction is made between heralds and the others. The term *angelos* bears the widest meaning and can be used to signify those who fulfilled the function of *presbeis*, but it was usual for Greek envoys to be referred to in literature and in documents as *presbeis* while it was more usual for non-Greek envoys to be described as *angeloi*. None of the three terms, however, has a significance which was originally or even principally concerned with diplomacy. Indeed, as has already been noted, the word *presbeis* means merely 'elders' and it has no singular form.

Heralds were the men who had the function to which was attached the oldest social and religious tradition. Before what is commonly recognized as the historical era, in primitive and archaic Greek society the heralds followed a recognized calling or profession which gave them a specific and honourable status in society. They performed a variety of tasks which ranged from acting as convenors of political meetings to pouring out the wine in the halls of the Homeric kings and princes. They also had a symbol of office, the herald's staff, unlike other envoys. As their calling was one which had its place in archaic Greek society and whose status had been sanctified by religious and ceremonial associations they, regarded as the offspring of Hermes the messenger of the gods, had an especially privileged position which went beyond the normal courtesies involved in receiving strangers and visitors. They enjoyed the protection of the gods, which in effect provided them with what amounted to a form of diplomatic immunity, which was not automatically extended to envoys in general.

Society and its institutions changed radically after the archaic period and although certain religious and ceremonial tasks were retained by successive generations of particular families diplomatic tasks were more especially political in nature and naturally they were assigned by election in political assemblies as the occasion required. Nevertheless the herald, irrespective of his function, retained his title and the religious protection that went with it. Society accordingly evolved its code of practice in respect of the name and function of a herald but not in respect of the more purely political elders or envoys (*presbeis*). Something of the former status of the heralds can be seen in two families, one in Sparta, the other in Athens. In Sparta the family of the *Talthybii*, named after Talthybius the herald of the legendary Agamemnon, traditionally performed heraldic tasks in the historical era. Similarly the family of the *Kerykes* (Heralds) in Athens performed such duties, especially in religious ceremonial. Among the most famous of their number was Callias, named The Torch-Bearer, a man of great significance also in the annals of Athenian diplomacy.

If a state of war existed between states then the despatch of a herald was the likeliest means of initial contact between them. If two armies had done battle on the field then traditionally the losing side sent a herald to ask for permission from the victors to recover the dead and the wounded. The presence of heralds in exchanges between states was a virtual acknowledgement that war existed even if it had not been declared. Before the start of the Peloponnesian War both sides tried, as far as was possible, to avoid responsibility for precipitating the actual outbreak of hostilities, even when war was unavoidable, and so in a preliminary naval encounter the Corinthians sent men in a boat with a herald's insignia, rather than a herald, for the despatch of a herald might have been taken by the Athenians to indicate that a state of war existed in the eyes of the Corinthians.[301] In war, if states wished to exchange full delegations of envoys for political discussions then the envoys would be preceded by a herald whose task it was to secure a safe passage. Thus before the negotiations opened between Athens and Philip of Macedon in 346 the Athenian politician Philocrates proposed that permission be given to Philip to despatch a herald and envoys.[302] Similarly in the truce established in the course of the Peloponnesian War for one year (423/2) the Athenians agreed that each side should be permitted to send a herald, envoys and attendants in any number to negotiate a settlement of the War.[303] It was most unusual for states to be unable to rely on contact even through heralds. In moments and moods of extreme bitterness and resolution a state could express its determination by decreeing that it would not receive a herald *and* embassy, as Pericles proposed at Athens in 431.[304] There was such a concept as 'heraldless' war, which could mean among other things that a war had been started without formal proclamation. It could also mean that the war would be fought to a decisive finish and that heralds would not be received. Such a procedure, however, was by way of an emotive, rather than a practical, gesture and was of temporary significance.

Unlike the herald who functioned alone, envoys (*presbeis*) generally worked in larger numbers. Their status, as their name indicates, was more political. Moreover, it had not been sanctified or codified by right of ancestral usage. Envoys passed readily between states which were not at war and relied on the traditional codes of conduct observed for strangers, but they did not possess freedom from arrest or immunity as such. When Spartan envoys were arrested in suspicious circumstances at the house of Callias in 378[305] they had no legitimate reason for complaint. It was, of course, a serious matter and a risky enterprise to abuse envoys. Even if their arrival was unwelcome or if they were dismissed they would expect to be given an ultimatum to depart by a fixed time. They could claim protection only if a herald first cleared the way. Furthermore envoys conducting business between two states had no general right of immunity from arrest or interception by a third party. In cases of doubt they would require permission to pass through the territory of third parties, but on the seas there was no such way of obtaining clearance. Thus in 430/29, a time of war, the Athenians caused to be arrested and put to death in Thrace Nicolaus and Aneristus, Spartan envoys on their way to Persia.[306] In time of nominal peace in 396/5 the Spartan naval commander Pharax arrested and had put to death an Athenian delegation on its way to Persia.[307]

When envoys did visit a state normally they would be free to pursue informal contacts in addition to their formal introduction to political councils and assemblies. In 421/0, for example, when Spartan envoys arrived in Athens they were engaged in private discussions by the Athenian politician Alcibiades.[308] Envoys were selected from the politically active circles and their task was to engage in political advocacy rather than in genuine negotiation, as we know it, or in bureaucratic exercises. Perhaps their position resembled rather that of twentieth-century delegates to the United Nations Organization than that of ambassadors or commissioners accredited to foreign states in modern times.

The size of embassies varied quite considerably not only from state to state but also from time to time in the case of any one state. The most consistent state was Sparta, which invariably sent three men on a mission, as she did to Athens in 378.[309] Athens regularly employed embassies of two, three, five, or ten men, but most commonly groups of three or ten are noted. No particular state or type of state rated the despatch of any fixed number of envoys nor did any particular kind of mission merit the despatch of a given number of envoys. Embassies of three, five and ten men were sent regularly to ratify treaties; a small embassy of only two men was sent from Athens to the King of Persia in 367,[310] whereas ten men were sent to Philip of Macedon in 346.

At Athens, where practice can be seen to vary quite clearly, the size of a delegation could be affected sometimes by its importance and perhaps more often by how many political groupings and politicians were interested in any given issue. The despatch of the embassy to make peace with Sparta in 371 seems to have involved three distinct political groups, that of Callias, who was favourably disposed to Sparta, that of Autocles, who was rather hostile, and that of Callistratus, who was prepared to judge issues on their merit in their immediate context.[311]

Strictly speaking, the envoys of the city-states as distinct from the Hellenistic monarchs were amateurs. They no more received financial reward for service on embassies than they did for being politicians or statesmen. The spur to serve was public recognition and fame, for election as envoy was one of the greater public distinctions. Such service could entail considerable private expenditure. If an envoy took his personal attendants or servants with him, then he had to bear the expense. He was liable to be away from home for an unforeseeable length of time and he might have to abandon other commitments. Few if any men, for example, could have predicted that Athenian envoys would have to spend more than two months on their mission to Philip of Macedon in 346.[312] One of these envoys was Aristodemus the actor, not a recognized politician, who was helped by the state to obtain the necessary release from acting contracts.[313] The financial compensation for election as envoy at Athens was a mere subsistence allowance which was by no means sufficient to keep envoys in the style to which they were accustomed. It amounted to a round sum in Classical times of about a drachma a day, or a little more – a sum which a soldier or an artisan expected to receive for a day's service. That level of payment ensured that public service was not undertaken for gain or profit but it also fitted in with the democratic ideal that a man should not be deterred by poverty from playing a full part in public life.

Whilst a man engaged in public life had to devote much of his time to it, a public figure was not engaged in full-time public employment. A man who was elected as envoy was elected solely for the duration of his mission. According to the degree of his political involvement and esteem he could be elected to few or many embassies. In Athens Demosthenes was almost continuously involved in debates on foreign policy in the 340s and he was repeatedly elected to embassies at that time. He is known to have gone to Macedon in 346, to the Peloponnese in 344/3[314] and 343/2[315] and to Thebes in 339/8.[316] Yet another orator of unknown identity claimed to have travelled as envoy to Thessaly, Macedonia, Molossia, Thresprotia, Italy and Sicily, reassuring friends, winning new friends and detaching others from enemies.[317]

From what is known of the diplomats who served the Greek states the Spartans appear to have cultivated the greatest degree of specialization of interest. Antalcidas, for example, seems to have held the stage for Sparta in all of her known negotiations with Persia until the failure of his final mission there and his consequent suicide. His diplomatic activities appear to have spanned more than two decades from 392/1 onward.[318] Then Euthycles seems to have taken over from him, as he went on the next two known important missions to Persia in 367 and 331.[319] Another Spartan who developed a similar degree of specialization was Philocharidas. He helped to arrange the truce with Athens in 423,[320] was present at the ratification of both the Peace of Nicias and the subsequent alliance with Athens in 421,[321] and by 408/7 he fulfilled two further missions to Athens.[322] For the Athenians it does not seem to have been the practice to maintain a similar continuity of representation, perhaps because there was greater contention in the political life of democratic Athens and there were more men from whom a choice could be made. Nevertheless Callias the elder was envoy to Persia *c.* 464/3 and went there again *c.* 449 to arrange the Peace which bore his name.[323] His grandson and namesake in the fourth century claimed to be visiting Sparta in 371 for the third time as an Athenian envoy.[324] The orator Aeschines maintained that there were Athenian politicians such as Thrason and Thrasybulus who in the fourth century were especially trusted in Thebes and consequently sent there often.[325]

There are but few instances where it could be maintained that the personality and disposition of any particular envoy were of greater significance than the brief which he held or the power which he represented. One possible instance of the overriding importance of the envoy chosen was that of Themistocles who was sent in 478 by the Athenians to Sparta, where he was trusted as was no one else.[326] His task there was to stall for time until the Athenians had completed the construction of their defensive walls, to which the Spartans objected so strongly. Nevertheless, the choice of individuals could give some indication of the serious intentions of a state in its diplomacy. Thucydides comments that after the Peace of Nicias began to founder the Spartans sent to Athens the men who were well disposed to Athens,[327] and Diodorus of Sicily stresses that in 377 the Athenians sent out the most illustrious men as envoys to seek co-operation against Sparta.[328] The careful selection of envoys could make even disagreement less unpleasant, for even though there was little prospect at the time of making effective the Peace of Nicias and the alliance with Sparta, the Athenians still sent their statesman and general Nicias there as the Spartans held him in high regard.[329]

Invariably men of fairly senior standing were sent on embassies, and so important was it for the state to exercise freedom of choice in election that men who already held official positions of state were not debarred from appointment. In Athens, for example, pluralism and re-election were avoided as far as possible in respect of most offices, but not where appointments to embassies were concerned. For election to embassies the same criteria and qualifications had to be met or satisfied as for election to general political offices. In Chalcis there was a law that no one under the age of fifty should serve as envoy or hold office[330] but in the majority of cases the minimum age qualification was nearer thirty. In 429, however, when the Athenians decided to send three envoys to Perdiccas of Macedon each of them had to be over fifty years old.[331] The personnel involved in diplomacy was drawn from the ranks of the politically and socially prominent figures in a state. Nearly every prominent Athenian is known to have served on diplomatic missions though, surprisingly, Pericles and Eubulus, two of the most influential statesmen in Athenian foreign policy in the fifth and fourth centuries respectively, were not among their number.

In Athens leading political figures such as Aristides, Cimon, Pericles, Nicias, Callias, Callistratus and Demosthenes were expected to come forward in political debates regardless of the subject, whether constitutional, financial, military or diplomatic issues were under consideration. The same applied to Sparta and other Greek states. Whilst admittedly there were times when influential orators tended to evade responsibility for the implementation of their proposals, it is generally true to maintain that those who were involved in the formulation of policy were also involved in the execution of policy. Aristides, Themistocles and Cimon were leading figures in the debates on Athenian external policy at the time of the Persian Wars and they consequently also acted as envoys to Sparta in 479 and 478.[332] In 346 Philocrates, who had proposed that negotiations be allowed to start between Athens and Philip of Macedon, was included in Athenian embassies to Macedon, as was Demosthenes, who supported Philocrates' proposal and had as much to say on Athenian foreign policy as any man. Similarly in 338 when Philip had overwhelmed the opposition at Chaeronea the Athenians sent out to him an embassy which included Aeschines and Demades.[333] The choice of those two men was particularly appropriate, for Aeschines' political influence had been diminished since 346 on the grounds of his alleged willingness to compromise with Philip, and Demades had openly advocated the necessity of coming to terms with Philip. In the fifth century the Peace of Callias with Persia and that of Nicias with Sparta were so named, as was the Peace of Philocrates, because the treaties were the fruit of the policies of these men. Callias himself went as envoy to Susa and Nicias was one of the ten negotiators and one of the seventeen commissioners for the oaths sworn for the Peace with Sparta. In the third century Chremonides was responsible both for promoting a policy of co-operation with Sparta against Macedon and for implementing it.[334]

A statesman who interested himself in external affairs might well find that his reputation and influence were in double jeopardy, in the first place in his own state and again in that other state which was the object of his policy and in which he might enjoy a certain regard. Themistocles, for example, was well regarded both in Athens and in Sparta, but his patriotism could serve to discredit him in Sparta and likewise his regard for Sparta could conceivably entail risk in Athens. Cimon exemplified a man whose regard for Sparta caused him political embarrassment in Athens. He had in any case his political rivals for domestic reasons and he incurred more hostility for the external policy which he advocated. For he sought a policy of co-operation between Athens and Sparta, and he maintained that Greek interests were best served by both a strong Sparta and a powerful Athens acting in tandem. There were those in Athens who saw Sparta less as a partner than an impediment and rival, and so when Sparta rebuffed Athenian support, offered at the instigation of Cimon at the time of the helot revolt in 462, Cimon and his policies were discredited and he suffered ostracism.[335] That, however, was not the end of his useful service as a politician and diplomat for Athens, for when it was thought desirable to end the war with Sparta c. 451 there was no one to whom discussions could be entrusted more appropriately than to Cimon, who proceeded to arrange a truce for five years.[336]

Nicias too risked his political reputation in dealings with Sparta. For some time before the Peace which bore his name was arranged the opposition to his policy was strong. A compromise between the opposing views resulted in the One Year Truce with Sparta in 423, but it was not extended and it was only upon the death of his personal and political rival, Cleon, that Nicias found his opportunity in 421. The arrangements to implement the Peace agreed in that year did not proceed smoothly, and after a fruitless embassy by Nicias to try to retrieve the situation in Sparta[337] the stage was set in Athens for a trial of political strength between Nicias and Alcibiades, who had assumed the role of arch-opponent of Sparta. An ostracism was organized and would have resulted in the enforced departure of one of the two rivals from Athens, had not political scheming by the two respective factions ensured instead the ostracism of Hyperbolus. Consequently the course of Athenian foreign policy remained ambiguous.

Of course men were identified with particular policies and also entrusted with their execution, but the risks involved were by no means invariably as great as those undertaken by Cimon and Nicias. The secret was to ensure that responsibility was shared and to maintain sufficient flexibility of approach. Callistratus, one of the leading figures in founding the Second Athenian Confederacy, was a powerful advocate of co-operation with Thebes against Sparta. Yet when Thebes had proved to be an unsatisfactory ally he could without loss of credibility advocate the end of war and conclusion of peace with Sparta in 371, and he was sent as an envoy to Sparta for that purpose.[338] Among his colleagues on that occasion were not only men of a disposition favourable to Sparta but also trenchant opponents of long standing. In 339/8 Demosthenes took the lead in securing Theban co-operation and gaining his own election as envoy to Thebes for that purpose.[339] He plunged ahead without caution on the ground that the situation was so desperate that a patriot ought not to stand back. He did not hold back with a view to finding others who would share the political risks and responsibility. Aeschines, on the contrary, who favoured a less intractable approach to Philip of Macedon in 346 tried to ensure that all of his colleagues on the embassy moved in step with him. When Philip offered gifts to the envoys Aeschines proposed that all of them should accept an equal amount, and in the later trial of Aeschines Demosthenes was quick to scotch any claim by Aeschines that there was collegiate or collective responsibility for what had occurred on the embassy.[340]

As we have seen, the Greeks appointed envoys as and when they were needed for tasks of a strictly limited duration. Nevertheless there was felt to be a need for more continuing and reliable contacts between states or individuals representing states. The institution of *proxenia* was the closest that the Greeks came to devising a form of permanent diplomatic representation. The system bears some resemblance to that which gave rise to the Venetian practice of appointing consular representatives and which is by no means unknown in the present era. For *proxenoi* were citizens of the states in which they resided, not of states whose interests they were appointed to represent. The Spartans, for example, appointed Cimon, the Athenian statesman, to look after their interests in Athens.[341] A *proxenos* could obtain his appointment either for recognition of, or in anticipation of, services or by inheriting the status from his father. Some continuity of representation was ensured by such hereditary transmission of an honorary and honorific status in a family. Among the clauses granting rights and privileges which were commonly contained in the decrees of appointment was specifically included the grant of proxeny to an individual and to his descendants. Thus Callias, who went as Athenian envoy to Sparta in 371, laid special emphasis on his status as *proxenos*, a position retained by his family since the time of his paternal grandfather, Callias.[342]

Whether or not the origins of proxeny are to be found in the activities of trade or religion, its significance in historical times was distinctly political, for the decree of appointment was a public political act and before the Hellenistic era it involved the appointment almost exclusively of leading political and social figures. Thereafter honorary appointments were showered upon individuals such as itinerant doctors and actors. That is not to argue that such individuals were all without their diplomatic significance, for in 346 the Athenians found it useful to include on their embassy to Macedon Aristodemus the actor. Among the most obvious obligations of a *proxenos* was to offer appropriate help and hospitality to private and public visitors from the state which he represented. In 391/0, for example, Pharax of Sparta, the *proxenos* of Thebes, offered to conduct the Theban envoys to the Spartan authorities;[343] and in 378, at the time when Sphodrias was raiding Athenian territory with a Spartan force, the visiting Spartan envoys were found in the house of Callias, their *proxenos* in Athens.[344]

In a world where social status and political standing frequently went together, often independently of mere possession of wealth, proxeny both involved obligations and conferred prestige. In common with most political appointments it brought little or no direct financial reward, although Cimon once remarked that unlike the *proxenoi* of other states he as *proxenos* of Sparta derived no lucre from his appointment.[345] The grant of proxeny signified that the political eminence of a man was recognized beyond the boundaries of his own state, and his authority within his own state could be increased correspondingly within the area of his special competence. For whenever Spartan affairs were discussed at Athens Cimon or Callias would expect to be heard; similarly in the fourth century a discussion of Boeotian affairs often would involve men such as Thrason and Demosthenes, Theban *proxenoi*, who were widely trusted in Thebes. Consequently it was as much to the advantage of Athens to possess such politicians who enjoyed repute in Thebes as it was to the advantage of the Thebans to be associated with such influential Athenian politicians. Lichas, the *proxenos* of Argos at Sparta, enjoyed a wide international reputation for his hospitality to strangers.[346] Not all *proxenoi* could aspire to a like reputation but such honours were keenly sought. Indeed Demosthenes charged his opponent Aeschines with being less intent on fulfilling his diplomatic role for Athens than on securing for himself appointments to proxeny.

But if reputations could be won in diplomacy equally they could be lost or put at risk. We have already noted how in Athens Cimon's stock rose or fell according to the success or failure of his policy.

In some ways *proxenoi* were especially vulnerable to attack, for aspersions could be, and were indeed, cast upon their loyalty and sense of patriotism. Amid the political and factional struggles such charges were made, as were those of bribery and corruption, almost as if by reflex action, but in Athens they were rarely justified and carried little weight. The discovery of the Spartan envoys at Callias' house in 378 is not known to have compromised his reputation. In 415 Nicias, the *proxenos* of Syracuse in Athens,[347] was chosen as commander of the Athenian expedition against Syracuse. There was, therefore, no need to doubt the loyalty of a *proxenos* to his own state. But it is easy to understand that a *proxenos* could find himself in a delicate or exposed position. In 374, for example, Polydamas of Pharsalus went to Sparta at a time when the growing power of Jason of Pherae was causing alarm and he prefaced his remarks as follows: 'Spartans, I, like all my ancestors of whom we have record, act as your *proxenos* in my own country and am honoured by you with the title "benefactor". It seems right then for me to come to you if I am in any difficulty and to let you know if things begin to be dangerous for you in Thessaly.'[348]

It was in states where political rivalry reached the point of civil war and revolution that the *proxenos* was most exposed to risk and was most assiduously courted by the external power, for his intelligence could help to determine the fate of an alliance. Xenias of Elis, the *proxenos* of the Spartans and the friend of their King Agis, was instrumental in the attempt to suppress the democratic faction and to align his city with Sparta.[349] Similarly in 428 when elements in Mytilene were planning to revolt from the Athenian alliance the Athenian *proxenoi* revealed to the Athenians the oligarchs' intentions, of which they would otherwise have been ignorant. In such circumstances *proxenoi*, in accepting their appointments, could expect at times certain implicit or explicit guarantees. For when *c.* 363 the people of Ceos took part in a revolt against Athens, Theban sympathizers murdered the Athenian *proxenos*. Consequently when the Athenian generals reduced the situation to order the ensuing treaty made it a capital offence to treat Athenian *proxenoi* in such a way.[350] There were many precedents for that, for in the previous century the Athenians had been heavily dependent on their *proxenoi* for the maintenance of links with the democratic factions of the subject states in holding together their alliance. Reassurance was given by guaranteeing for the *proxenoi* protection in Athens and throughout allied territory.

When *proxenoi* were obliged to leave their own state of residence on account of the domestic political situation in the fluctuations of internal political warfare they could often be sure of asylum in the alien state with which they were associated. Amyntor of Thasos, for example, was exiled on a charge of 'Atticism' and fled to Athens.[351] Conversely political revolution in the city which had appointed the *proxenos* could result in termination of the appointment and its privileges. It is accepted that such cancellations were made by the revolutionary oligarchic régime at Athens in 404/3; later, reinstatements were made after the restoration of the democratic constitution and among the beneficiaries were Amyntor of Thasos and his four brothers.[352]

War and breaches of alliance by no means necessarily led to the cancellation of appointments of proxeny. The seal was often set on alliances by the appointment as *proxenoi* of men who had been instrumental in drawing them up, but the proxeny was made as a permanent and hereditary arrangement which was not dependent upon the existence of the alliance. Indeed one of the commonest privileges accorded to a *proxenos* was immunity by land and by sea both in war and in peace.

In the preceding description of the personnel and their function in what may be termed 'ambassadorial' and 'consular' diplomacy, we have seen that although certain practices were normal the working of the system was not based upon established routines and departments of state but upon individuals and upon decisions which were taken as the occasion arose. Consequently little courtly etiquette surrounded the despatch and reception of envoys or representatives. Such developments were reserved for the Romans and Byzantines.

If envoys were proceeding to a hostile state they could naturally gain advance clearance by sending ahead a herald, who was inviolate; otherwise they proceeded without ado. On arrival they presented themselves to the appropriate authorities. At Athens at any given time they were likely to present themselves to the presiding committee of the council. Thereupon the council could deliberate upon their mission before recommending either that the envoys be turned away or that they be introduced to the next statutory meeting of the public assembly. At Sparta envoys presented themselves for preliminary meetings with the authorities. In 405 Theramenes and his nine colleagues on their first embassy from Athens to Sparta encountered there the five leading officials, the ephors, who demanded to know their terms of reference. The ephors were not satisfied and sent the envoys back to Athens, suggesting that they return with different terms of reference.[353]

It was a serious affront to turn away an envoy abruptly. The Athenians in a mood of trenchant opposition to Persia sent away Murychides, the Persians' Hellespontine envoy c. 480, and refused him access to public discussion.[354] Similarly after the Battle of Leuctra in 371 the Thebans sent a garlanded messenger to formally announce in Athens their victory over Sparta. At the time the Athenian council happened to be meeting on the Acropolis, but after the councillors heard of the events it was clear that the news was far from welcome. They did not offer the herald any hospitality, and they said nothing in reply to his request for aid. Thereupon he left Athens.[355] It was unusual for an envoy to receive such a cold reception, for even when there was a complete failure to establish any diplomatic rapport, it was usual to observe the customary niceties. In 344/3 there was complete disagreement in principle between the Athenians and Philip's envoys, yet the courtesies of hospitality were extended.[356] When a firm rebuke was intended envoys could be formally requested to leave within a specified period, as when Spartan envoys in 404 received an ultimatum to depart from Argos before sundown.[357]

A state had little obligation to provide hospitality for visiting envoys. Normally they fended for themselves, staying at an inn or resorting to their *proxenos*, as did the Spartan envoys to Athens in 378. When a conclusion was reached in the business upon which the envoys had been sent, by a formal resolution attached to the main proposal on the business an invitation was issued to the visiting envoys to dine at public expense on the morrow or the day after that. Athens, for example, extended invitations to envoys from Segesta in 458/7[358] and from Selymbria in 407.[359] Such invitations could include more than a mere dinner, for in 346 Philip's envoys were given reserved seats, on a proposal made in the council, at the Dionysian Festival.[360]

In the reception of guests it was an old and chivalrous custom of the Greeks to exchange gifts, but it seems that envoys eschewed such practices and the reception of envoys by a state was not to be compared with reception by a personal host. In any case the risk of bribery or the appearance of bribery presented an obvious problem. That problem became the more acute when envoys encountered the hospitality of a ruler such as the king of Macedon or Persia. In 394 the Athenians sent two envoys, Epicrates and Phormisius, to Persia, where they were presented with gifts. The matter was raised in the assembly on their return home, but they were able to laugh it off by suggesting in jest that instead of appointing nine archons every year the Athenians should elect nine of their poorest citizens as envoys to Persia.[361] Timagoras was not so lucky on his embassy from Athens to Persia in 367, for he accepted imprudently lavish gifts and was condemned to death after his return.[362] Embassies to such rulers were naturally expected to observe certain procedures of etiquette at court. Instances of the rather more direct and personal, if formal, contact can be seen in the exchange of 'tokens' or symbols of formal recognition of the right to receive, and the obligation to bestow, hospitality. The Athenians in according honours to King Strato of Sidon *c.* 367 decreed that the council should see to the provision of a set of tokens which the envoys of Athens should present when visiting Sidon, and vice versa.[363] Similar provision seems to have been made in the agreement between Athens and the satrap Orontes in 348,[364] but such an exchange of tokens was not a necessary part of proceedings.

If one state wished to make a gesture to another by assuring attention to its envoys at all times, a clause could be appended to a principal decree dealing with the business in hand to the effect that thenceforth envoys would be received by the council and granted introduction to the assembly within a fixed period. In 446/5, for example, the Athenians guaranteed to offer Chalcidian envoys access to the council and assembly within ten days.[365] Where individual representatives were concerned the host state could make known its pleasure by passing a formal resolution specifically praising envoys, as the Athenians did in the case of the envoys of Amyntas of Macedon (375–3)[366] and of Mytilene (367).[367]

The political power and responsibility for dealing with external policy and diplomacy lay directly in the hands of the sovereign institution of a state, normally the public assembly. In Athens the assembly was under a statutory obligation to meet every nine or ten days or so. Its agenda was to some extent predetermined, for, irrespective of what other pressing business there might be, certain issues had to be raised in a fixed order even if only as a formality. Among the issues which at Athens were prescribed for automatic and regular attention were the supply of corn and defence.[368] It is true that the main business and resolutions were prepared by the council before the meeting of the assembly, but in the assembly there was freedom to deal with amendments and pressing matters. In any event it was not possible so to manage business as to confine issues and debates to a predictable course, and as time went on it became easier for the initiative to be taken by the assembly as occasion demanded.

Naturally enough it was recognized that a meeting of a large public assembly was not the ideal occasion for instigating initial discussion of detailed proposals which could have wider implications. Furthermore, even though in Athens the Council of Five Hundred had a general responsibility for preparing business for discussion in the public assembly, a committee of the five hundred councillors would receive news and act as agents for summoning full meetings of the council and assembly to discuss matters upon which preparatory work had been done. There was always in session a committee of fifty of the councillors, who acted in turn for one-tenth of the year. It was the normal practice for the decrees of the assembly to be passed in accordance with the terms of a preliminary resolution (*probouleuma*) of the council, and for the texts of most treaties and resolutions concerning diplomats and diplomacy to be produced in that way. Typically, for example, the inscription set up by the Athenians to record the treaty with Thessaly in 361/0 opens with the phrase 'By the resolution of the Council and Assembly',[369] and an identical phrase is to be found on the inscription set up by Arcesine in Amorgus to honour its Athenian governor Androtion.[370] Of the amendments and riders which were proposed in the assembly the majority seem to have been relatively minor. For example when the Athenian assembly passed a resolution formulated by the council concerning relations with Mytilene a rider was added to commend the Athenian envoys concerned and to invite them to a public dinner.[371] Occasionally, however, an amendment of greater substance was introduced. The Athenian council passed a preliminary resolution *c.* 342 to honour Arybbas the Molossian, but the assembly voted in addition to offer him and his children protection and to instruct the generals to restore his ancestral realm if need be.[372]

In Athens, and many other communities, on account of the nature of the composition of the council and its standing committee, whose membership was determined by lot and by rotation, it was always possible that there were not enough suitable men with adequate knowledge to discuss any given topic. But the system ensured the preponderance of the wealthier and more leisured classes, who were able to give more time to politics and public affairs. Certainly it has been noted how in the fourth century those who were most likely to want, and were best equipped to fill, a place in the council at Athens managed to secure it for themselves. But even if the requisite expertise was not there in the council or its committee, individuals had access and could be consulted, and the generals always had the right of access to discussions. The board of Ten Generals, certainly in the fifth century even if to a lesser extent subsequently, was composed of major political figures who were elected by no means merely for their military skill. They were elected for their political authority and expertise. They were men who knew much of the financial and military affairs of state and they were leaders of opinion. They too had a general executive responsibility for the strategic welfare of the state and their voice could not be ignored by the council.

In debates on diplomacy and foreign policy the public assembly was much more at the mercy of its leaders – and of its emotions – than it would be where general constitutional issues or matters of purely internal financial importance and civic welfare were being discussed. For the majority of citizens had little direct acquaintance with affairs beyond their own immediate environment. Foreign travel and the consumption of printed books and instant news were not part of the experience of the ordinary citizen. Public opinion then was not necessarily informed, even inadequately, of affairs in other states. The main political protection in a state such as Athens was that there was a nucleus of men, expert in their field even if political rivals, and that argument and debate between political rivals would expose issues. The plausibility of the factions would be challenged and their ideas assessed by a shrewd electorate, which was familiar, through acquaintance, with its leaders.

In communities such as ancient Athens it was easier than in modern times for leaders to present themselves more constantly and consistently before the public eye. For in many modern democracies a leader may alternate between periods in office and government, when he has power and responsibility, and periods of political opposition, when he has no power and little but moral responsibility; perhaps following one significant defeat a modern politician or statesman may be inclined to retire from public life. In the ancient world such alternation between office and formal opposition was nothing like as significant. Since policies evolved in the course of public debate and were not necessarily proposed by a holder of office an individual had greater incentive to remain consistently in public life. Indeed it was always possible that a man who held office had to operate a policy of which he disapproved. Such an official was nevertheless fully accountable for his conduct in office whilst the man who was responsible for initiating or proposing the policy was not accountable if he did not hold office.

To the extent that there was scope for private contact and initiatives the exercise of control over policy by public institutions and officials was not complete. It was, for example, widely believed that in 446/5 the situation between Athens and Sparta was so manipulated in the field by Pericles and the Spartan King Pleistoanax as to avoid a military clash and to smooth the way for the Thirty Years' Peace.[373] Pericles was apprehensive lest the start of the great Peloponnesian War took on the form of a 'phoney' war, thereby arousing suspicion that an understanding existed between him and the Spartan King Archidamus.[374] Similarly Alcibiades made full use of his private external contacts when out to manipulate relations between Athens and Argos. He had personal friends and influence in Argos, and he attempted to sabotage the Peace of Nicias and cause the Athenians to ally with Argos instead.[375] When the Spartan envoys came to Athens in 421/0 to attempt to salvage the Peace he succeeded in wrecking their attempt. The Spartan envoys introduced themselves and stated in the Athenian council that they had come with full powers to settle the issues outstanding. Then Alcibiades, fearing that they might succeed in their mission, sought a meeting with them, at which he pretended to help expedite their business. Accordingly he managed to persuade them to deny before the Athenian assembly that they had come with full powers on the grounds that in the assembly the Athenians would attempt to wring excessive diplomatic concessions from the Spartans. The result was that the Spartan envoys were discredited. In the meantime, still acting in a private capacity, Alcibiades had sent a message to the Argives informing them of developments in Athens and urging them not to take any further thought for the Argive envoys who had been sent to Sparta but to send envoys instead to Athens. When Nicias returned virtually empty-handed from an embassy to Sparta, upon which he made a last despairing attempt to retrieve the situation, the Argive envoys were already at hand in Athens, where they were introduced by Alcibiades. As a result the Athenians made an alliance with the Argives and their allies, the Mantineans and Eleans.[376] Demosthenes too in the following century was not without his private contacts and sources of information in other states. In 346 he was said to have concerted plans with Callias of Chalcis in making proposals to put before the assembly concerning Philip of Macedon.[377]

Although situations and relations between states and persons could be manipulated by individuals it was quite difficult for private initiatives to be carried through and put into effect without public approval. As far as the formal relations between states and their representatives went, the greatest scope for initiative was afforded to commanders in the field by breaking off military engagements and concluding truces, but commanders were always held subsequently accountable at home for their actions. In 418, for example, the Spartans and their allies having assembled what was, according to Thucydides, the finest Greek army ever brought together up to that time for action against the Argives, completely surrounded the Argive forces and cut them off from their city. Then Thrasylus, one of the five Argive generals, and Alciphron, a leading Argive politician who was *proxenos* of the Spartans, on their own initiative approached King Agis, the Spartan commander, and asked him to restrain his attack as the Argives were ready to submit to arbitration any complaints which the Spartans might have against Argos. Agis granted a truce for four months to allow diplomacy its scope. But not only was Thrasylus reviled and almost stoned to death at home before gaining sanctuary at an altar, but Agis for his part encountered such serious opposition at home that although he promised to atone by further military service there were attached to him ten counsellors, without whose agreement he was to have no authority to lead out an army.[378]

It was difficult alike for individuals, boards of officials or councils to commit themselves or their states without public approval. The college of the five Spartan ephors could signify or lead a shift in the policy of state, as did Xenares and his colleagues in 420, who were less inclined than were their predecessors to try to compromise with the Athenians in an attempt to preserve their alliance and the Peace of Nicias. The ephors by themselves could not make treaties or even binding commitments of lasting significance. They could offer to other communities assurances which were of some value as mere statements of intention and which had some force for so long as they were in office, a period of one year only. The Spartans were supposed to have secretly offered help to Thasos in its struggle with Athens[379] and we are told that in 432 the 'Spartan authorities' promised to invade Attica if the Athenians proceeded against Potidaea,[380] but no formal treaty or protocol seems to have been involved and the Spartans did not fulfil the promise. Techniques were clearly somewhat different in the case of the Hellenistic leagues and monarchs. For monarchs would deal through the officials of their royal courts and not have to be concerned with popular debates on policy. Debates too were perhaps less of a feature of the working of the leagues. The Achaean League, for example, had a central authority and its leader could act on its behalf. The Aetolian League, however, required formal discussion and a vote by its representatives to approve diplomatic

measures. The historian Polybius is almost certainly in error in referring to a secret treaty between Sparta and the Aetolians in 220, for
neither party had the constitutional mechanism for such an arrangement and probably no more than an understanding was reached
between Spartan and Aetolian leaders of the time.[381] Even if monarchs
could circumvent lengthy constitutional processes in their diplomacy
by issuing decrees and publishing letters, their agreements with other
states would be subject to the normal constitutional processes of that
state, and in any event it was as well for them to place on record
agreements between rulers. In 311, for example, the Macedonian
leaders Antigonus, Cassander, Lysimachus and Ptolemy reached an
agreement which was nominally of great significance in its provision
of guarantees for the independence of the Greeks. The agreement
was formally published in the form of a letter to the Greek states and
a copy of it, inscribed on marble, was discovered at Kursunlu Tepe,
the ancient Scepsis, in Asia Minor.[382]

In Athens the council could do much in the field of diplomacy
and many matters were by custom left to its discretion. The council
and its committees had the charge of keeping official records. It
received visiting envoys and was responsible not only for introducing
them to the assembly but also for formulating a resolution or recommendation to the assembly for discussion of the business of the envoys.
An Athenian inscription of 355 shows how when two envoys arrived
from Neapolis the council resolved that the envoys be introduced at
the next meeting of the assembly together with the recommendation
of the council on the matter.[383] The council or its committee also
received returning envoys and heard their reports before discussion
was held in the assembly. The council could then act as a clearing-
house for information, and as a small body charged with responsibility
for administration of detail it was clearly a focus of influence. Its role
was far from being confined to matters of procedure and bureaucracy;
its membership, determined by lot, was composed of a broad section
of public opinion and it could be expected to reflect or take into
account the political susceptibilities of the assembly or of groups
within it. In the decrees of the fifth and fourth centuries there are
many instances where amendments to the proposals of the council
were carried in the assembly, but there appears to have been no
tendency for clashes to occur between the council and the assembly,
even though the council sometimes went beyond dealing with procedure and policy to make recommendations of men to serve as
envoys.

Under extreme stress of war and in extraordinary circumstances the initiative could pass from the assembly or council to individuals or other groups. For example, early in the great Peloponnesian War Pericles appears to have prevented the assembly from meeting for unusually long periods; in 413 the Athenians appointed ten senior citizens as *probouloi*, or special commissioners, with wide powers to organize finance and the war-effort more efficiently, and in the last period of the War the conduct of the council was not above suspicion. But even if the council could take the initiative in discussion and policy it could not pursue its own policy. In 396/5 the Athenian general Demaenetus, after confidential discussions and in collusion with the council, launched an attack on Milo, the Spartan harmost stationed on Aegina.[384] The attack symbolized, but did not begin, Athens' naval revival and assertion of independence from Spartan control of her foreign policy. The attempt failed and following Spartan complaints the assembly wisely took into account the balance of forces and disclaimed any responsibility. The attempt of Demaenetus, like that of Sphodrias for the Spartans against Athens in 378,[385] was conceived no doubt on the basis of the old Spartan adage that in success the state assumed the responsibility and credit whilst in failure blame attached to the individual.

In the Athenian constitution not all matters were decided according to the votes of the council and assembly, for judicial procedures were invoked for political ends: indeed justice was political. The courts of law of course could not act as a positive stimulant to certain policies but they could act as a check on men and proposals. A variety of procedures was open covering various charges ranging from unconstitutional procedure to bribery and corruption. Such use of the law courts was a normal and important extension of the ground over which personal and political battles were fought between the orators. It was a perfectly legitimate means of blocking proposals or discrediting politicians, and it could be used as an extra line of defence or attack after the votes of council and assembly had been recorded.

Such cases were an accepted part of the life of a politician. Aristophon, the Athenian general and politician of the fourth century, proudly claimed that he had been accused of unconstitutional procedure by the process of *graphê paranomon* no less than seventy-five times and that on each occasion he had been acquitted.[386] Demosthenes had severe problems in overcoming constitutional limitations in his fight to find an effective military force with which Athens could combat Philip of Macedon. Funds were needed urgently to equip a force but the Athenians were unable or unwilling to supply them. Accordingly in 349 Demosthenes proposed that surplus money from the Theoric Fund, a fund instituted in the Periclean era and used to subsidize public attendance at dramatic festivals, should be appropriated for military purposes. His opponents, less belligerent than he, blocked his proposal by the device of *graphē paranomon*, but ten years later he achieved the conversion of the use of the money in organizing the final confrontation with Philip.

On many other occasions the resolution of disputes over foreign policy turned on the votes or verdicts of jurors. In 392/1 the Athenians elected ten men as envoys to Sparta, including Andocides, who was a powerful advocate of a rapprochement with Sparta. On their return they made their proposals but they were charged with misconduct of their embassy by Callistratus,[387] who judged that it was best for Athens to align herself with Thebes. Andocides and his colleagues fled into exile and so a man of many years' standing in Athenian public life was removed from Athens. In 367 there was a keen dispute on the question of whether the Athenians were to align with Sparta or with Thebes and Persia. Following the Theban diplomatic success with the Persians and the attempt of the Athenian envoy Timagoras to draw Athens closer to Thebes and Persia, his political opponents accused him of misconduct on the embassy and had him condemned to death. Soon afterwards the Thebans chalked up another success against Athens by gaining control of Oropus. Callistratus and the general Chabrias were acquitted on a charge of treason arising from that event, but the action was part of a successful campaign to discredit them. Similarly in the events from 346 in respect of Athenian policy toward Macedon the law courts were an arena in which the political battles were fought and certain politicians and their policies were rendered ineffective. After the Athenian failure to secure the implementation of the Peace of Philocrates on terms favourable to Athens the political repercussions were felt in the courts. For Philocrates, who was the architect of the treaty with Philip, was condemned to death for treason, although he had had the prescience to escape that sentence by flight into exile.[388] Thereafter he took no further part in Athenian diplomacy. Aeschines too was prosecuted for misconduct on the embassy to Philip in 346, and although he counter-attacked Demosthenes and his colleagues with enough success to secure acquittal the margin was narrow. Thereafter men of a stronger antipathy to Macedon rose to the fore and Aeschines' influence was temporarily impaired, but it was useful for Athens to have him available when envoys of a suitable disposition were required to arrange terms with a victorious Philip in 338 after the Battle of Chaeronea.[389]

From the late fifth century onward the Athenians no longer favoured the device of ostracism, which had at times helped to secure some degree of at least temporary continuity of policy. Pericles, for example, was relieved of the main opposition to his imperial policy by the ostracism of Thucydides, son of Melesias, for ten years in 443. But in times of war and crisis it was not necessarily beneficial to a state to have leading statesmen in exile where they could symbolize the disunion of a state or act as a focus for subversion. In 480 the Athenians were aware of such risks and made a conscious attempt to secure political unity. That was demonstrated by the recall from exile of Aristides to co-operate with his former opponent Themistocles against the Persians. After the Peace of Nicias ostracism did not resolve the main issue of the day, which was to maintain peace or resume war with Sparta. For Hyperbolus' exile left the diametrically opposed Nicias and Alcibiades exactly where they had been.

In Sparta too differences over foreign policy were reflected in both political and legal procedures. The change in the diplomatic situation after the break-down of the Peace of Nicias was accompanied by the election of ephors, Cleobulus and Xenares, who were opposed to the peace.[390] Sparta is represented as a community which bore an authoritarian régime, but there were full discussions on policy. Polydamus of Pharsalus, for example, waited until the third day in 374 for a Spartan reply to his request.[391] In addition to the public bodies for debate at Sparta there was the factor of the two kings. At times differences between them could be exploited but the emergence of a powerful figure could contribute a degree of continuity to policy. The influence of King Agesilaus, punctuated though it was by his colleague King Cleombrotus, helped to ensure a continuing hostility to Thebes for many years after 396. The kings were not immune from political challenge. In 446 King Pleistoanax withdrew his forces from Attica and being suspected of engaging in collusion with Pericles he was found guilty on a charge of corruption.[392] King Agis found that his attempt in 418/7 to achieve a diplomatic, rather than a military, coup by collusion with pre-Spartan elements in Argos brought the Spartans close to punishing him by pulling down his house and fining him ten thousand drachmas.[393] In 403 after the policy of the admiral Lysander had been called into question and his authority had been weakened by verdicts of treason and embezzlement recorded against two of his associates, Clearchus and Thorax, King Pausanias superseded him and reversed the policy of supporting extreme oligarchic movements, especially in Athens. In his turn Pausanias found himself charged, and barely acquitted, with allowing the restoration of democracy in Athens, a charge which was revived eight years later when in 394 he was impeached both for failing to link up on time when campaigning with Lysander's force at Haliartus and for arranging a truce with the Thebans.[394]

So far we have dealt with the evolution of policy through the formal and informal institutions of state but we have said little of the extent to which this was based upon informed discussion and calculation. Apart from the *proxenoi* there was no clearly identifiable body of men upon whom a state could rely for its information. No state possessed sufficient apparatus for the systematic collection of information, and neither the bureaucracy nor even the physical means of communication existed to facilitate it. In communities where the production of wealth and military efficiency were not constantly improved by developments and inventions of technology, there were few secrets to be kept. When important developments were effected, such as the strengthening of the prows of the Athenian ships to ram the enemy vessels at Syracuse in 415, it required the experience of only one encounter for the opposing side to learn what had been done. Much of the statistical information on the wealth and man-power of a community was sufficiently common knowledge in that community for men to know of such things not so much from documents as from common talk and informed debate. Even so it sometimes took some effort to compile the appropriate facts and figures to enable decisions to be made. In 374, for example, when Polydamas of Pharsalus approached the Spartans for help it took them two days to reckon up the number of regiments which were serving abroad and the number which were operating against Athens and on their own frontiers. Where knowledge could be gained for the asking and where no organized apparatus existed for its collation internally there was little incentive for men to collate intelligence on an international scale. In an environment where change was slow that might not matter to any great degree, but it was possible for men to assume that things had remained the same when in fact many factors had changed. Athens in the age of Demosthenes might have been better served by the preservation of, and willingness to consult, objective records of basic data. For many were inclined to regard most factors as constant but to consider as the principal variant the

morale and will-power of the citizens. Similarly notions about
Spartan power remained constant and so it came as a surprise to the
Greeks to learn of Sparta's defeat at Leuctra, whereas a knowledge
of the size of the Spartan citizen population and that of the army in
successive campaigns might have given some indication of what was
to come.

Socrates teased an aspiring young politician, asking him if he knew
the financial resources and man-power of his own state and if he
could say what were those of the other leading states of Greece. For
he argued that any statesman ought to be that well-informed to guide
his state in advising on its policies. In crude terms leading politicians
would have a fair idea of what military and diplomatic opportunities
were open to their states. They generally recognized that success or
failure in warfare depended upon the inferiority or superiority of
numbers on one side or the other. Accounts of wars, whether in
Homer, Thucydides or Xenophon, are accompanied frequently by
catalogues of the respective alliances. To some extent the experience
of the Greeks both in their campaigns against Persia and during the
long period of Spartan predominance pointed to the importance of
sound strategy and careful military training and exercise. But even
so in the fifth and fourth centuries the Spartans were slow to fight
against Athens without the support of Thebes, and the Athenians
realized that they needed Theban support to stand a good chance
of military success against Sparta, and each of those three states knew
that if it was outnumbered by the other two the best chance of redressing the balance of power lay in calling in the Persians and appealing to their sense of self-interest. In earlier times most disputes were
essentially local and between neighbouring states, but the Athenians
complicated international life by gaining diplomatic and military
support from unprecedently wide areas, for they were able to exercise
their naval power, which rested not upon the control of a mainland
but upon control of great numbers of island and maritime communities.

Consequently when crises arose over issues which were not merely
local disputes and when appropriately detailed calculations had to
be made, then a state could easily find itself at a loss. The Athenians
were remarkably ill-informed about affairs in Sicily before the despatch of their expedition in 415, although they had by then long-
standing treaties with Rhegium and Leontini and during the Peloponnesian War they had already sent out naval detachments to western
waters. When Leontini asked for help against Syracuse the Athenians
had virtually no idea of how much local support they would find,[395]

and in spite of their attempts to obtain this information, it was not until the despatch of their unprecedentedly large expedition that they discovered how little support there actually was. In 411 when men of Chios suggested to the Spartans that it would be in their interest to co-operate against Athens on the ground that Chios had one of the largest navies, a useful factor in combating Athens, the Spartans sent out Phrynis to see if Chios really did have a large navy.[396] It might have been expected that since Chios possessed one of the few navies which were independent of Athens the Spartans would either have known about it, or made it their business to find out in the two preceding decades of warfare. For the support of such a navy was likely to be as important a factor in Spartan strategy as was that of Corcyra's navy to Athens just over twenty years before.

Generally the collection of information was a haphazard affair. It was, for example, by chance that Herodas of Syracuse visited Phoenicia in 396 in company with a ship-owner. He observed the presence of Phoenician ships and heard that some three hundred had been assembled. Without delay he boarded the first available boat so that he could inform the Spartans of his intelligence.[397] The Spartans were glad to receive the information, for it was probable that the ships were being prepared for action against them. Nevertheless armies in the field did make it their business to collect information. The work of Aeneas the Tactician in the fourth century shows a preoccupation with measures to be taken to deal with envoys and strangers who might come on missions of espionage or sabotage. Philip of Macedon was reputed to have a good system of intelligence which enabled him to find out within hours what his arch-opponent Demosthenes had said in his speeches in Athens.

The unerring accuracy with which Greek states were often able to anticipate the moves of others in times of crisis is quite surprising. The Athenians intercepted Spartan envoys to Persia on their way through Thrace in 430/29[398] and they intercepted a Persian messenger on his way to Persia in 425/4.[399] Similarly the Spartans intercepted an Athenian embassy to Persia in 396/5[400]. In 392 the Athenians sent envoys to Persia to counter the Spartan envoys who had already been despatched there[401] and in 367 the Athenians, Spartans and Thebans all sent embassies or counter-embassies to Persia.[402] At those times Persian support was critical in the balance of power in Greece, and the swift counter-action may have been taken either on the basis of positive intelligence or because at any given point the diplomatic moves of Athens, Sparta and Thebes were fairly predictable.

When it came to the point and a state had to concert its policy it could not rely on the reports of functionaries or professional specialists, and the knowledge which was at the disposal of a state was contained not so much in files as in the heads of its leading political figures. For sound and informed advice the Athenians would look to a Cimon or Callias concerning Sparta, to Demosthenes concerning Thebes and to Nicias concerning Syracuse, just as the Spartans would look to Philocharidas or Endius before dealing with Athens and to Lichas in dealing with Argos. No individual had an unchallengeable knowledge of any particular sphere but small numbers of men, whether in or out of office, were expected to provide the appropriate political leadership. If their advice was soundly based then they earned credit, or even if it was not they could be lucky, as was the Athenian Cleon on campaign at Pylos in 425. Otherwise the political leader paid the penalty and was discredited, as was Cimon at Athens after Sparta's refusal of his help in 462/1.

In view of the nature of Greek government and its propensity to avoid bureaucratic procedures one would hardly expect to find much evidence of careful archive administration or preservation of records. The Athenians, for example, had well-established constitutional practices before the late fifth century, yet when the closing years of that century saw two sequences of oligarchic revolution and democratic counter-revolution it is doubtful if anyone, whether he was an honest or a fraudulent man, could say exactly what were the provisions of the 'Ancestral Constitution'. In political speeches and pamphlets men were guilty of perpetrating the grossest errors and perversions of history, whether recent or distant events were under discussion. It is plain that even where records did exist they were not consulted as much as they could have been, even if only because politicians were not so much deliberately dishonest or idle as inclined to rely on memory.

In Athens at least from the middle of the fifth century permanent records were made with increasing frequency. The earliest surviving Athenian inscription on stone which concerns inter-state affairs relates to dealings with Erythrae at some time after 465,[403] and the earliest inscribed Athenian treaty is that signed with Segesta, dated by some scholars to 458/7.[404] It was the normal practice that when a measure had been passed or a treaty had been approved by the Athenian assembly the terms should be formally inscribed on stone and the *stele* erected. Of course such inscription was expensive, especially if it was on marble as at Athens, and the wealth of Athens from the fifth century may explain the greater number of inscriptions which are found there by comparison with other states. The Athenians set aside funds for the publication of such records and the passage of a decree was regularly accompanied by a rider directing the appropriate officials to publish it at the charge of such funds. The Athenians did not, however, pay for the inscription of all the decrees recorded and inscribed, for in cases where a request was made by another state for fresh arrangements to be instituted or for existing arrangements to be modified it was common for the Athenians to discuss the matter, make their resolution and to order publication to be made in Athens at the expense of the other state. In 446/5, for example, when the Athenians had discussed the request of the Chalcidians they ordered publication of the inscription in Athens at the expense of Chalcis.[405] Similarly when the Athenians granted the request of Phaselis for standing arrangements to be made for adjudicating disputes between citizens of the two states the people of Phaselis had to pay for the inscription at Athens.[406]

Treaties could be published in places other than the states which were signatories. The treaty signed between the Metapians and Anaitoi in the sixth century was inscribed in bronze at Olympia[407] as was the treaty signed between Elis and Heraea.[408] It was fashionable c. 420 for the treaties made by Sparta to be recorded at religious centres. The Peace of Nicias in 421 was to be recorded on *stelai* not only on the Athenian Acropolis and in the temple of Amycla in Sparta but also at the religious centres of Olympia, Delphi and the Isthmus.[409] Similarly in 420 the treaty between Athens, Argos, Elis and Mantinea was to be recorded by each party on the Athenian Acropolis, the Argive temple of Apollo and the Mantinean temple of Zeus, and they were all jointly to erect a commemorative bronze pillar at the Olympic Games of that year.[410] Such publication at Olympia was not so much for public information as part of the solemn ritual of witnessing a binding agreement at a religious centre.

The decrees of appointment of *proxenoi* also provided for publication of the record on stone. As in the case of treaties the expense was not always borne by the authorities responsible for passing the decree. Soon after the Peloponnesian War, when the newly reinstated democratic régime at Athens restored the proxeny decrees which had been cancelled by the oligarchs, five men of Thasos, including Eurypylus, were recorded as *proxenoi* of Athens and the clerk of the council was bidden to see to the inscription at Eurypylus' expense.[411] Evidently if one wanted an honour one had to be prepared to pay for it.

Many other kinds of records of a more or less permanent nature could be kept. Increasing numbers of catalogues of military and naval resources were commonly inscribed in Athens from the middle years of the fourth century. Similarly the publication of the financial accounts of officials and of the various treasuries was made annually. Accordingly if a statesman wished to review available resources in evaluating policy then it was open to him to do so. The working of the Delian League can be traced in considerable detail since there have survived documents known as the Athenian Tribute Lists, which record the financial transactions and the proportion of the annual contributions to the League which were paid to the treasury of Athena. The payments for the first fifteen years after the treasury was moved to Athens were recorded on a large block of marble of which one hundred and eighty fragments survive. Payments for the next eight years were recorded on another block of which over seventy fragments have been found. Thereafter inscriptions, of which some survive in part, were separately and annually set up to maintain the records. In the series dealings with almost three hundred and fifty states are recorded.

In view of their size and material the stone inscriptions were not the easiest documents to handle, consult or even preserve in the short term. It would not, for example, be the most convenient course to track down and look at several dozen inscriptions to ascertain the membership roll of the Second Athenian Confederacy. Consequently there was kept the main inscription, made at the time when the nucleus of the alliance was formed, and the names of other members were listed by addition in the margin,[412] even when a subsequent inscription separately recorded their accretion to the Confederacy. Two inscriptions, for example, from the year 375 record alliance between Corcyra[413] and the Athenian Confederacy, yet in addition the Corcyraeans were listed in the margin of the decree of the alliance which was set up in 377.

The officials and policy-makers of Greek states comprised at all times figures who were in the public eye and constantly in a position of having to justify and account for their activities in public debate. Matters were not handled in such a way that most issues were settled behind the scenes whilst only the crises caused public discussion. However much committees and councils explored possibilities, solutions and answers to diplomatic questions, their resolutions were submitted subsequently for public ratification. The relationship between policy-makers or advisers and the popular assembly was a

direct one. Political figures co-operated and acted in concert, but
generally they put forward proposals in their own names. Only
infrequently do we find adopted the procedure which Demosthenes
used in his later career of putting forward proposals in the name of
other men lest his own ideas were discredited by their mere association
with his name. Only in quite extraordinary circumstances do we
find in Athens avoidance of public debate, as happened early in the
Peloponnesian War. Then Pericles had such personal prestige and
political eminence to add to his elected position as general that for
a time when he caused a defensive strategy to be pursued he was able
to avoid calling meetings of the public assembly. But even he could
not maintain his position indefinitely, for he was prosecuted and
heavily fined.

Demosthenes' complaint was that a community such as Athens,
which rigorously maintained its constitutional procedures and public
control over policy, was at a constant disadvantage in its foreign
policy. As issues of external policy were as much political as anything
else, opponents, or rogues and scoundrels as Demosthenes put it,
had first to be overcome in debate. That enabled opposing states to
find out what was going on and to gauge their political and military
strategy accordingly, and it slowed down the response of Athens.
If all the states involved had similar institutions then in that respect
all were on roughly equal terms, but where it was a case of dealing
with states controlled by monarchs or narrowly based oligarchies
the conditions were not equal. The result was, claimed Demosthenes,
that Athens tended to react to the policies of Philip of Macedon rather
than to take the initiative against a man who had the sole direction
of affairs in his hands.

In 413, after suffering their greatest disaster of all time in the Sicilian
Expedition, the Athenians were shocked into attempting to modify
their institutions to meet the demands of running a war in what was
virtually a struggle for survival, let alone for victory. There were
political operators who merely sought a chance to subvert the democracy but there was a majority of honest voters who thought it better
to surrender their control of financial and military affairs to a special
commission of ten elders. The arrangements were perverted and led
to an oligarchic *coup d'état*, and the episode served to illustrate the
risks involved in modifying institutions merely to satisfy the needs of
war and external policy.

The impact of events upon the political mood of an ancient state
was more immediate than in the case of a modern state, especially at

a time of disaster. News was not conveyed exclusively or most quickly along official channels. Therefore there was no opportunity for it to be digested by an official body which could then carefully prepare its release or manipulate public opinion. Public emotion was therefore much more keenly aroused on matters of foreign policy. Often, of course, external affairs would loom larger in an ancient state since proportionately there was likely to be less other serious business. An ancient state, for example, did not deal comprehensively with the management of economic affairs or social policy; inter-mittently constitutional issues of great moment would arise, but in general there would be too little other business of significance to allow matters of peace, war and alliances to be obscured. News of the Athenian disaster in Sicily percolated gradually through the barbers' shops in the Piraeus, and the arrival of important news in such a manner was conducive to an irrational reaction. The reaction of the populace was one of fear and of anger at the orators who had advocated policies which had turned out disastrously.[414] Before the expedition the populace had heard the initial debates on policy and voted accord-ing to its own choice. No minister, functionary or bureaucrat could be pinpointed as the one to be blamed, tried or dismissed. The atmosphere was one of complete confusion, loss of confidence and frustrated anger.

A passage from one of Demosthenes' speeches[415] gives as well as any other in ancient literature an insight into the emotional and political condition of a populace confronted with a diplomatic crisis. It was in 338 just before the decisive Battle of Chaeronea when Philip of Macedon had occupied Elatea astride the principal route to Thebes and Athens and was poised to strike. 'It was evening in Athens and a messenger came to the presiding committee of the council with the news that Elatea had been captured. The members of the committee immediately got up in the middle of their dinner, cleared the people away from their market-stalls and burned the litter. Others sent for the generals and called out the trumpeter; the city was a scene of commotion. On the following morning at the break of day the presiding committee summoned the council into session and a meeting of the assembly was called, and the people were already in their seats before the council had reviewed the business and formulated a resolu-tion. When the councillors entered the assembly and the presiding committee had reported the news the messenger repeated his announce-ment in person and the herald formally put the question "Who wishes to address the assembly?" But no one came forward. Even though the question was repeated many times no one was the more inclined to come forward although all the orators and all the generals were present and our state was crying out with one voice for someone to speak for our salvation. . . . And yet if all who wished the city to be rescued had been obliged to step forward, you and all the Athenians would have left your seats and proceeded to the speaker's rostrum. . . . But that crisis and that day called for a man who not only was of sound disposition and wealth but had also kept track of events right from the start and who had correctly fathomed Philip's motives and objectives. The man who had no such knowledge or had not made a careful study of the history of the developments could neither discern the correct course nor dispense good advice.' The man who eventually came forward was, of course, Demosthenes.

CHAPTER XVII

THE INSTITUTIONS
OF DIPLOMACY

DEMETRIUS OF PHALERUM, whose life spanned the later fourth and early third centuries, was supposed to have written a treatise on inter-state relations. Nothing of it, however, or any similar historical survey or theoretical analysis survives. Nevertheless every indication which we have of the relations between states from the earliest times suggests that they were conducted on a rational basis. Even if the work of Demetrius had survived we would not have found in it clear statements of International Law and comprehensive codes, for addicted though the Greeks were to the creation of constitutions their codes of law were never the clear and comprehensive collections such as emanated from the Roman world.

In the Homeric poems there emerges quite clearly the idea of a justifiable war of revenge and of the obligations of alliance and assistance. There emerges too quite clearly a code by which envoys and strangers could be received in war and peace. The gods intervene in human affairs, and in all periods of Greek history the sanction of religion has some force. Messengers are of the divine stock of Zeus himself and compacts between men and states are sealed by due religious ceremonial. Thus treaties even in later times are described as *Horkoi* (oaths) or *Spondai* (libations).

The historian Herodotus quoted the saying of Pindar, the Theban poet, that custom is the ruler of all things.[416] In the pages of the history books there is a break in the continuity of the record between the world of Mycenae and Homer and of that which emerges after the 'Dark Ages'. Nevertheless it is hard to imagine that there was not a certain continuity of development which found no authority to record it. From the fifth century there are many references in the Greek writers to the common customs of all the Greeks. When Xerxes, for example, offered alliance to the Athenians, at the instigation of Aristides they replied that there was insufficient gold on earth, no land wealthy or rich enough, nor anything at all which could

tempt them to espouse the Persian cause in the enslavement of Greece.
For as the Hellenes were of the same blood, spoke the same tongue and
maintained the same gods, temples, sacrifices, customs and observances,
it would be a shameful act of betrayal.[417] Furthermore, although the
Greeks collectively were beset by excessive egocentricity it was not
altogether left to the Greek writers Polybius and Diodorus of Sicily
under Roman influence to ponder on the common customs of mankind and the problems of the unity of Mediterranean history. For
Xerxes in protesting at the treatment of his envoys by the Greeks
declared that he would not contravene the accepted laws of mankind
by similar violation.[418]

   The lack of formal codification of customs by no means reduced
their moral force. No code was sufficient to cover all possibilities
and even within a state when there was a law apposite to certain
circumstances it was commonly argued that Unwritten Laws were
of greater force than the constitutional contrivances of men. Such
arguments are found in a variety of works from Sophoclean tragedy
to Aristotelian political theory. It was obviously reasonable that limits
should be set to legitimate hostility, that unprovoked aggression
should be avoided, and that war should be formally declared rather
than instigated by surprise. At the outbreak of wars states often staged
an elaborate minuet in which each party tried to place itself in a
position of moral ascendancy, if not to claim the support of the gods.
Before the Peloponnesian War Corcyra challenged Corinth to accept
the arbitration of any suitable Peloponnesian authority or Delphi, and
the Athenians challenged Sparta to arbitration. Sparta in her turn
demanded that the Athenians expel the Alcmaeonidae, including
Pericles, who had been for long under a divine curse. Before proceeding to war states were in the habit of resorting to the Delphic Oracle
not only for some forecast of the result but also to extract some element
of justification. At the start of a campaign all the best military authorities dwell upon the necessity of convincing an army that it has divine
approval. Conversely one had to be careful not to excite divine
disapproval and so the Spartans were notorious for finding difficulties
in rendering military assistance at times of religious celebrations, which
were frequent in any Greek calendar. When the Spartans met with
their first serious reverse at Pylos in 425 they began to suffer lack of
confidence in fearing that divine disapproval was being visited upon
them for having launched the Peloponnesian War with inadequate
justification. After the Athenian disaster in Sicily in 413 public wrath
was turned against the oracle-mongers and soothsayers.

Divine guidance might be hard to find but religious observance and fear pervaded public life and argument from it was reinforced by appeal not only to recent history but also to archaic precedent. At the turn of the seventh and sixth centuries the possession of Salamis was disputed between Athens and Megara. The parties resorted to arbitration by Sparta and each tried to reinforce its claim by appeal to the authority of Homer in quoting the Catalogue of Allies and each accused the other of misquotation. The dispute turned in favour of Athens on two grounds: there were Delphic oracles which described Salamis as Ionian, and Philaeus and Eurysaces, sons of the Salaminian hero Ajax the son of Telamon, had accepted citizenship of Athens and handed Salamis to their new city, where the Philaid deme continued to observe Philaeus as its eponymous ancestor.[419] In the fourth century reference continued to be made to archaic precedent in the search for justification of argument or conduct which was, however, based on other and more realistic grounds. Aeschines, as Athenian envoy to Macedon in 346, attempted to justify the Athenian claim to Amphipolis by relating how one of the sons of King Theseus, Acamas, received the district as his wife's dowry. The orator himself declared that ancient legend was of less significance than recent events in determining ownership.[420] Just as an inveterate rivalry had existed between Sparta and Argos from the second millennium so too ancient passions existed between Thebes and Orchomenus. Sparta and Argos managed to control their rivalry and to recognize the legitimacy of war between strictly confined limits over disputed areas. Epaminondas, the Theban statesman, in 371 managed to control reaction to the support which Thebes' rival gave to Sparta, but seven years later Orchomenus was obliterated, for Theban resentment had fed upon the legend of how in the Heroic Age Thebes had been obliged to pay tribute to the Minyae.[421] Perhaps such considerations based on arguments from ancient precedent or justice carried less weight than more immediate issues but they were important in conditioning the attitudes of rulers and communities, and we see that the Athenian orators were constantly at pains to demonstrate that what is just is nonetheless expedient for the state.

What many would accept as the earliest historical evidence for the inter-state affairs of Greece relates to the Olympic Games, which were instituted in 776. It is remarkable that such a Panhellenic festival was instituted, for it had a significance which transcended a mere interest in athletics and involved a common agreement to proclaim a holy truce and to suspend all hostilities for the duration of the festival.

Of course there are cases of violations and alleged violations of such
truces, but it is most significant that the Athenians were represented
even at the Isthmian Games held at Corinth in 412 immediately after
they had suffered such a terrible defeat as was engineered for them in
Sicily by Sparta and Corinth.[422] The local religious leagues, or
Amphictyonies, are the earliest manifestations of inter-state organiza-
tions, which were essentially based on a common cult. Their business,
however, did involve inter-state disputes, and they could impose
religious sanctions or even declare Sacred War upon delinquents.
The best-known Amphictyony is that based on Delphi, which
assumed considerable military and strategic importance in the middle
of the fourth century, but there were many others of no little antiquity,
including one based on the cult of the sea-god Poseidon in the Peloponnese at Calauria, a place which had a significant alternative name
Eirene (Peace). Members of the Delphic Amphictyony from of old
were bound by oaths to refrain from the destruction of member-
states and from interruption of supplies of running water either in
peace or in war. Any city which transgressed was liable to be razed
to the ground.[423]

Greek attitudes to law, government and bureaucracy were not
conducive to the adoption of specialized terms and formulas, but
even though we cannot trace in great detail the diplomatic inheritance
of Classical Greece a remarkable variety of treaties and diplomatic
institutions comes to light from the fifth century. There are clearly
expressed agreements, if not terms, providing not only for arbitration,
friendship, non-aggression, neutrality, treaties of defence, and all-
embracing treaties of defence and offence between states but also for
the regulation of the rights of strangers and traders.

There were many treaties whose purpose was not so much to
regulate or co-ordinate the public policies of states as to facilitate
the dealings of the citizen of one state with those of another. Such
treaties correspond in some respects to modern consular conventions
and were especially useful to those who were active in trade. The
common term used to describe many such conventions was *symbolai*.
Such *symbolai* dealt with all aspects of legal relationships which affected
the rights of a citizen in an alien state and they were not necessarily
confined to cases which arose from business agreements. In the fifth
century Athens is known to have had such agreements with Chios,
Phaselis, Selymbria, Mytilene and Samos, for which there is documentary evidence.[424] It is, however, somewhat tantalizing that none
of that series of inscriptions sets out the full details of the treaties.

The inscription mentioning the treaty between Athens and Phaselis contains only an amendment to it concerning the hearing of disputes and it was evidently made at the request of Phaselis. Provision was made for any dispute arising out of a contract made at Athens by a Phaselite to be heard before the Polemarch at Athens. An Athenian decree of 405 merely provides for disputes arising between Samians and Athenians to be settled according to the *symbolai*. Other such agreements were made by Athens in the fourth century with Troezen, Cretan communities and Siphnos.[425] Part of the inscription which records the treaty with Siphnos survives and shows that Siphnos guaranteed not to prosecute or put to death any Athenian without consulting Athens and that no Athenian would be put to death without due trial. In the treaty concluded *c.* 350 with Naxos arrangements were made for appeals to be heard.[426]

The existence of such *symbolai* in no way implied the subordination of the interests of one state to those of another. For although Athens had a series of agreements with members of the Delian League and experienced political difficulties with many of them, reference to the agreements with Selymbria and Samos was made in 409 and 405 respectively, occasions on which the Athenians were intent on stressing the sovereignty and independence of those two communities. The conclusion of such arrangements did not necessarily imply the existence of an alliance or any formal expression of friendship between two communities, but if feelings of hostility were aroused, as between Athens and Philip of Macedon, then the chances of arranging a convention were clearly slimmer. Equally it was possible, if by no means a common practice, to include clauses concerning private disputes in a fuller document of inter-state alliance. In 418 in the treaty between Argos and Sparta after the clause which provided for arbitration in disputes between the states there followed another to the effect that private parties should settle their disputes according to the traditional procedures.[427] From that it may be implied that *symbolai* were commonly concluded between members of the Peloponnesian alliance.

Commerce was generally in the hands of private contractors and the state as such tended not to intervene. There were, however, some exceptions to the general practice, especially in the case of certain strategic supplies and coinage. Early in the fourth century Mytilene and Phocaea concluded a currency agreement.[428] In the military alliance concluded *c.* 393 between Amyntas III of Macedon and Chalcis there was a clause regulating the export of timber and pitch, according to which a proper declaration and payment of duty had to be made.[429]

Part of an inscription recording an alliance between Erythrae and Hermeias of Atarneus, inscribed and found at Erythrae, covered the transit of goods in time of war. Each party was entitled in wartime to deposit property with the other for safe-keeping. No duty was to be incurred on it or on offspring born to slaves or livestock in deposit provided that property was retrieved within thirty days of the conclusion of peace and was not disposed of, otherwise the normal two per cent tax was payable.[430]

Terms for the export of ruddle from Ceos were imposed by the Athenians in the mid-fourth century. Then in answer to the demands of Athenian envoys three communities of Ceos, namely Carthaea, Coressus and Iulis, passed decrees that ruddle was to be exported solely to Athens;[431] in the event of anyone attempting any other outlet the goods and the freightship were to be publicly confiscated and half of the proceeds delivered to the informant. If the informant was a slave then he was to be granted his freedom. Export of the ruddle was to be in a vessel authorized by the Athenians and any further decisions of the Athenians were to have immediate effect. The Athenians were able to behave in such an authoritarian manner because they had exercised close supervision over political conditions in Ceos after their generals restored its communities to the Athenian alliance following the revolt c. 362.[432] In the case of a treaty for the import of Crimean corn the Athenians were much more 'correct' in their behaviour. They did not have a military alliance with King Leucon of the Bosporus, but they did have a commercial treaty with him from 357.[433] He gave them the first option on supplies and granted them exemption from export duty. In return Leucon and his sons were honoured with the privileges of Athenian citizenship but exempted from its obligations. A further Athenian decree was enacted in 346 to continue the arrangements when Leucon's sons sent envoys to Athens to discuss Athenian debts and to request permission to recruit naval crews in Athens.[434]

Many conventions between both large and small states gave limited rights and protection to individuals. For example, the treaty between Oeantheia and Chaleion in the mid-fifth century limited the opportunities for reprisals by permitting seizure only on the high seas, not on land or in port.[435] In the event of illegal seizure goods were to be restored within ten days and a fine was to be levied according to the decision of a tribunal. The wholesale exchange of civic or political rights between communities was quite unusual in Classical Greece. In the case of neighbouring communities, political unions or fully-

fledged federations there were naturally rights held in common. Far
less common was the kind of treaty which existed between Ceos
and Eretria from early in the fourth century.[436] This provided for
the enrolment by the Eretrian Board of Generals in a tribe and deme
of anyone from Ceos who wished to settle in Eretria and for the
enrolment by the *Thesmophylakes* in Ceos of any Eretrian who wished
to settle there and enjoy full political rights. In the late third century
too Ceos offered citizenship to the Aetolians in return for certain
guarantees against the seizure of its citizens even in the event of an
Amphictyonic dispute.[437] In the latter third of the fifth century the
Athenians cultivated the Samian democrats and rewarded their outstanding loyalty to the alliance by a block grant of citizenship at the
end of the Peloponnesian War, but it was not anticipated that the
gesture would have much practical effect. It was only in the Hellenistic
era that such arrangements commonly were made on a reciprocal
basis as part of a treaty of alliance or friendship. Thus in the third
century there was agreed an exchange of rights between Messenia
and Phigalia on terms which were to hold good for as long as both
parties maintained the formally declared state of friendship.[438] There
was a similar exchange of political rights in the third century on the
part of Smyrna and Magnesia, between whom was concluded a formal
treaty of friendship and alliance.[439]

In Classical Greece the most comprehensive form of treaty was
that of offensive and defensive alliance. The phrase which was commonly used to signify such an alliance was 'to have the same friends
and enemies'. If the obligation was taken seriously and literally then
it did involve some surrender of sovereignty and an entry into an
open-ended commitment. For a state might be drawn unwillingly
and unexpectedly into a war which could not be terminated without
the concurrence of the allies. The first known alliance where the
phrase was used was the Delian Confederacy,[440] where it was important
to have a pledge of complete loyalty to face imminent and conceivably
long-standing danger from the Persians. Of the many communities
which seceded from the Confederacy certain Bottiaean cities made a
full reconciliation with Athens and rejoined in 422, swearing to have
the same friends and enemies as the Athenians.[441]

As the extent of such a commitment was virtually without limit,
demands for action in accordance with the terms were a fertile source
of dispute. If one party differed from the other in its interpretation
then the way was open for accusations of bad faith and the imposition
of sanctions or direct action to force compliance. Peithias, the popular

leader in Corcyra, proposed in 427 that Corcyra should extend its defensive agreement with Athens to an offensive and defensive alliance.[442] The situation was one in which the democrats and oligarchs of Corcyra saw their long-continuing feud approaching a climax. No doubt Peithias realized that the best hope of the democrats was to make an alliance offering to Athens a total commitment which the Athenians could use as a pretext for intervening in support of the democrats in Corcyra.

The formula was rarely employed between two communities of equal standing, but even so, in the light of the diplomacy in founding the Delian Confederacy and the return of the Bottiaeans to the Athenian alliance, it did not necessarily imply the subordination of one party to another. Nevertheless the way in which the greater powers operated and exercised leadership within their respective spheres made such terms valuable diplomatic weapons for them to employ. When, for example, the Athenians surrendered to Sparta in 404 and were deprived of their defences and armaments they were not deprived of their sovereignty but they were compelled to have the same friends and enemies as Sparta.[443] The oath in that respect could be reciprocal but there was no doubt as to who had the power of initiative and the force to compel compliance. After that treaty the Athenians took virtually no serious diplomatic initiative for almost a decade. They did send envoys to Persia in 396/5, but these were arrested and put to death by the Spartans, apparently without any Athenian protest. When in 395 the Athenians made their first effective and positive post-war diplomatic decision it was to agree to the Theban initiative for an alliance, in which emphasis was placed on its defensive nature when the case was argued in the Athenian assembly.[444] Then in 379 after beating Olynthus into submission the Spartans demanded the despatch of envoys with full powers from Olynthus to agree to an alliance which involved respecting the same friends and enemies.[445] An equally clear case of the marked supremacy of one power in such an agreement was that involving Boeotia in 368 when the Macedonian ruler gave his son Philoxenus and fifty Companions as hostages to the Boeotians.[446]

In 302 when the League of Corinth was reconstituted as the Hellenic League by Demetrius Poliorcetes and Antigonus, members were bound, as in the Delian League, to have the same friends and enemies, and as in the case of the earlier League a Council was constituted to determine common policy.[447] Thereafter the principle was incorporated in various agreements of the Hellenistic period.

As opposed to alliances which committed states to support each other in battle (*symmachia*) there were other alliances in which the parties were obliged to render assistance only if one suffered an attack (*epimachia*). The terms used to describe each kind of alliance could be quite distinct but the Greek attitude to this kind of terminology was such that both regularly were described as *symmachia*. The first known instance of a purely defensive alliance was that concluded between Athens and Corcyra in the summer of 433. After hearing the representations of Corinthian and Corcyraean delegations the Athenians agreed to the Corcyraean request for alliance, but not on terms which would commit them to have the same friends and enemies. The alliance was on purely defensive terms, which could not be used by Corcyra to involve the Athenians in an attack on Corinth and which were compatible with the Thirty Years' Peace signed by the Athenians, Spartans and their respective allies.[448] That alliance, however, was sufficient to maintain Corcyra's resistance to Corinth and to prevent her naval assets from accruing to the Peloponnesians. Later when the Athenians stationed their vessels for the defence of Corcyra the Corinthians sent men in a boat to test the Athenian intentions. The Corcyraeans exhorted the Athenians to kill them, but the Athenians merely told the Peloponnesians that neither were they beginning war nor infringing the Peace, for they were there to help their allies. No obstacles, they continued, would be placed in the way of the Corinthians if they sailed elsewhere than against Corcyra or her possessions.[449]

In 420 the Corinthians were fully aware of the room for manoeuvre which was afforded by a defensive alliance. They had at some time previously concluded a defensive alliance (*epimachia*) with Argos.[450] Argos, Elis and Mantinea subsequently concluded a fuller alliance by which they were bound to make peace and war in concert, but the Corinthians did not join in, nor did they join the same three states when they extended their alliance to Athens in 420.[451] The Corinthians maintained that they were adequately protected by the first treaty, which bound them by guarantees of mutual assistance in repelling invasions but did not bind them to participate in offensive measures. In 370 the Phocians made a defensive alliance with Boeotia, and when in 362 Epaminondas led out the Boeotians, Euboeans and Thessalians against the Peloponnese the Phocians refused to follow. For they maintained that according to the treaty they were bound to offer assistance if anyone attacked Thebes but they were not obliged to go on an expedition against others.[452]

There were, of course, many other alliances which were formed purely for defensive purposes. Sometimes, however, the issues were less clear cut. Some alliances were essentially defensive or protective in origin but had wider implications. The alliance of the Greeks against Persia in 481/0 and the Second Athenian Confederacy, formed in 378/7 to compel the Spartans to allow the rest of the Greeks to live in freedom, are cases in point. Those two alliances were formed to combat a known menace and did involve their members with their full knowledge, awareness and anticipation in joint expeditions to beat the oppressor into accepting submission or terms. In some instances the potential enemy might not always be known, although in most cases he was, and a defensive alliance could involve joint punitive action against an aggressor.

In 420 when the Athenians, Argives, Mantineans and Eleans concluded their alliance for one hundred years they promised not to bear arms against each other or their allies, but if the territory of any party were attacked then they were all to provide assistance as the victim requested. But the arrangements went further than that, for it was agreed not only that an invader should be treated as a common enemy but also that no peace should be concluded except by common consent. Furthermore, even if the invader withdrew after ravaging territory, war was still to be maintained against the aggressor, until all agreed upon peace. So long as the fighting was on the territory of one of the parties that party was to exercise military command, but if a common expedition was mounted then the command was to be shared. Somewhat similar terms were included in the alliance made between Athens and Sparta in the previous year, by which an invader of one was automatically considered the enemy of the other until both agreed to conclude peace.[453] There was also a clause to the effect that even if the invader withdrew after ravaging and plundering territory punishment was to be meted out by both.

In the fourth century there was developed a basic form of alliance which was adopted as a fairly standard model. It is first seen in the document which records the perpetual alliance between Athens and Boeotia, for which the text reads as follows: 'If anyone proceeds to war against the Athenians either by land or by sea, the Boeotians are to render assistance with all their strength to the utmost of their ability as the Athenians may request. And if anyone proceeds to war against the Boeotians either by land or by sea the Athenians are to render assistance with all their strength to the utmost of their ability as the Boeotians may request.' Similar wording was used in the treaty also concluded in 395 between Athens and Locris.[454] The same formulas also appeared in the treaty of 384 between Athens and Chios,[455] which was itself the pattern for the alliance concluded in 378 with Byzantium.[456] Then it was formally adopted in the document which set out the terms of the Second Athenian Confederacy in 377. With minor variations it was used in Athenian treaties with Corcyra (375), Dionysius of Syracuse (367), Thessaly (361/0) and Eretria (341). The formula was also partly adopted in the treaty between the Illyrians and Chalcidians (357).[457]

One considerable advantage which states derived from adopting the new pattern in the fourth century was that they were less likely to be involved automatically in a war by the action of another party, whereas if they did wish to intervene then their freedom of action was not impaired. At times it might also be possible to make a sensible choice between two apparently conflicting obligations, such as in 366 when Athens found herself allied both to Sparta and Arcadia, who were at war with one another.[458]

When an alliance was made at a time when its military terms were likely to be invoked it was natural that there should be some discussion on the terms for supplying forces and allocating the command. The earliest document to give detailed information on such points is that of the alliance made in 420 between Athens, Argos, Elis and Mantinea. As we have seen, each party was to exercise command of allied forces in action on its own territory, but if a joint expedition were made anywhere then the command was to be shared. The method of sharing was not specified, but to judge from other arrangements made in Greek battle order it is likely that each in turn would exercise command for a short period. If a force was sent out in answer to a request for help then the despatcher was to provision and supply the troops both on outward and return journeys and for up to thirty days in the field–a reasonable period for a limited campaign leading up to a decisive battle. If the force was needed for longer, then the recipient undertook responsibility for any period above the thirty days. The alliances between Athens, Arcadia, Achaea, Elis and Phlius (362/1[459]) and between Mantinea and Sparta (362/1[460]) also provided for the supreme command to be held by each party on its own territory.

In 369 there was some political argument over the terms upon which the military command should be shared in the alliance between Athens and Sparta. Xenophon refers to pressure not only from Athenians but also from many foreigners for the alliance to be on strictly equal terms. The Athenian council passed a resolution, for approval by the assembly, that in any joint action the command at sea should be exercised by Athens while Sparta should be given the command on land. In some ways it was logical enough that each should exercise its own particular special skill in such a manner, and it was exactly this kind of division that the Athenians had hoped for just over a century earlier against Persia. But on this occasion it was argued that the main action was likely to be on land in the Peloponnese and that therefore in order to achieve a fair division the supreme combined command by land and by sea should alternate between the two powers for five days.[461] In 339, however, the principle of separate commands by land and sea was incorporated in a modified fashion in the alliance between Athens and Thebes. Then the Athenians were to bear two-thirds of the cost of campaigning by land and the entire cost of naval operations, and they were to share the naval command with Thebes, whereas the Thebans were granted undivided command by land.[462] In that emergency the action was mainly by land on territory nearer to Thebes, which had a larger army but a lesser ability to pay. Demosthenes argued that the emergency was such that Athens could not afford to hesitate and had no alternative but to offer generous terms to induce her former enemy to stand against Philip of Macedon.

The test of whether the parties to an agreement were bound and obligated equally depended often not so much on the terms stated as on the attitudes of the parties, their relative power and the way in which the arrangements worked in practice. But on many occasions treaties of an unequal nature were imposed. The imposition usually resulted from war or the use of force to compel a delinquent ally to observe the terms of an earlier agreement. Invariably the details of the imposition were spelled out, for even if adverse publicity or reputation accrued to the usurper he was keen to have stated clearly in documentary form an instrument to regularize relations. The nature of Greek warfare and the formal way in which a petition was made to retrieve the dead from battle, either in concession of defeat or acknowledgement of supremacy, was conducive to an attitude of mind requiring a situation to be clearly defined. Thus on many occasions when it would have been easy to end inconclusive hostilities by a withdrawal, a formal instrument of truce or peace was drawn up. When, for example, the Athenians recognized that they could no longer coerce allies who had seceded from their naval confederacy they not only ceased military and naval operations but in 355 concluded a formal peace with the secessionists and formally recognized their autonomy and independence.[463]

As may be imagined, some of the stiffest terms to be found in treaties concern states which revolted from an alliance and were brought back into the fold by military intervention and coercion. The clearest and most obvious examples of such arrangements and treaties which survive in any detail are in a series of documents relating to the Athenians and their allies in the middle years of the fifth century. The states concerned are Miletus, Chalcis, Eretria, Colophon, Erythrae and Samos.

The earliest example in that series concerns Erythrae, which had evidently fallen into the political power of a small group favouring adhesion to Persia instead of the Delian League. Consequently Athens intervened to arrange a political settlement by expelling the ruling faction and installing a democratic régime, whose position was guaranteed by the presence of an Athenian garrison. Members of the new Erythraean council were required to swear loyalty not only to the Erythraean democracy but also to the Athenian democracy and to the allies of Athens. Furthermore the Athenians were to be consulted in the matter of any political expulsions or restorations.[464] In spite of those limitations imposed upon Erythrae the Athenians seem to have been concerned to maintain a working relationship with a political régime rather than to secure a pretext for continuous political supervision and to impose punitive terms on a wayward ally. The oaths of the Colophonians, who were restored to Athens' alliance at about the same time, show that they swore to maintain a democratic régime in Colophon, to remain loyal to Athens, and to hold the Athenian democracy in regard.[465]

In 446/5 the Athenians dealt with two allies, Eretria and Chalcis, which had participated in the general secession of Euboean communities from the Delian League. In bringing them back into the fold the Athenian decrees made little pretence of action within the framework of the general alliance. The relations of the two communities are mentioned only in respect of their obligations to Athens. The Eretrians swore not to revolt from Athens by any artifice or device either in word or in deed and they promised to denounce any dissident to the Athenians.[466] Chalcis gave similar assurances to the Athenians and promised to assist them in case of need and to accept their leadership. The Athenians for their part guaranteed not to expel inhabitants of Chalcis or destroy the city, in contrast to their treatment of Hestiaea, and promised not to exact summary justice in respect of property or persons of Chalcis.[467] In spite of the dignified language and politeness of the Athenian resolutions the determination of the Athenians and the strength of their position is evident. In reply to a Chalcidian request for the release of hostages the Athenians stated that for the moment it seemed best to them to leave matters as they stood, but at an opportune moment they were prepared to consult and act as seemed appropriate to the Athenians and Chalcidians.

The mood of the Athenians, however, in 439 towards the Samians was ostensibly more charitable in spite of the costly and protracted siege which had to be mounted before Samian resistance was broken. In the settlement the Samians were obliged to surrender their fleet, pull down their walls and pay for the cost of the Athenian operations. They promised to follow Athenian initiatives and to remain loyal to the Athenians and their allies. For their part the Athenians promised that in action, words and counsel they would assist the Samian democracy according to the advice of the Samian officials and Athenian generals.[468] The Athenians had no doctrinaire attachment to a policy of universal imposition of democracy in other states, but generally in allied states the opponents of democracy stirred up hostility towards Athens, and so it was useful for the Athenians to work through the popular factions. Certainly their endorsement and support of the Samian democrats in 439 paid off, for the Samians proved to be the most loyal allies to the end of the Peloponnesian War, when they were the subject of complimentary decrees at Athens.

In Greek warfare the last stages of campaign almost always led up to a diplomatic encounter, for it was not the normal procedure to indulge in total destruction of a state. Terrible measures could be considered and implemented, such as the Melian decree of the Athenians, but the measures contemplated against Melos, the destruction of Hestiaea for revolt from Athens, and the demolition of Methone in 354 by Philip and of Thebes by Alexander the Great in 335 stand out as occasional reminders of the excesses to which opponents could be driven either in their fury or in their calculation. When a state capitulated it was common for its defences to be dismantled as one of the conditions for accepting surrender in order to prevent a quick resumption of war. The Spartans in 404 systematically destroyed the defensive walls of Athens, walls which had ensured her impregnability by land. That was an indignity which the Athenians had inflicted upon others, for in 463 when Thasos surrendered after a three years' siege the Athenians pulled down the walls,[469] as they did at Samos in 439[470] and Nisaea in 424.[471] A surrender of arms and ships was required of Thasos, Samos and Nisaea by Athens, and in 404 Athens suffered a similar blow, having to surrender all but ten or twelve ships to Sparta.[472] It was also common practice to agree terms upon which the political and economic life of the capitulated state was to continue. The victor could impose terms which compensated him for the expenses of war, as in the case of the Athenian siege of Samos in 439. Nisaea paid a ransom for each man and in 354 Philip gave to the Macedonians the land confiscated from Methone.[473] In the case of Thasos Athens took over mines and territory, and after the Athenian defeat in Sicily Nicias offered reparations.[474] On the other hand guarantees were sometimes given that existing owners of property should continue to exercise their rights. In 424 Nicias agreed that Cythera should retain its lands, although the Athenians then spent seven days in ravaging the territory.[475] In the capture of Amphipolis in the same year the Spartan commander, Brasidas, allowed not only the Amphipolitans but also the Athenians who remained there to enjoy their property.[476] Similarly in 322 when Antipater imposed a garrison and harsh political measures upon the Athenians they were allowed to retain their property.[477]

Hostages were taken to guarantee subservient or correct conduct. In 446/5 the Athenians, as we have seen, decided to retain hostages from Chalcis and they took hostages from Samos in 439. Undesirable persons or factions could be excluded. In 424, for example, one of the conditions of Cythera's surrender to Athens was that some individuals should be taken away to prevent them causing difficulty.[478] The voluntary departure of persons who were unwilling to live under new conditions or régimes was sometimes permitted, and no doubt that enabled the captors rather to avoid trouble than to establish a reputation for magnanimity. In 346, for example, in the surrender of Phocis Phalaecus and his soldiers were permitted by the Macedonians to go whither they wished[479] and in 404 the Spartans permitted free people to depart from Samos, taking with them one cloak each.[480] Conversely, captors often found it politically desirable to ensure the return of political exiles to a community, where they would help to promote a politically suitable climate if not an actual change of régime. The Athenians promoted the interests of the democratic faction in Samos, and to undo that policy the Spartans restored oligarchic exiles to Samos in 404,[481] giving them the property of those who had been allowed to depart. The same year similar imposition by Sparta of terms for the return of exiles to Athens helped to tilt the political balance in favour of oligarchy and in 322 the Athenian surrender to

Macedon involved the installation of an oligarchy protected by a garrison.

Personal guarantees could be demanded and granted. In 427 Mytilene surrendered to the Athenian general Paches on condition that no one was imprisoned, enslaved or put to death until an embassy had been despatched to, and received back from, Athens.[482] That represented about the least concession which could be granted, for the Athenian general Demosthenes surrendered his forces in Sicily on condition that no deaths occurred by force, imprisonment or starvation.[483] Far more insidious were the Spartan terms offered to Plataea in 427, whereby the Plataeans suffered the imposition of a Spartan tribunal which was to ensure that the 'guilty' were punished but that no one was to be punished contrary to the law.[484] The Plataeans were in no condition to resist the Spartans, but equally the Spartans wished rather to persuade the Plataeans to accept terms than to have to carry the city by storm. For, according to Thucydides, the Spartans were using diplomatic methods against the day when it came to making a full settlement of the Peloponnesian War. If in such a wider settlement it turned out that one of the conditions was for the return of places captured in the war then it would be advantageous to be able to maintain that Plataea had not been captured but had changed sides voluntarily. The Spartan sense of diplomacy can also be seen at work in 424 when Acanthus was encouraged to capitulate and to go over to Brasidas on the understanding that Brasidas' oath of office at Sparta guaranteed the autonomy of Sparta's allies.[485]

In general the capitulating state does not seem to have been able to arrange any guarantees for allied forces or for other foreigners on its territory. In 435 when Epidamnus surrendered to Corcyra Corinthians were to be taken prisoner and other aliens sold,[486] and in the surrender of Nisaea to Athens in 424 the treatment of Spartans there was left to the discretion of the Athenians.[487] However, when Amphipolis surrendered to Sparta in the same year and the Spartans were intent on creating a reputation for moderation, Athenians were treated on the same terms as the Amphipolitans.[488]

If negotiations were not possible or were considered unnecessary or undesirable by the victor, then on occasions the expulsion of the population was ordered. In 429 the Athenians expelled the Potidaeans, men, women, children and auxiliaries,[489] just thirty years after Sparta ordered the expulsion of Messenians from the Peloponnese.[490] The Potidaean women were allowed to take two cloaks, others one, besides their journey-money, and they departed to Chalcidice or wherever they could. When the Thebans *c.* 373 expelled the Plataeans with their movables they allowed the women to take two cloaks, the men one,[491] and in 354 those who were expelled from Methone by Philip were allowed to take only one cloak with them.[492]

Truces of various kinds were observed in the relations of the ancient Greeks. Some were contracted directly between belligerent parties, others were wider in scope and were proclaimed typically, as we have seen, at times of religious festivals without specific reference or application to conflicts with which they happened to coincide. The most widely observed truces occurred at the times of the great Panhellenic festivals. According to Isocrates their institution was conducive not only to a Panhellenic sentiment but also to the resolution of conflict and the conclusion of treaties.[493] When the time of the festival approached the supervising authorities sent out truce-bearers (*spondophoroi*) to proclaim a sacred truce in the various communities. Once the holy month (*hieromenia*) had been declared in a community, it was bound to desist from hostilities. It was the complaint of the Plataeans that in 431 the Thebans attacked them not only in time of peace but also in a holy month.[494] To that the Thebans retorted that such an invasion in time of peace and at a festival would have been a crime indeed, but that they were not guilty, for so far were they from harming anyone that they had successfully invited the Plataeans to join them in a Boeotian venture.[495] At the Olympic Games of 420 the Eleans barred the Spartans from the temple and thereby disqualified them from taking part in the Games on the grounds that they had failed to pay a fine for attacking the fort at Phyrcus and sending troops to Lepreum during the Olympic truce. The Spartans claimed that they were innocent as the truce then had not yet been proclaimed in Sparta.[496]

In addition to the major Panhellenic festivals there were others which had more local significance but which nevertheless had their effect on the inter-state dealings of the Greek communities. In 367 the Athenians proclaimed the fifty-five-day truce of the Greater Eleusinian Mysteries. Although, the Athenians claimed, the sacred truce had been accepted by the Aetolian League, one of its members, Trichoneia, seized two Athenian representatives who had been sent to make the proclamation, and so a herald was sent from Athens to complain to the League about the alleged outrage, which had been committed in violation of the accepted customs of all the Greeks.[497]

The existence of such truces was both a cause of, and a pretext for, diplomatic and military inactivity. In 480 the Carnean festival hindered the Spartans from making prompt moves against the Persian advance on Thermopylae. A little later the Hyacinthian festival caused a similar delay.[498] In 419 a religious festival caused the Spartans to hold back an attack on Argos. Although the Argives nevertheless persisted in their attack on Epidaurus her allies either refused assistance or sent forces only to the frontier.[499] Thirty-one years later the Argives themselves tried to claim the protection of a holy truce when they felt that they could not withstand the Spartan attack led by King Agesipolis. The Spartans then went to Olympia and obtained the authority of Zeus and the Delphic Oracle against recognition of what the Argives claimed to be an ancestral truce established among the Dorians of old.[500]

Other truces were more specifically bilateral and were arranged for purely military or political reasons. The common words for truce were *ekekheiria* (a restraining of the hand) or *spondai* (libation). Libations were drunk commonly to set the seal on an agreement and of the two terms *spondai* was the more common, but it could be used properly of all agreements, of whatever nature and duration, and took its meaning from the context in which it was used. At the shortest the arrangements were made by the commanders in the field when one side was ready to acknowledge defeat by sending a herald to seek the opponent's permission to pick up the casualties under truce. It was such an agreement that King Pausanias made at Haliartus in 394,[501] and the humiliation felt at Sparta, especially by the supporters of the dead Lysander, led to his vilification. Truces were also arranged frequently to last for considerable periods. In 367 when Epaminondas was sent out from Thebes to deal with the hostile Alexander of Pherae the latter sent envoys to him, but Epaminondas did not conclude peace and friendship with him, establishing only a truce for thirty days.[502] After the Battle of Tanagra the defeated Athenians drew up a truce for four months with the Spartans[503] and their allies, and in 395 King Artaxerxes concluded a six months' truce for the Persians with Agesilaus of Sparta.[504]

Such truces were not necessarily concluded as an end in themselves. After the Battle of Pylos the Athenians arranged a truce which was specifically arranged to last until Spartan envoys should go to Athens concerning a settlement and then return.[505] Two years later in 423 the Athenians and Spartans agreed to cease fighting for one year. The Athenians thought that such an interval would prevent the intrigues of Brasidas and that they would be able to prepare for a further general agreement and settlement of the war.[506] During the year free passage was guaranteed by land and sea between Athens and the Peloponnese to heralds and embassies for settling the war. Ostensibly a year was the period prescribed to allow time to negotiate a lasting agreement, but the Spartans thought that the length of the period would enable the Athenians to appreciate the advantages of peace and to allow hostile opinion to be assuaged. In 418 when the two Argives, Thrasylus the general and Alciphron the *proxenos* of Sparta, appealed to the Spartan King Agesilaus not to attack on the grounds that Argos was prepared to accept arbitration and to make a treaty, a truce was concluded for four months.[507] If a general in the field did not have instructions or sufficient authority in the matter of concluding a truce with an eye to a longer settlement, then he could act in the manner of the Spartan general Dercylidas in 397. On this occasion the satrap Tissaphernes requested a conference to stop the fighting in Asia Minor and started negotiations. Each side accordingly arranged a truce to last for as long as it took to report back to Sparta and to the Persian King.[508]

Occasionally formal or informal truces could be arranged or recognized between two parties who were unable to agree upon terms of peace but who were not disposed, perhaps out of deference to allies, to take an issue to war. After the Peace of Nicias, for example, both the Boeotians and the Corinthians were dissatisfied with the terms which the Spartans had negotiated with Athens. As a result the Boeotians had a ten-day truce (*anokokhe*), probably an arrangement concluded for ten days and terminable at ten days' notice.[509] The Corinthians then requested Boeotian diplomatic support for a similar arrangement for themselves. The Athenians refused but acknowledged an informal truce (*anokokhe aspondos*).[510]

In 424 the Boeotians behaved unusually, at first refusing a truce to the Athenians after the Battle of Delium on the grounds that they had been guilty of impiety to the temple there. The area in dispute between the parties was Oropus and the Boeotians maintained that if the Athenians were in Boeotian territory then they must depart before picking up the dead or that if they were on Athenian territory no truce was needed. Eventually the Boeotians gave their consent.[511] Occasionally wars were described as 'heraldless' or 'truceless' or both, but such descriptions had more emotional than legalistic significance. At the outset of the Peloponnesian War Pericles caused the Athenians to pass a decree forbidding the reception in Athens of heralds and embassies once the Spartans had marched out into the field.[512] Accordingly the Spartan herald Melesippus was refused admission to the

city, ordered to depart on the same day and escorted back to the
frontier. A short time later the Athenians came off worse in a minor
cavalry engagement at Phrygia and retrieved their dead without first
requesting a truce.[513] But it was not impossible to arrange contacts
between belligerents when there was no truce. Envoys needed the
protection of a truce but heralds did not. Certain others such as
proxenoi who had the requisite privileges did not need such a protection.
There survives, for example, a Rhodian decree, passed *c.* 410, which
in appointing a *proxenos* guaranteed to him and to his descendants
right of passage without truce in peace and war.[514] In spite of the
intentions of the Athenians early in the Peloponnesian War the
Spartans did send envoys after their defeat at Pylos to sue for peace
and they, if not their arguments, were received in Athens.[515] A
declaration that heralds would not be accepted could not be maintained for more than a limited period of time. Thus a resolution
that the Ten Thousand would wage war without heralds was qualified
by the phrase 'for so long as they are on enemy territory'.[516] After
the murder of their herald Anthemocritus in Megara the Athenians
decreed that truceless and heraldless hostility should endure against
Megara. In itself that decree implied the rejection of any herald sent
by Megara, but did not imply that reprisal would be taken, and so
to the decree was attached a clause that any Megarian who set foot
in Attica would be put to death.[517] At his trial Aeschines declared
that Athens might find its wars truceless and heraldless, not for
diplomatic reasons but for imposing intolerable conditions upon
envoys, since men would be unwilling to serve as heralds or envoys.[518]

Although surprise attacks were made it was the habit of the Greeks
to make a formal declaration of war. The Persian Mardonius remarked
upon the air of formality of Greek warfare whereby after a preliminary declaration the opposing parties proceeded to a set-piece
battle on a suitably level location.[519] In 435 after the Corinthians had
rejected the proposals of Corcyra and their allies had assembled, they
sent on a herald to make a formal announcement of war. Similarly
before their siege of Epidamnus the Corcyraeans first proclaimed that
any natives or aliens could either depart unharmed or remain and
be treated as enemies.[520] Contrary to the normal practice Aegina and
Athens are thought to have waged war early in the fifth century
without any formal declaration, for there had been a long and bitter
hatred between them. The Spartans and the Messenians too had a
long history of embittered relations in the Peloponnese. Accordingly
when the Spartans complained to Pyrrhus of Epirus on account of

his surprise attack he politely reminded them of their infliction of war upon the Messenians without any formal declaration.[521]

It was possible for states to drift into war in a sequence of hostile events, none of which in themselves was sufficient justification or pretext for war. It was equally possible in such a situation that either or both sides wished to escape the actual responsibility for declaring war. When the Athenian naval reinforcements went to help the hard-pressed Corcyraeans against the Corinthians at Sybota in accordance with the terms of the defensive alliance, the Corinthians put men without the insignia of a herald into a boat to make an announcement to the Athenians, accusing them of contravening the treaty and starting war. The men challenged the Athenians to treat them as enemies if their intentions were deliberately hostile. The Athenians, however, avoided provocation and replied that they intended to defend Corcyra but would not hinder Corinthians in any other way.[522] The Athenians and the Peloponnesians continued to maintain contact for some time after that without using heralds,[523] but the situation was uneasy as there continued to occur incidents which amounted to breaches of treaty and cause for war. But at the beginning of his second book Thucydides wrote, 'this is the starting point of the war between the Athenians and the Peloponnesians in which they no longer made contacts without heralds'. War broke out indirectly between Thebes and Plataea, which afforded the first overt breach; we read, moreover, that no formal declaration was made before the Spartan forces moved and the Athenians refused to admit the Spartan herald to their city.

When treaties were signed the documents were drawn up in answer to a specific problem or situation, whether that was defined or not. It was rare for treaties to be contracted to counter some distant threat or remote contingency or to fulfil a general need for collective security. Generally, therefore, the more specific the expressed aims and terms of an alliance or treaty, the better were its chances of immediately successful implementation. On the other hand if the terms and aims were expressed in a more general way, the better were its chances of enduring through adaptation to changed circumstances. The Delian League was the classic example of a voluntary alliance where many states faced an immediate threat and spontaneously joined together under a leader. Their aim was to remove the Persian threat, yet to remain allies until the lumps of lead, over which the oaths were sworn, floated on the waters.[524] No one seriously questioned in advance whether the Persian threat would finally disappear or what would happen to the League if the threat did disappear. In the longer-term view of historical perspective it can be said that the Persian threat did not disappear until Alexander the Great conquered the Persian Empire. But in the intervening one hundred and fifty years there were occasions when Persian defeats apparently diminished the danger, and for several periods of many consecutive years there was no overt threat. Yet the various problems and diversions of the Persian monarch and his susceptibility to invitations to intervene were beyond the control of any individual state in Greece.

The Delian League outlived its usefulness and became an instrument of Athenian foreign policy, providing Athens with resources which were used against Sparta. The Second Athenian Confederacy suffered from similar problems in the definition of its aims. It was a permanent and general defensive alliance but it was created specifically to deal with the threat to the freedom of the Greek states posed by Spartan intervention in their affairs. That Spartan threat was clearly and swiftly ended within the decade by the Battle of Leuctra in 371. What was then to become of the alliance? If no further immediate aim could be found the likelihood was that it too would become an instrument of Athenian foreign policy without any particular focus, as happened to the Delian League after, if not before, the Peace of Callias. At all times in history it has been easier to create an alliance against some party than to maintain it in a positive cause.

Such difficulties were more keenly experienced in the case of alliances which covered many states scattered over wide areas and where communications had to be maintained by sea. Local alliances, which covered more limited and identifiable tracts of territory were easier to maintain. The Spartans found it a practical proposition in the Peloponnese to maintain communities in an alliance with her in the Peloponnesian League. There it was relatively easy for the Spartans to maintain constant contact and to give more immediate help to classes which supported them in allied states. Sparta and her allies promised mutual assistance, but locally the Spartans were the decisively preponderant power, the alliances came about on her initiative, and the Peloponnesian League existed quite obviously for the defence of Sparta, whose peculiarly stratified social and political system presented her enemies both within and outside the Peloponnese an opportunity for subversion. Until the time of Lysander Sparta undertook major operations outside the Peloponnese only under duress.

Two treaties which were unusually comprehensive, both in the numbers of states included and in the nature of their terms, were the King's Peace of 387/6[525] and the alliance which constituted the League of Corinth under Philip of Macedon in 338/7.[526] In the case of the King's Peace the guarantee of autonomy was accepted as a praiseworthy principle but its application and interpretation were erratic and unpredictable. In the absence of direct action on the part of the Persian King its general concepts were perverted to support or justify the specific local policies of states, such as the dissolution of leagues by Sparta and the subversion of Sparta by Theban support for Messenian independence. There was no machinery or recognized forum where such matters could be reviewed or controlled. Unlike the Peace of 387/6 the arrangement of 338/7 constituted a semblance of an agreement rather than the mere imposition or acceptance of terms. There was a council of members and probably some arrangement for the proportional representation of members. The League of Corinth offered far-reaching and binding guarantees for the defence of member-states against external attack and guaranteed states against attempts to stir up political dissension from outside. It was, however, a hegemonial alliance contracted by Philip for himself and his successors and it was dependent upon the power and the continuity of the Macedonian monarchy. Its general terms could be used by the leader in support of his specific policies, whether they involved a Panhellenic crusade to liberate Asia Minor or a campaign to conquer Persia. On the other hand its resources in practice could not be so used by any other of the contracting states.

To some extent it is inevitable that there should be a disparity between the aims expressed in a treaty and the details of their application, but perhaps what caused an element of unpredictability in the Greek world was the lack of a bureaucracy which could speak in similar terms in each state, impose some caution or restraint in the political arena, and encourage a certain continuity or stability in affairs. Greek generals and diplomats had always recognized the need for astute propaganda and the need to justify actions by some criteria. That tendency was taken much further by the great Peloponnesian War and the King's Peace, but no state could be adequately protected by it from the baser instincts of others.

So far in discussing treaties we have dealt with arrangements which involved positive measures, such as rendering assistance to states or individuals, or making arrangements for peace or war. Other less tangible kinds of relationship, such as those of friendship, non-aggression and neutrality, were also expressed, directly, or indirectly, in treaty form.

A formal pact of friendship (*philia*) was by no means unusual but most commonly such a declaration was made as part of a wider arrangement and no specific obligations of friendship were defined. An unusual treaty of friendship for fifty years was concluded between the Anaitoi and Metapioi *c.* 550. No obligations were specified on the bronze tablet from Olympia but the priests of Olympia were to adjudicate in cases of alleged breaches.[527] Thereafter many instances are found of the conclusion of both friendship and alliance. The Chalcidians and Amyntas III of Macedon *c.* 393 concluded friendship and alliance in a treaty by which the parties undertook not to conclude friendship with the Amphipolitans and other named communities except by joint agreement.[528]

The contract of friendship, even if it involved intangible obligations, was sometimes more than a mere gesture. In 346, for example, the renewal of the alliance between Athens and Mytilene involved a formal renewal of friendship in which the political sympathy of the two democracies was stressed.[529] Communities which attempted to renew their former good relations after a period of discord or hostility could set the seal on their practical diplomatic arrangements with a profession of good will. Thus in 422 the Athenians concluded friendship and alliance with Bottiaean communities after a lapse of ten years since their revolt from the Athenian alliance.[530] Similarly, following the changes in Theban fortunes and internal politics by 387/6 Thebes was drawn back into alliance and friendship with her old ally Sparta after some two decades of hostile or indifferent relations.[531] In cases too where an agreement was made between monarchs it was perfectly proper for a formal relationship to be declared, and so when Perdiccas II of Macedon and Arrhabaeus of Lyncestus ceased fighting in 423/2 there was negotiation of *philia*.[532]

States which came together for the first time in alliance and wished to exploit their common interests may have found a formal declaration of friendship more reassuring than a bald diplomatic convention. The alliances between Athens and Carthage in 406[533] and between Athens and Egypt *c.* 390[534] opened up great possibilities for each party, but they were not preceded by previous close or lasting associations and co-operation. Perhaps the Athenians hoped for continuing favours in the supply of cereals, a matter which could not so conveniently be made explicit in treaty form. Equally, however, the Greeks could enter into professions of friendship which amounted to something less than they appeared. The King's Peace of 387/6 was a peace accompanied by professions of friendship to all parties.

It could hardly be expected that Athens, Sparta and Thebes, among others could all experience feelings of positive friendship towards each other, but the Peace had its merits which many were content to recognize or eager to maintain. In 384 the Athenians were sufficiently ready or punctilious to include a reference to friendship in the inscription of the alliance with Chios.[535] At the least the declaration of friendship with the King's Peace symbolized an obligation of non-aggression. On other occasions 'friendship' meant little, if anything, more than neutrality. In 420, for example, when the Thirty Years' Peace between Argos and Sparta expired overtures were made for a renewal.[536] The Argives, who had remained neutral in the ten years since the outbreak of the Peloponnesian War, were anxious to avoid diplomatic isolation and so they were ready to conclude a new treaty with Sparta. The Spartans were ready to renew the Thirty Years' Peace on the same terms as before and made a concession to the Argives, for, says Thucydides, they were keen on having the *friendship* of Argos.

Neutrality was a concept which was fully accepted by the Greeks, although it was not one that was regularly incorporated in the form of a treaty. It was a status which, if not clearly and juridically defined, did confer some protection, for, as the Athenians reminded the Spartans in 430, whereas it was justifiable to seize enemy men and material in time of war those who were on neither side should remain unmolested.[537] Neutrality could result from the mere fact that a state was not concerned in a dispute between two other parties. On the other hand neutrality could be the deliberate goal of a policy aimed at steering clear of commitment or it could be affirmed by a formal declaration. Before Xerxes launched his invasion of Greece he sent an envoy to Argos to argue that as the Persians originated from Argive stock it was neither right for the Persians to proceed against Argos nor for the Argives to join the Greek coalition against Persia. The Argives did remain neutral, but for other reasons.

Melos attempted to remain neutral between Athens and Sparta, although it had been colonized by Sparta. The Athenians in 426 attempted without success to bring over Melos in their efforts to weaken the Peloponnesians, then in 418 further Athenian incursions aroused Melian hostility. After a conference the Melians in vain invited Athens to conclude a treaty and withdraw, allowing the Melians to be friends of Athens and foes of neither side.[538] Eleven years earlier the Spartans, following Plataean protests against infringement of their sovereignty, invited the Plataeans either to join the

Peloponnesians or to be inactive (i.e. stand neutral).[539] Then in 427 when the Spartans inflicted the death penalty on Plataean prisoners, they claimed that they did so because the Plataeans had not remained inactive.

In the two treaties of peace which were concluded between Athens and Sparta in 446/5 and 421 respectively attention was given to neutral states. In the earlier treaty it was laid down that whichever states were not enrolled in either alliance should be permitted to join either alliance.[540] Then in the Peace of Nicias it was agreed that six specified cities, Argilus, Stagirus, Acanthus, Scolus, Olynthus and Spartolus, should be neutral, allies neither of the Spartans nor of the Athenians, but if those cities so wished they could be enrolled as Athenian allies.[541] The Corcyraeans made a principle of standing aloof from diplomatic entanglements before their differences arose with Corinth over Epidamnus, when they were made to acknowledge the failure of what had seemed to be a wise policy of not contracting alliances with other states lest they were involved in risks. Then when Corcyra appealed to Athens for help she stressed that she was a neutral state and could join in alliance with either Athens or Sparta without causing a breach of the Thirty Years' Peace between those two states. Corcyra, as we have seen, gained a defensive alliance with Athens and gave a little help to Athens at the beginning of the Peloponnesian War, but at a time of internal crisis in 427 the Corcyraeans claimed to be both allies of the Athenians and 'friends as before' of the Peloponnesians.[542]

The word 'friendship' was one which could easily be overworked and devalued in diplomatic exchanges. At best it could signify a positive relationship and at the least it meant little, if anything, more than non-aggression or non-belligerency between powers which might or might not have contracted any formal relationship by treaty. In 384 when Athens and Chios concluded an alliance reference was made to the preservation of the peace and friendship which had been sworn as part of the arrangements in the King's Peace, friendship which amounted to no more than enforcement of peace. At some time perhaps between 430 and 420 the Athenians contracted an agreement with an unknown party which pledged friendship to Athens. So far as can be seen from the fragment of the relevant inscription that friendship involved little if any more than a promise to refrain from piratical or military enterprises against Athens.[543]

A typical example of an exchange of promises of non-aggression was continued in the perpetual alliance made in 367 between Athens and Dionysius of Syracuse. The treaty was set out according to the standard terms of alliance of that period, guarantecing assistance in case of attack by land or by sea. Then before the usual arrangements for the oaths there was an insertion to the effect that it was not permissible for Dionysius or his successors to bear arms against Athenian territory either by land or by sea. Similarly the Athenians were to refrain from bearing arms by land or sea against Dionysius, his descendants and his dominion.[544] Similar arrangements were made by the members of the League of Corinth in 338/7 when they swore that they would not only abide by the Peace and refrain from infringing the treaty with Philip of Macedon but also refrain from bearing arms by land or sea against those who stood by their oaths, and that they would by no stratagem or device seize a city, fort or harbour with hostile intent against those who abided by the peace.

Such guarantees were, of course, not worth much more than most promises made in Greek diplomacy, but they by no means constituted mere empty verbiage. They did signify the firm resolve of the parties to turn over a new leaf, if necessary, in their relations. In the two instances quoted in the previous paragraph Athens and Syracuse attempted to wipe clean the slate of many years' hostility, and in founding the League of Corinth Philip not only looked after his own interests but also attempted a policy of reconciliation between the Greeks and tried to exploit the best of the diplomatic practices and traditions that had evolved in the fourth century. Indeed the terminology of those two treaties reflects that which had developed in the fifth century. For in 421 under the terms of the Peace of Nicias the Athenians, the Spartans and their respective allies were forbidden to take up arms against each other with hostile intent by any stratagem or device. For the alliance of 420 between Athens, Argos, Elis and Mantinea it appears that identical terms were incorporated in the inscription set up at Athens. It may appear strange that a treaty of alliance which lays down terms for mutual assistance should also contain clauses committing each party to refrain from aggression against the other, but in 424/3 the Athenians, who were concerned with the problem of piracy, made a treaty of friendship and alliance with Halieis on such conditions.[545] Each party guaranteed to help the other against attack, but in addition Halieis promised neither to harbour pirates nor themselves to engage in piracy, not to join in an expedition with enemies against Athens, not to help an enemy force or provide money for enemies, and not to receive a garrison within their defences to the detriment of Athens.

Arbitration was a well-established feature both in the internal and in the external life of the Greek states. Tradition had it that Bias of Priene, one of the seven sages, was called in to arbitrate between Priene and Samos. In the late seventh or early sixth century Periander, tyrant of Corinth, reconciled Athens and Mytilene by arbitration over the title to Sigeum, and Sparta arbitrated in the dispute between Athens and Megara over Salamis. Then before the Battle of Marathon Corinth was invited by Thebes and Plataea to settle the extent to which Theban authority extended over other communities in Boeotia. In those cases the dispute arose first and then the means of settlement were proposed. It was, of course, the mark of a civilized approach that arbitration was a recognized method of achieving solutions but, more significantly, it was from the middle years of the fifth century that provision was made in advance for settling disputes before they arose by inserting appropriate clauses in treaties. In the treaty of the sixth century between the Anaitoi and Metapioi there was provision for the reference of infringements to the religious authorities at Olympia,[546] but in the surviving records that is an isolated case until we come to the Thirty Years' Peace of 446/5. In 432/1 when Peloponnesian allies lodged complaints at Sparta against the Athenians and were urging the Spartans to take military action, Athenian envoys, who happened to be present on other business, urged the Spartans to submit the issues in dispute to arbitration in accordance with the treaty of 446/5.[547] Archidamus, the Spartan king, in vain counselled caution and declared that it was not lawful to proceed against a party which offered arbitration as if against a transgressor. The Spartan refusal of arbitration was then used by Pericles to justify the policy which he advocated in Athens; for he declared that since the Spartans never made any offer of arbitration nor accepted any such proposal according to the terms of the treaty, it was clear that they wished to settle matters rather by war than by negotiation. In reply to Spartan envoys who arrived immediately before the outbreak of war the Athenians repeated their readiness to submit to arbitration, but the envoys left Athens and did not return. Later on, we are told, after losses at Pylos and other reverses there was recognition at Sparta that the Peloponnesians had been put in the wrong both by the Theban attack launched on Plataea in time of peace and by the refusal of the Athenian offer of arbitration in accordance with the clause in the treaty.[548] Accordingly in the One-Year Truce of 423 between Athens and Sparta it was stated that disputes should be settled by legal means and without recourse to war. Then in the Peace of Nicias in 421 the Athenians and Spartans and their respective allies accepted that it would be unlawful for either side to take up arms against the other and that differences should be settled by such legal process as might be acceptable to the parties. By 413, however, the alliance between Athens and Sparta had become a dead letter, if it had ever been anything else, and so too did the Spartans regard the Peace of Nicias. The Athenians consistently refused Spartan offers of arbitration on points of difference in interpreting the treaty, and so the Spartans made preparation for war. The fifty-year treaty of 418 between Sparta and Argos also provided for arbitration. After the expiry of the thirty-year agreement between them in 421 the Argives suggested another arrangement for fifty years which provided for arbitration over the disputed Cynurian frontier territory. Then in 418 when the two states made peace and alliance it was stated that all disputes should be settled by fair and impartial arbitration.

As in much of Greek diplomacy there was at times an element of gamesmanship in an appeal to arbitration. Such an appeal was used automatically as a first line of defence by the weaker party or it could be seen as a device to present opponents in an unfavourable light. The Spartans in 431 and the Athenians from 420 declined arbitration when each party thought it held the advantage. In 431 Sthenelaidas, the Spartan ephor, appealed to the honour of Sparta against the surrender of good allies to the Athenians or consent to the settlement of issues by words and legal process on the grounds that lengthy arbitration and a war of words were for those who prepared to perpetrate injustice.[549] Earlier, in the dispute between Corinth and Corcyra over Epidamnus Corcyra proposed to Corinth a settlement by arbitration. Corinth, not wishing to put herself blatantly in the wrong, accepted the proposal on condition that her troops were allowed in the meantime to remain in Epidamnus and that Corcyra withdrew her forces. Accordingly when Corcyra claimed the help of Athens she made the point that Corinth chose to resolve matters rather by war than by arbitration.

Offers of arbitration by no means were invariably made from calculations of strength or weakness. Corcyra immediately won a naval victory over Corinth, although she was far from confident of maintaining her position. After the Peace of Philocrates began to break down Philip of Macedon, not out of weakness but from a desire not to antagonize Athens needlessly, offered arbitration over Halonnesus and over disputes in Cardia,[550] but Athens, who forced the Thasians and Maronites to arbitration over Stryme, refused.

Demosthenes maintained the absolute justice of the Athenian case, and according to Aeschines he always claimed that no impartial arbitrator could be found when Philip was willing to go to arbitration.[551]

Invariably that was the nub of the problem. Who could be trusted to arbitrate fairly? For within states justice knew few absolutes and public processes were settled by political means. The professional jurist existed hardly any more than did the professional diplomat. Occasionally an individual had sufficient prestige for his word to be accepted, as was Periander's between Athens and Mytilene[552] or Themistocles' between Corinth and Corcyra,[553] but not even the Delphic Oracle could be relied upon for her impartiality. Certainly Corcyra achieved no response from Corinth following her suggestion of Delphic arbitration. In the time of King Agesipolis Megara offered to mediate between Athens and Sparta, but the Spartan retort was that the Megarians were hardly likely to know more about justice than did Athens or Sparta.[554]

The cynic could ask how many troops had the Delphic Oracle. The matter of the power of the arbitrator, as well as of his influence, and the sanctions which could be employed to enforce his judgement were of some importance. Demosthenes declared that it was the mark of a leading power to be invited to arbitrate disputes,[555] although that statement should be accepted with considerable reserve. A clear case of the use of force by an arbitrator occurred in 421 when the dispute between Lepreum and Elis was submitted to Sparta for arbitration. The Eleans suspected the impartiality of the arbitrators and attempted to withdraw the reference. The Spartans nevertheless gave their judgement in favour of Lepreum and sent in a garrison of hoplites to protect her.[556]

The larger powers were often in danger of being drawn into a conflict which involved allies or other minor parties who looked to them for aid. The consequences of intervention in such cases could be as incalculable as they were unwelcome. If the major power therefore was unwilling to intervene for those reasons, then an exhortation to arbitration was both honourable and convenient. In the dispute early in the fourth century between Phocis, traditionally supported by Sparta, and Locris, traditionally supported by Thebes, the Spartans called upon the Phocians to submit their case to arbitration.[557] At about the same time the Athenians sent envoys to Sparta to urge the settlement of her dispute with Thebes by arbitration.[558]

Irrespective of the power and authority of the arbitrators and of the intentions of the parties to a dispute, the machinery of arbitration was not firmly established. Treaties and leagues which prescribed arbitration for disputes had no detailed or standing arrangements to be applied automatically or speedily. The Peace of Nicias provided merely for arbitration as might be agreed between the parties. Then in 420 the Argives suggested to Sparta a reference to the arbitration merely of some state or individual of the dispute over Cynuria. In the subsequent treaty between them in 418 arbitration in conformity with their national customs was mentioned. Concerning disputes between allies in the Peloponnesian League, the same treaty stipulated reference to a third state considered impartial by both parties.

Such generally worded provisions appear rather vague, but the nature of the reference, tribunal or judges could not easily be anticipated. An appeal to Sparta was likely, if accepted, to result in the special appointment of five commissioners, as in the dispute between Athens and Aegina. An appeal to Athens could result in the case being heard by the Council of the Areopagus. In Classical Greece it was probably only in the case of the Amphictyonic Council at Delphi that a state could anticipate the procedure to be followed. There delegates would argue the merits of a case put to it by the parties in dispute and the Amphictyons gave their verdict. Membership of a league was conducive to agreement on measures for arbitration. As we have seen, the practice seems to have been accepted quite normally within the Peloponnesian League. The League of Corinth, too, made arrangements for arbitration. In 336, for example, in accordance with a resolution of that League, Argos arbitrated between Melos and Cimolus.[559] Members of the Achaean League, who could send envoys to other communities only with federal permission, were obliged to submit their disputes to the League. In a dispute in the middle of the third century between Corinth and Epidaurus the League appointed Megara to arbitrate. The Corinthians did not accept the original verdict of the one hundred and fifty-one Megarian judges who inspected the disputed territory, but after an appeal they were compelled to accept confirmation of the judgement made by a sub-commission of thirty-one of the judges.[560] After a territorial dispute arose between Miletus and Myus c. 390, which resulted in an appeal to the Persian King, the Persian satrap of Ionia invited the Ionian League to arbitrate. The ten members of the League other than Miletus and Myus each supplied one member for a tribunal, whose verdict was accepted by the satrap.[561]

Little is known of the precise judicial procedures and of the substance of the arguments in such cases, but had they survived they probably would not have shed much light on standards of International Law and morality. For most cases involved territorial disputes where evidence of priority of ownership had to be shown. In the dispute between Athens and Aegina evidence from Homer, Delphic responses and modes of burial was adduced.[562] In the dispute between Thebes and Plataea there was an early instance of the so-called doctrine of unimpeded sovereignty when Corinth declared that any Boeotian community which did not wish to participate in Boeotian institutions should be left alone.[563]

There were few sanctions that could be applied if the results of arbitration were rejected. In the arbitration by Pelopidas of Thebes in the dispute between Ptolemy and Alexander of Macedon, who were at war, Pelopidas settled the issues and brought back hostages, including Philip of Macedon, as guarantees.[564] It was not, however, a regular feature of arbitration to offer hostages. The physical strength and prestige of the arbitrating authority were the surest guarantees of compliance with judgements, but the threat of intervention was not one which the arbitrating authority necessarily would issue lightly. In the dispute between Lepreum and Elis when the latter, as the more powerful state, refused to accept the decision of Sparta's arbitration, Sparta did not act directly against Elis but merely sent a garrison as protection for Lepreum. In the case of a league being involved collective action could be mounted against a delinquent party, as happened in 340/39 when the Amphissaeans were censured for cultivating the Crisaean plain contrary to their oaths. Then the Amphictyons, with the help of Philip of Macedon, marched out to enforce their ruling.[565]

In the absence of a codified body of International Law, developed legal practices or inter-state political organs, it is difficult to see how the Greeks could have progressed further. Their achievements were by no means minimal, for they established firm traditions which the Romans encountered and adopted when they came into contact with the Greeks. One of the most significant documents in Greek inter-state affairs, dating from c. 362, announced the common decision of the Greeks to refuse help to satraps in revolt from the Persian King on the grounds that they had resolved their own conflicts and arranged for territorial disputes to be settled by arbitration.[566] Where more progress would have been welcome was in the definition and interpretation of the terms of treaties.

The published terms of treaties were, at least until the Hellenistic era, surprisingly brief and the steps in the conclusion of treaties were few. Contingencies were not spelled out or anticipated in great detail.

In a state after the appropriate debates had been held and resolutions on policy made, if it seemed right to make overtures to another state for a treaty, an embassy was appointed with suitable instructions. Then after its despatch and arrival at its destination the embassy presented itself to the appropriate authorities. At Athens, for example, embassies were received by the council or its presiding committee. At Sparta the credentials of Theramenes and his colleagues from Athens were first examined by the ephors in 405/4. After the preliminary hearing of their purpose and terms of reference the envoys were either turned away or allowed to present themselves to the sovereign authorities.

If one party to the negotiations wished to gain concessions from another but either found it difficult to devise a suitable policy or did not wish to disclose its stance in advance, it could send envoys merely to ask questions. Thus in 391/0 the Thebans sent envoys to the Spartans with instructions merely to ask what they were to do in order to obtain peace.[567] No doubt in private discussions with political figures the envoys would have been able to give some indication of what was likely to be acceptable in Thebes. In states where decisions followed due political or parliamentary processes envoys had opportunity for private discussion with political figures, as did the Spartan envoys with Alcibiades in 421/0, and even apart from mere service on embassies political figures maintained personal contacts in other states, as Alcibiades of Athens did in Argos. Matters could be more delicate in the case of a monarchy, for then a direct approach had to be made to the man who held power. In such a case even a non-committal approach to discussions was more akin to a negotiation in conference than the Greeks generally were accustomed to accept. In 346 the Athenians elected the first of their embassies to Philip of Macedon merely 'to converse with Philip concerning peace'.[568] On other occasions, or later in the process, one party would formulate a public resolution, perhaps producing a draft for a treaty, which envoys would then convey to another state to advocate its acceptance. One of the clearest instances of the system at work is the One-Year Truce agreed between Athens and Sparta in 423. Thucydides gives the terms resolved and proposed by the Spartans and their allies; then the wording of the official motion which he gives as being put before the Athenian assembly indicates acceptance of the Spartan proposal.[569] Several Athenian decrees of the fourth century which have been preserved on stone show the close relationship between the proposals made to the assembly and the decrees that were passed in consequence. The decree of 377 admitting Methymna to the Second Athenian

Confederacy begins with the phrase 'with reference to what the Methymneans say . . . '[570] Prefatory remarks of a like nature preceded the decree granting Athenian alliance to Thessaly in 361/0.[571] Similarly a decree passed in the late fifth century in connexion with the alliance between Histiaea and Eretria recommends alliance on the terms of the written draft document.[572] In 425/4 indeed the Athenians complained that the Spartans made proposals but reduced none of them to a written text.

Nearly always the sovereign authorities of each state closely supervised the details of diplomatic procedures, for no diplomatic moves had any validity unless they were publicly approved, and a man who took a personal initiative on a mission put himself in a personally and politically exposed position. The diplomatic dialogue essentially was conducted between the corresponding political bodies, the councils and assemblies. Documents containing public resolutions were borne by envoys who were influential statesmen and acted as advisers and advocates but not overtly as negotiators in a conference. In 420 when the Argive envoys, apparently on their own initiative, made proposals for a fifty-year peace at Sparta on the condition that either party might challenge the other to fight over the disputed territory of Cynuria whilst each should forgo the right of pursuit beyond Cynuria, the Spartans were eager to accept those proposals but first sent the Argive envoys home to see if the terms really were acceptable to their people.[573] It was only in circumstances when the detailed implementation of a general settlement required careful attention that anything like negotiation by conference was likely to be attempted. The negotiating commission which was established, consisting of ten Spartans and ten Athenians, for the Peace of Nicias[574] was most unusual.

Once the terms of a treaty had been approved by the political authorities, it remained for the formalities of the oaths to be concluded before the arrangements came into force. Those formalities usually involved an exchange of embassies which administered the oaths to the appropriate domestic authorities in the contracting states. The content and form of the oaths varied quite considerably. At the fullest they comprised three parts, a complete repetition or paraphrase of the clauses of the treaty, a general imprecation for those who kept or broke oaths, and the invocation of deities.

The treaty between Athens and Corcyra concluded in 375 was accompanied by an oath which was one of the fullest in form. The surviving inscription, entitled 'Alliance of Corcyra and Athens in perpetuity', proceeds to set out the terms in documentary form as follows: 'If anyone proceeds to war against the territory or democracy of the Corcyraeans, the Athenians are to render assistance with all their might and to the utmost of their ability in accordance with any request made by the Corcyraeans.' Then comes the corresponding obligation of the Corcyraeans to assist Athens, followed by a clause to the effect that it was not permissible for the Corcyraeans to make peace or war without the Athenians and the majority of their allies. After those terms the corresponding oaths of the Athenians and Corcyraeans repeat the provisions in the first person as follows: 'I shall assist the Athenian/Corcyraean people with all my strength to the utmost of my ability if anyone proceeds to war either by land or by sea against the territory of the Athenians/Corcyraeans as they request, and with respect to peace and war I shall act in accordance with the decision of/the Athenians and/the majority of the allies of the Athenians, and in other respects I shall act in accordance with the resolutions/of the Athenians and/of the allies.'[575] In 361/0 the perpetual alliance concluded between Athens and Thessaly was accompanied by a brief oath which did not summarize all of the details that had been agreed. Then the Athenians swore as follows: 'I shall render assistance with all my might to the utmost of my ability if anyone proceeds to war against the Thessalian League or the Archon elected by the Thessalians or if anyone establishes a tyrant in Thessaly.' Similarly the Thessalians swore the following oath: 'I shall render assistance with all my strength to the utmost of my ability if anyone goes to war against the city of Athens or subverts the democracy of the Athenians.'[576] In cases where the treaty was long and contained a large number of provisions it was obviously not practicable to include or summarize all the terms in the oath. In 421 for the Peace of Nicias the Athenians and the Peloponnesians swore merely as follows: 'I shall abide justly and honestly by the agreements and this treaty.'

When treaties were drawn up between parties which acted as equals their respective oaths corresponded closely, but on other occasions quite different oaths could be prescribed for each party as was suitable in the circumstances. Thus in 422 rather different oaths were sworn by the two parties in the alliance between Athens and the Bottiaean Cities when the latter rejoined the alliance ten years after their secession. The Athenian oath was: 'I shall defend the Bottiaeans who are parties to the alliance and I shall faithfully and honestly preserve the alliance with the Bottiaeans zealously according to the terms of the agreement. And I shall not bear malice for past events.' The Bottiaean oath was, 'We will faithfully and honestly be friends and allies to the Athenians and we will recognize the same friends and enemies as the Athenians and will refrain entirely from assisting the enemies of the Athenians with either material or men. And I shall not bear malice for past events.'[577] In 362 when Ceos was brought back into the Athenian Confederacy and the Athenians restored those who had been exiles from Ceos in revolution, there were three different oaths taken respectively by the Athenians, the Ceans and the restored Ceans, containing provisions and promises additional to the basic terms involved in membership of the Confederacy.[578]

The diplomatic content of the promise was followed frequently by a general imprecation that evil should befall anyone who forswore himself and a prayer that good fortune should attend those abiding by their oaths. Such phrases are found, for example, in the treaties between Athens and Macedon (423/2), Halieis (424/3) and Ceos (362) and between Chalcis and Grabus of Illyria (357) and Philip of Macedon (357/6[579]). In those cases the forms of words used by each party were identical, but the same deities did not have a similar standing in all states or on all occasions and so different formulas sometimes were used in making the invocations. In the treaty between Athens and Argos in 420 each party swore in the same terms to abide by its provisions, but each was to make the most binding invocation peculiar to its state. Similarly in the alliances made by Athens with Syracuse (367), Thessaly (361/0) and Eretria (341/0) provision was made for 'the customary invocation' to be made by each party. In 362 both Athens and Ceos invoked Zeus, Athena, Poseidon and Demeter for their oaths; in 357/6 the Macedonians invoked Zeus, Gê, Helios and Poseidon in their oaths with Chalcis, and in 356 the Athenians swore their oaths to Cetriporis of Thrace by six deities, Zeus, Gê, Helios, Poseidon, Athena and Ares. The inscription recording a treaty of the mid-fourth century between Erythrae and Hermias of Atarneus provides for the invocation of 'gods pertaining to oaths'.[580] The religious nature of the ceremony for the oaths would be enhanced by the accompanying sacrifices, which are mentioned, for example, in connexion with the alliances of Athens with Elis, Argos and Mantinea in 420 and of Chalcis with Philip of Macedon in 357/6.

Each party nominated its own representatives to administer the oaths to the other party. The embassies which were sent for the purpose varied in size, for the Athenians sent three men to administer oaths for the agreement with Cetriporis in 356,[581] five men to Eretria in 341 and ten men to Eretria in 394.[582] The embassies were composed of the political personalities who were prominent in policy-making, and in 346 the ten Athenian envoys who went to administer the oaths to Philip of Macedon were those who had earlier carried out the negotiations. Just as the embassies elected to administer the oaths varied in size and composition, so too did the groups of officials who swore the oaths in each state. In the agreement with the Bottiaean Cities in 422 the Athenian Council, Generals and other officers swore the oaths; in the agreement with Argos, Elis and Mantinea in 420 the oaths were taken by the Council and domestic officials under the supervision of the Prytaneis; in the alliance with Eretria in 394 by the Athenian Generals, Council and Knights; in the alliance of 361/0 with Thessaly by the Athenian Generals, Council, Hipparchs and Knights. Where such boards and groups of officials were stipulated the occasion would clearly be one of significant formality and involve public activity by a number of socially and politically significant persons. Only in the case of the two treaties of peace and alliance between Athens and Sparta in 421 do we have a full list of the names of persons who swore the oaths. In those two instances Thucydides appears to give accounts based on Spartan records, which list seventeen Spartans, including the two kings, five ephors, ten negotiators, and a corresponding number of Athenians. The basis for the choice of those who were to swear, as opposed to administer, the oaths is not certain, but it may be that a contracting party had the right to nominate those officials or individuals who were to swear the oaths for the other state. In the alliance of 357/6 between Philip of Macedon and Chalcis it was stated that Philip of Macedon and those whom the Chalcidians required should swear the oaths, and in the fourth-century alliance between Phaselis and Mausolus of Caria those whomever Mausolus required were to swear the oaths in Phaselis.[583]

The procedure to be followed in swearing and administering oaths was simple in the case of treaties directly arranged between only two states, but if either of the parties was a member of a wider association such as a league or a federation, then matters were more complicated. In the Peace of Nicias Sparta and her allies all took the oaths separately, partly to avoid upsetting unduly some allies who accepted the situation grudgingly and partly because the Peloponnesian allies were concentrated in a geographically confined area. The Athenians, who assumed more direct responsibility for their empire and whose subject allies were spread over an extensive maritime area, concluded the treaty on behalf of their whole alliance. In 420 when the Athenians joined the alliance which already existed between Argos, Mantinea and Elis the oaths were to be sworn individually in each state.

It cannot be argued that a necessary attribute of independent sovereignty was the power of a state to swear individually to any treaty which committed it, as is shown by the history of the Delian and Peloponnesian Leagues, the Second Athenian Confederacy and the Hellenistic leagues, but such attributes and powers were of some significance. In 346 the Athenian envoys who were elected to administer the oaths for the Peace of Philocrates were supposed, according to the decrees quoted by Demosthenes, to administer them to Philip and then separately to the officials of each of his allies. The purpose was to cultivate those allies and to make them aware individually of the difficulties inherent in the situation. Philip prevaricated, took the oaths himself at Pherae and permitted the Athenian envoys to administer oaths only to such allied representatives as he brought to them.[584] He wished to retain full diplomatic control over his own allies and could point to the fact that three Macedonian representatives had administered the oaths collectively to all the representatives of the Athenian allies in the office of the Board of Generals.[585] In 387/6, conversely, when the Thebans wished to secure diplomatic recognition for the Boeotian Federation and their supremacy within it by themselves swearing the oaths in the name of the Boeotians, the Spartans refused to countenance that. The Spartans wanted to weaken Thebes' position and demanded that Thebans swear only for Thebes. A similar crisis occurred in 371 when the Spartan King Agesilaus refused the claim of the Thebans to have taken the oaths for Boeotia. In the Common Peace agreed at Sparta in that year the Athenians, who at the head of their new Confederacy fought in the name of freedom and autonomy, and their allies swore the oaths individually, whereas the Spartans concluded on behalf of themselves and their allies.[586]

Xenophon's account gives no further details of who administered and swore oaths for all the Athenian allies in 371. It would certainly have been a considerable undertaking to organize the despatch of envoys or to synchronize arrangements for so many communities. In the ordinary working of the Confederacy simplified arrangements could be worked out, as we have seen in connexion with the affairs of 346. In the Confederacy members swore to abide by the decisions of the majority of the Council of the Allies in respect of peace and war, and allied *synedroi* constantly were present in Athens. When Methymna applied to join the alliance in 377 the Methymnean envoys were to swear to the allied *synedroi*, the Athenian Generals and Hipparchs the same oaths as the other allies, and the allied *synedroi*, the Athenian Generals and Hipparchs were to swear in similar terms to the Methymneans. In that way detailed reference to the domestic authorities of each state was avoided. Presumably similar arrangements were made in 375 when the allies gave oaths to three new members of the Confederacy, Corcyra, Acarnania and Cephallenia.[587] Certainly there were joint consultations between the Athenian assembly and the allied council over the despatch of envoys to administer oaths to the new members.

Without a doubt, in view of the physical state of communications and of the constitutional processes of each state, the conclusion of an agreement on even fairly simple matters could be a protracted affair. Such considerations seem to have led to some modification of practice in one or two instances in the fourth century when an embassy went to Athens to petition for an alliance on standard terms which had already been granted to others and when the request was hardly unexpected. When Methymna sent envoys to Athens to apply for membership of the Confederacy those envoys were to swear oaths to the allied councillors and Athenian Generals and Hipparchs, but arrangements were made in addition for the domestic authorities of Methymna to swear oaths. In 361/0 the Thessalian envoys who came to Athens to seek alliance also swore oaths in the Athenian council; the authorities were likewise to swear the oaths in Thessaly.

The duration of treaties was sometimes specified and sometimes not, and they were arranged to last for a variety of terms. In the sixth century the Serdaioi and Sybaris concluded their treaty in perpetuity,[588] and in 478/7 members of the Delian League swore an oath of alliance and cast iron ingots into the sea, indicating that their oaths held good until the iron floated upon the waves. Two other treaties contracted in the fifth century by the Athenians with Rhegium and Leontini (433/2) may have been sworn in perpetuity,[589] and in 424 Hermocrates of Syracuse at the Congress of Gela urged the Sicilians to conclude a pact in perpetuity or, failing that, for as long as possible.[590] Apart from those instances it seems to have been the general practice up to the end of the fifth century to specify a term for the duration of a treaty. The longest specified terms were for the treaties between the Eleans and Heraeans in the sixth century,[591] between Athens, Argos, Elis and Mantinea (420[592]) and between the Acarnanians, Amphilochians and Ambraciots (426[593]), which were concluded for one hundred years. Arrangements were made between

Sparta and Athens in 421 and between Sparta and Argos in 418 for fifty years, and for thirty years in the treaties which Sparta concluded with Argos (451/0), Athens (446/5) and Mantinea (418/7[594]). In the fourth century, perhaps from a desire to infuse greater stability into affairs or from a recognition that peace rather than war was a normal state of affairs, it became the regular practice to conclude treaties to last for ever. Apart from the treaty concluded for fifty years between Macedon and the Chalcidic League c. 393 no limited term is prescribed for any treaty except the short truces between belligerents.

The arrangement of contracts in perpetuity seems to have had little marked effect on their practical duration. Members revolted from their perpetual alliance with Athens in the fourth century just as they had done in the fifth, and other alliances displayed the same degree of instability. Political subversion or a change in régime in one of the contracting states was a major factor in the breach or abrogation of treaties. There was no effective way to obviate such tendencies except to incorporate some arrangement to guarantee the continued existence of the régime which secured the treaty. The longevity of a treaty generally depended upon the will and determination as well as the sheer military strength of the leading party both to maintain its own obligations and to compel others to do so. Thus in the fifth century in the decree regulating relations with Erythrae (c. 455) the Athenians made detailed provision for the establishment and preservation of democracy, which would maintain its links with the democracies of Athens and her allies. Such procedures were open to abuse and caused unpopularity, to such an extent that Athens' interference in the internal affairs of her allies gave the Spartans a pretext for campaigning in the Peloponnesian War in the cause of Greek liberty. Consequently in the fourth century it became standard practice to guarantee the sovereignty of allied communities by avoiding such intervention and that principle was enshrined in the terms of the Second Athenian Confederacy. On the other hand some attempt was made to achieve stability by an exchange of guarantees made by the contracting parties to help preserve the political régimes existing at the time of the contract. Accordingly in the alliances between Athens and Corcyra (375[595]) and between Athens, Arcadia, Achaea, Elis and Phlius (362/1[596]) the treaties not only guaranteed assistance in repelling attacks on territory but also in maintaining the current political régime in each state.

In the event of a unilateral abrogation of a treaty or alliance there was no accepted theory that the sovereignty of a state overrode its obligations by a treaty to another. Obligations could be construed as absolutely binding. Consequently there was nothing necessarily or inherently immoral in the coercion of states into continuing their membership of alliances. In the mid-fourth century Chios, Cos, Rhodes and Byzantium joined in the secession from the Second Athenian Confederacy although they had sworn to abide by their agreements in perpetuity. Athens had also sworn not to interfere in their internal affairs, yet changes in régime caused changes in their external policy. The natural reaction of Athens was to take military action to restore their membership, but the orator and pamphleteer Isocrates argued that such action would be harmful to Athens' interests by launching her on the path of imperialism which had contributed to her defeat and the downfall of her democracy in the fifth century.[597] The cost of the Social War with the allies mounted and so on purely practical grounds the alliances were allowed to lapse.

Even where treaties were concluded for a limited term they regularly failed to last the full course for which they were designed. They and perpetual treaties tended to lapse into obsolescence or to be superseded by fresh arrangements either made between the parties or dictated to them by an outside party. Some treaties were formally abrogated. The clearest method of signifying an unequivocal abrogation was to tear down the pillar on which it was inscribed. Thus the final break in relations between Athens and Philip of Macedon in 340 was symbolized by the acceptance of a proposal at Athens to pull down the pillar on which was recorded the Peace of Philocrates.[598] In 361/0 when the Athenians concluded a perpetual alliance with Thessaly the enemy whom both parties had in common was Alexander of Pherae, who had molested Athenian allies although he was nominally their ally. Consequently the alliance between Athens and Thessaly was accompanied at Athens by the destruction of the record of the treaty with Alexander,[599] although it probably had been concluded for ever.

The abrogation of a treaty did not necessarily involve destruction of the record. Demosthenes argued indeed that the Athenian behaviour in repudiating the treaty with Leucon of the Bosporus was the worse because the pillars still stood, for by the failure of the Athenians to remove them traducers of Athens' reputation would the more easily find ammunition.[600] Pausanias saw the record of the Thirty Years' Peace of 445 six hundred years later[601] although the Peace had endured only until 431 and it had been superseded by several other treaties between Athens and Sparta. After the Peace of Nicias had broken down and the Argives complained that the Athenians had been lax in forcing the Spartans to implement its terms, the Athenians were not ready to denounce the Peace but on Alcibiades' proposal they inscribed at the base of the pillar a record of the infraction by the Spartans of their oaths.[602] A short time before, Alcibiades and his supporters had clearly come out in favour of abrogation of the treaty,[603] but neither Athens nor Sparta had moved to cancel their alliance after the conclusion of the treaty between Athens and Argos.

Failure by one party to fulfil the terms of an agreement could be construed as grounds for its termination by another. In 389, for example, the Achaeans sent envoys to Sparta complaining of the Spartan failure to render assistance.[604] They threatened either to abandon the campaign in the Peloponnese or to make peace on whatever terms they could and leave their alliance. In view of this the Spartans organized a supporting expedition. In at least one treaty, however, it is virtually implied that a breach would not constitute so much grounds for termination as for the imposition of sanctions. For in the alliance of c. 400 between Hestiaea and Eretria it was stipulated that whichever party infringed it should pay a fine of ten talents.[605] Certainly, as we have seen, in the Social War Athens was obliged to recognize the alliance of Chios, Cos, Rhodes and Byzantium with Mausolus of Caria[606] and their effective secession from the Confederacy only because she could not prevent it. If she had possessed the strength and capacity there is little doubt that her instincts would have led to the same methods and results as in dealing with the revolts from the Delian League which led to the imposition of terms on such communities as Samos and Mytilene.

Treaties could be nullified effectively by the conclusion of others which were directly contrary or apparently incompatible, as we have seen in the case of those of Athens with Thessaly and Alexander of Pherae. An earlier and clear instance occurred in 418, when after internal political changes in Argos the pattern of external relations changed accordingly. The Argives voted for the alliance with Sparta and the ascendant party in Argos secured renunciation of the alliance with Mantinea, Elis and Athens.[607] Similarly in dealing with the appeal of the Megalopolitans at Athens in 353 Demosthenes and others argued that the Arcadians should renounce their alliance with Thebes before concluding an alliance with Athens.[608] It must be remembered, however, that alliances could be undertaken in apparent conflict with those which already existed but which the parties intended to maintain. The signal example of such apparently conflicting obligations occurred, of course, in 366, when the Athenians were led to contract the alliance with Arcadia.[609] When Lycomedes, the Arcadian, heard that the Athenians were disturbed at the lack of support rendered by their allies he persuaded the Ten Thousand to negotiate for an alliance with Athens. At first some Athenians were concerned at the thought of allying with a state which was hostile to Sparta, with whom they themselves were friendly and had an alliance. Ultimately they were convinced that it was to the benefit of both of them to ally with Arcadia and keep out of the area the Thebans, who otherwise could acquire too great an influence. The Athenians were, however, careful to avoid provocative action and, as we have seen, the ostensibly defensive nature of treaties enabled states to face, as it were, two ways at once. A certain degree of flexibility was both necessary and desirable in Greek political conditions, and to that extent many agreements contained permissive rather than mandatory clauses. In the terms of the King's Peace, for example, it was stated that the King would wage war together with those who were willing, against those who refused, to accept the Peace. Then in the renewal of the Common Peace at the first conference of 371, held in Sparta, it was explicitly stated that those who did not wish to involve themselves in common actions of enforcement need not do so.[610] At the second conference of 371, however, held at Athens, such involvement was held to be obligatory.[611]

If treaties did become obsolete, or if certain terms were rendered inappropriate by the passage of events, it was an accepted idea that the treaties need not be terminated but could be subject to amendment. In the Peace of Nicias the last clause provided for both the Athenians and the Spartans to make good any deficiency which appeared in the terms. More specifically the ensuing alliance between them had as its final provision a clause stating that the Spartans and the Athenians could by agreement between them add or erase terms. Shortly afterwards the Athenians, Argives, Mantineans and Eleans included in their treaty of alliance provision for the addition of clauses which had the consent of all parties. In 407 Neapolis secured revision (*epanorthosis*) of an earlier Athenian decree referring to relations with Athens.[612] Then in 344 when the Athenians wished to reopen negotiations on the terms of the Peace of Philocrates it seems that Philip sent a letter to Athens stating that revision was possible. But what the Athenians wanted amounted in that case not so much to an amendment as to a revision of the basis of the treaty. Supplementary terms were known as *epispondai*, although in the one instance where that term is used by

Thucydides it refers to the ten-day truce between Athens and Boeotia, which was not so much supplementary to any agreement between Athens and Boeotia as to the treaty between Athens and Sparta and their respective allies.[613]

Wider diplomatic settlements, such as the conclusion of major wars, were taken as superseding all earlier arrangements without detailed or explicit amendments or renunciations. When the Athenians lost the great Peloponnesian War and became subordinate allies of the Spartans, agreeing to have the same friends and enemies, that effectively terminated the existing network of alliances in the Delian League. Similarly the Second Athenian Confederacy was dissolved,[614] if not already defunct, after the victory of Philip at Chaeronea and the foundation of the League of Corinth in 338/7. The King's Peace of 387/6 also had its ramifications for alliances which existed between states. Athens, for example, had concluded an alliance with the Boeotian League in 395, but by the terms of the King's Peace and according to the subsequent interpretation and guarantees of autonomy the League was deemed to exist no longer and by 382 the Thebans themselves no longer recognized the alliance.[615] Likewise the rather one-sided arrangements which the Athenians had recently made with Clazomenae and with the Eteocarpathians lapsed as they were thought to constitute an infringement of autonomy.

CHAPTER XVIII

THE INSTRUMENTS
OF DIPLOMACY

IN SEEKING TO MAINTAIN its status and influence a Greek state had only one way of buttressing its position; that way was to contract an alliance with either one or several states. If it could find sufficient common cause and reason to merge its identity with another state then some form of political union or federation was sometimes possible. Essentially, however, it was by diplomatic means that a state could ensure its survival and the execution of its will. Skill in warfare did count for much, but basically in war the factor which counted for most was the number of ships or men which could be deployed. Of course skill in the use and deployment of those forces was important: Greek military history is strewn with episodes in which 'few stood against many' heroically and even successfully, but the state of weaponry and technology was such that revolutionary inventions and devices of war were not introduced regularly. Tactical innovations, whether of the Athenian navy or of Epaminondas' Theban troops, had their initial impact, but could be learned and imitated by others after brief acquaintance. The famous Homeric catalogue of Greek allies who fought against Troy may or may not be based on fact, but at least its invention and repetition indicated that the calculations of the numerical strength of alliances were made. Thucydides' attention to the list of allies on each side at the outbreak of the Peloponnesian War was symptomatic of Greek attitudes. So too were the constant appeals to crude calculation of power when states petitioned others for alliance. Such calculations were decidedly in evidence in the presentation of requests to Athens for alliance made by Corcyra in 433 and by Thebes in 395.

Fundamentally the political history of Greece is the story of the posture of the polis in maintaining its own isolated and independent sovereignty and its inability to depend upon its own resources. Traditional attitudes rendered the control and leadership of alliances most difficult to manage, and it was not until the rise of Macedon in the fourth century that some more or less permanent resolution of these conflicting attitudes and needs was dictated by the force of circumstances.

There were many moderating forces and influences in the form both of ideas and institutions in the context of which diplomacy was practised. As has been remarked, a state often wished to find some reassurance of the moral acceptability of its stance for its effect both on its own citizens and on its friends or even its enemies. In that respect Delphi and other religious centres assumed some importance. Delphi came into prominence for its oracular responses in the period of intensive colonization, when it was consulted regularly. Thereafter its opinions were sought often, in matters of both internal politics and diplomacy, in order either that proper guidance might be given or that justification might be found for a contemplated course of action. Before the Peloponnesian War envoys from Corcyra went to Corinth and in the presence of representatives from Sparta and Sicyon offered to submit to the arbitration either of agreed Peloponnesian cities or of the Delphic Oracle. There was, however, some revulsion of feeling against seeking the advice of Delphi for action against another Greek state. Delphi provided the justification for the attitudes of Greek states at the outset of Xerxes' invasion of Greece. The Oracle, perhaps being excessively cautious or merely bribed by the Persians, told the Spartans that in opposing Persia they would be acting contrary to the will of Zeus and that they would incur great risk. Athenian enquirers too received a prophecy of impending doom and Argos received a response sufficient to justify its attitude of neutrality. Gelon of Syracuse despatched an agent to Delphi in order to await the course of the invasion and to enable him to make the appropriate gestures from his seat of neutrality.

Before the formal outbreak of the Peloponnesian War the Spartans obtained the approval of Delphi for their cause and secured a reassurance that victory would be theirs.[616] In 346 Philip of Macedon was glad to have Delphi on his side and to be able to act as its champion against Phocis. That position certainly gave him a pretext to intervene in central Greece, provided him with moral authority, and made it easier for other states such as Athens to acquiesce in his policy. Delphi was neither infallible nor beyond corruption, but the right of prior consultation (*promanteia*) was eagerly sought, for Greek attitudes to religious matters were ambivalent. Greeks could rarely be dissuaded from their intentions by religious arguments, but hesitations and delay could be caused. The Spartans achieved a certain notoriety by their hesitation in sending an army beyond their frontiers and their slowness to act, even in military emergencies, during religious festivals. In the Persian Wars their inclination was to sacrifice Greece beyond the Isthmus of Corinth. Before the Battle of Marathon they were inclined to delay action until the arrival of the Full Moon,[617] at the time of the campaign of Leonidas at Thermopylae the festival of the Carnea delayed them,[618] and in the campaign leading up to Plataea the Hyacinthia intervened.[619] Even when events were pressing nearer home in the Peloponnese at the time of the Athenian activities at Epidaurus in 418 the Hyacinthia caused a delay in reaction, but it should not be thought that the Spartans were entirely selfish or inclined to use religion as a pretext for inactivity, for they, or at any rate especially those of them who came from Amyclae, were habitually inclined to return home from campaign for the Hyacinthia.[620]

The role of religion in the substance as well as in the ceremonial of diplomacy in general should be fully recognized, for, as in many aspects of ancient life, there was not a clear division between the secular and the religious. Of the personnel of diplomacy heralds were treated as agents of Zeus and Hermes, and they were regarded as inviolable. Generally envoys did not enjoy similar privileges but at least they experienced the scrupulous attention traditionally offered to strangers. The conclusion of a truce or treaty was accompanied by a libation to the gods, *spondai*, a term which, as we have seen, itself came to mean truce or treaty. The affirmation of the arrangement was by oaths, *horkoi*, a term which was regularly used for the treaty itself.

The religious centres where the Panhellenic festivals were held provided suitable locations to deposit copies of treaties and to solemnize or renew treaties. The occasion of the festivals provided suitable opportunities to ventilate disputes, to issue challenges and to make propaganda for peace. In fact the earliest forms of inter-state organization were religious leagues or Amphictyonies. Several Amphictyonies are known, although relatively little can be said about any of them. Their purpose was ostensibly religious and they had no overtly political role or powers, although they could become centres of political and military disputes. Essentially they were local or regional associations with a communal religious centre. Twelve Ionian communities of Asia Minor maintained an Amphictyony with its common cult centre of Panionium in Priene, north of Mt Mycale, associated with the worship of Poseidon. Excavation has shown the existence of an altar, sixty feet in length, and the chamber where the

delegates met. Another Ionian centre was Delos, where the Amphictyony was associated with the cult of Apollo. Still another such cult
centre was based on the island of Calauria, off the Argolid coast,
where the Amphictyons maintained the cult of Poseidon, presumably
on account of their maritime interests.

It can be seen from the locality and the composition of the Amphictyonies mentioned above that it was likely that members would find
that they had certain political or diplomatic interests in common.
Indeed we have mentioned that Calauria went under another name,
Eirene or 'Peace'. One of the earliest statements of acceptance of
some form of code regulating the conduct of states toward each
other can be seen in the oath sworn by members of the Delphic
Amphictyony. They swore that they would neither destroy any
member city nor shut off its water supply either in war or in peace.
If any party violated the oath the rest of the members were pledged
to march against and to destroy him. If anyone violated the shrine
or holy places, the rest were pledged to punish him with hand and
foot and voice and all their power.

The twelve tribes of the Delphic Amphictyony appointed officials
to take charge of the care and maintenance of the centre, but twice a
year a formal meeting of representatives was summoned. If the
meeting was likely to have political or diplomatic ramifications,
then the appointed representatives were chosen decidedly on political
criteria. Aeschines on one occasion was originally elected by Athens
to present her case for taking over the temple of Apollo on Delos,
but he was replaced by Hyperides, whose anti-Macedonian stance
proved more acceptable to the mood of Athens.[621] Then in 340/39
Aeschines was appointed as Athenian representative, or *Pylagoras*,
together with Meidias and Thrasycles. He used his rhetorical powers
to turn the tables on the Amphissaeans, who, as friends of Thebes,
accused the Athenians of committing sacrilege by their dedication
of shields in the temple to commemorate the Greek victory gained
about one hundred and fifty years before over the Persians, with
whom the Thebans had collaborated. Then the occasion was one of
crisis, for sanctions, probably including military action, were likely
to be invoked against the party found guilty.

In the Amphictyonies theoretically the relationship between members was founded strictly on a basis of equality. Aeschines stressed
that of the members of the Delphic Amphictyony each tribe had
equal voting power, the greatest being equal to the least.[622] Each
tribe had two votes; of the Dorians the delegate representing Dorion

and Cytinion had authority equal to that of the Spartans, the Ionian representatives from Eretria and Priene had authority equal to those from Athens. Common action could be taken against defaulters, both individuals and communities, but there was little limitation of sovereignty involved. Members pledged themselves to observe certain decencies toward each other but they were not committed to peace or war in any respect except in matters which concerned their oath. There was no leader to apply compulsion to defaulters or offenders against the common cause; the guarantees were in the oaths to punish transgressors and in the solemn curse pronounced against transgressors and defaulters. The notion of the sovereignty of each state was entirely compatible with Amphictyonic membership.

The alliance which Sparta developed within the Peloponnese from the middle years of the sixth century was one of the earliest and most effective diplomatic institutions in Classical Greece. Certainly it proved to be one of the most durable diplomatic associations in history, and although it was based upon the Peloponnese, it came to take in members from outside and lasted until its dissolution in 366. For her own interests Sparta concluded with other communities a number of bilateral agreements, of which the earliest known was with Tegea,[623] and before long the association of the Lacedaemonians and their allies, as the Greeks called the alliance, became the most formidable power in the Greek world. By clever exploitation of the trend against tyranny in many states and by her activity in the cause of Greek freedom Sparta managed to find a common interest with many other communities. Her own need was to protect her own community from subversion by internal and external enemies within the region. Territorial expansion, with the political problems entailed, would have been incompatible with her own domestic institutions. Accordingly security from external threat was best achieved through alliances with neighbouring communities, and Spartan authorities were left with a free hand to deal with threats from Messenians and helots without interference from outside. By offering assistance to oligarchic groups in other communities against tyrants Sparta helped political friends into power in those communities, which then had an interest in maintaining, and an obligation to maintain, the ties that had been created. Her policy also succeeded in isolating her most serious military rival within the Peloponnese, Argos.

The alliance of the Lacedaemonians and their allies was not a sudden creation and it was not founded as a direct response to a common external threat. New allies were recruited gradually. If we are careful to bear in mind those considerations, it is easier to appreciate the nature of the diplomatic association which in modern times has become known as the Peloponnesian League. A league might well be expected to embody clearly defined political principles and to employ explicit constitutional procedures, if not an actual charter, as was the case with the Second Athenian Confederacy. No such charter is known in the case of the Peloponnesian League and the terms of only a few of the treaties survive, but sufficient is known of the bilateral treaties made by Sparta to enable us to say that there was no standard diplomatic instrument which all prospective members first had to accept. Treaties were drawn up to deal with individual cases, and although they might refer to certain common practices they related essentially to the needs of the moment.

From the start Sparta's diplomatic and military pre-eminence was recognized and it was never challenged by members. Her policy and her wisdom could be challenged but her position was secure until the later years. The treaties were not concluded as between parties of equal standing and Sparta was established as leader or *hegemon*; she automatically assumed leadership in any common military action and the so-called Peloponnesian League was the earliest kind of hegemonial alliance. In the case of the earliest known ally, Tegea, the treaty followed a Spartan military victory. In contrast to her earlier behaviour Sparta followed up her military action by constructive diplomacy, making an alliance with, not incorporating, Tegea. Spartan interests were maintained by the Tegean promise to co-operate in restricting the activities of the dissident Messenians. Subsequent allies were beholden by diplomatic favour or by the bonds of military necessity.

The alliance was of continuing significance, for it provided the base of Sparta's military superiority in Greece, but its activities were only spasmodic. The advantage gained thereby was that Sparta did not need to make frequent demands upon her allies and that they did not regard the alliance, at least in the first century or so, as an organization which impinged on their freedom. There was correspondingly a diminished need for a precise definition of the position of Sparta in relation to her allies. Provided that she retained their loyalty or respect and did not appear to neglect or ignore their interests, enough was being done to ensure the working of the alliance, and her position was such that by 481/0 her standing within the Peloponnese ensured that no other Greek power could be contemplated seriously as a candidate to lead Greek resistance to Persia either by land or by sea.

The position of Sparta was enhanced by the spasmodic nature of the activities of the alliance. For there was little need of any formal organization or bureaucracy, and, in the absence of such machinery, when action was needed Sparta, possessing the most powerful army and the most capable commanders, was indispensable as the leader in the field. Generally she retained the diplomatic initiative, but even if another state such as Corinth did seize it, little could be achieved without Spartan involvement. Equally, when an outsider wished to deal with the Peloponnesian alliance it would find it most expeditious to deal first with the Spartan authorities. Thus the attitude both of members and non-members caused Sparta to wield a predominant influence and to exercise executive control. It is much to Sparta's credit that until the Peloponnesian War, which caused her to take over the Athenian empire and induced a change of outlook, she did consult, and listen to, her allies more than others might have done.

Effective action depended upon agreement in decisions made on the one hand by Sparta and on the other hand by the allies. In the sixth century when the Spartans decided to regulate the affairs of Athens to suit their own ends and to achieve that by reimposing a tyrant, Hippias, upon Athens, the Peloponnesian allies were summoned and presented with the proposal. Sosicles of Corinth denounced it at the assembly of the allies and he was acclaimed by the rest of those present, who had hitherto remained silent.[624] Accordingly the Spartan proposal lapsed. In 432/1 the situation was rather different, for Sparta initially was inactive but was galvanized into action by a skilful diplomatic campaign which was mounted by some of her allies. Again, however, we see that positive action depended upon two separate decisions taken in harmony by the Spartans on the one hand and by her allies on the other. Corinth vigorously lobbied the Peloponnesian allies and others who had a grievance against Athens, and sent envoys to Sparta to make the case against her. The Spartan assembly was summoned to hear the grievances of the Corinthians, Aeginetans and Megarians, and by a decisive majority the Spartan assembly decided that the Thirty Years' Peace had been broken by the Athenians and that war ought to be declared.[625] Of the Spartans' decision Thucydides pointedly observed that they were not so much moved by the arguments of their allies as by fear of the growing power of Athens. After the meeting of the Spartan assembly the Delphic Oracle was consulted on the propriety of declaring war and a meeting of the allies was summoned, at which the Spartans heard their opinion and took their vote. Of the allies the majority of those present voted in order, great and small alike, for war.[626]

The separate votes of Sparta and her allies took them into war.[627] Thereafter Sparta assumed a more positive role. She sent orders to her allies for the requisition of troops to invade Attica. When the force was gathered King Archidamus of Sparta, its commander, summoned the generals and other leading men of all the states to an address, which he concluded by telling them of the benefits to be gained by maintaining unity of discipline. The proportion of the levy to be raised by each state was ordered by Sparta and at the start two-thirds of the army of each state was mobilized. When ships were needed Sparta also required her allies in Italy and Sicily to supply five hundred and a sum of money according to a quota determined by the size of each state. Until those preparations were completed, Sparta commanded those states to remain neutral and even to allow single Athenian warships to put in at their ports.

The lack of a large standing force of the League did weaken Sparta's authority in dealing quickly with diplomatic and military emergencies. The Spartan requirement of five hundred ships from her allies was not something that could be fulfilled quickly and efficiently. Similarly the requisition for a muster of allied contingents proceeded slowly on occasions. In 428, for example, the Spartans were induced to disengage at Mytilene partly because they were in difficulties through the failure of their allies to muster.

When many allies had common grievances against a state and war was contemplated, a feeling of unity was more easily engendered and the military and diplomatic initiatives of the *hegemon* were accepted. But the pressures of war were such that over a long period adequate consultation on policy was far from easy, and, as has been found so often, it was difficult to satisfy allies in arranging terms of peace. Few of Sparta's allies were likely to quarrel when before the Peloponnesian War Sparta herself turned aside overtures from Lesbos to join the Spartan alliance and secede from Athens:[628] in any case Sparta thereby avoided a breach of the Thirty Years' Peace. Furthermore few allies of Sparta were likely to be worried when Athens, in dire straits, sent envoys to sue for peace in 405 – only to have them turned away by the Spartan ephors for coming with insufficient authority to make concessions. But after their reverse at Pylos the Spartans were very discreet in their overtures to Athens in order to avoid complications with the allies; the Athenians, for their part, attempted to embarrass the Spartans on that account by pressing them to make their proposals in public rather than in private conclave.[629] By 421, however, the Spartans and most of their allies were in agreement on the need to end the war and on the principles upon which this should be done. The Spartan wish for terms was approved by a majority of the allies, and each city swore oaths in its own right to indicate its acceptance of the treaty of peace.[630] Some of the most important allies, Boeotia, Corinth, Elis and Megara, declined to accept the decision of the majority, and although Sparta claimed that they were bound by that decision she could do little to coerce them. Boeotia and Corinth were also aggrieved by, and spoke against, the terms which Sparta concluded with Athens in 404 at the end of the Peloponnesian War.[631]

The extent to which the *hegemon* could act on behalf of its allies was almost certainly not a matter for prescription so much as for regulation by judgement and sentiment in the light of circumstances. In 421 each ally ratified the treaty of peace individually, as has been seen. In the Peace arranged at Sparta in 371 the Spartans ratified on behalf of their allies,[632] in contrast to the procedure adopted by Athens and her allies, but at the conference which was held at Athens later in 371, when Elis dissented, it was arranged that all states should take the oaths separately.[633]

Sparta's outlook and attitude changed in the late fifth century. Her system of alliances altered from one which met an essentially local or regional need into one which was designed to incorporate the Athenian empire. Whereas some states had been able to trust Spartan assurances of respect for autonomy and agreements to respect ancestral constitutions, Sparta now exploited the situation to quibble over what constituted an autonomous unit and over what was the legitimate ancestral constitution. Her resort to Persia for renewed support damaged her prestige; her failure to retain Persian support both permitted an Athenian naval revival which curtailed her maritime power, and allowed a strengthened Thebes to prise the Peloponnese from her grasp.

The Delian League was quite different from the Peloponnesian alliance in many ways. For in contrast to the position of Sparta Athens found herself placed at the head of an alliance which she did not create and she was at the head of one which was kept continuously in commission. After the great victories over Persia in 479 Spartan interest in issues that did not immediately concern her declined and Sparta's reputation suffered in the events which led to the recall of her regent, Pausanias, the Greek commander. Consequently the

Greeks from the coast of Asia Minor, the northern coast of the Aegean and the Aegean islands took the initiative in asking Athens, whose prestige had grown in the Persian Wars, to head a new alliance.

The confederates swore to have the same friends and enemies, indicating their offensive and defensive intentions, for they intended not only to protect themselves from Persian encroachment but also to wreak vengeance upon Persia. The members of the alliance came from a geographically wide-spread area, thus making it rather different from the more closely confined Peloponnesian League, and although it did not take in all the members of the anti-Persian coalition of 481/0 there were those who referred to the allies as the 'Hellenes',[634] emphasizing the wider association. Immediately the members had a common purpose and task in which they were already involved. They needed a leader and appointed one. Athens therefore was not put in the position of creating an alliance but Athenian diplomacy was nonetheless skilful. The League was based on the traditional Ionian religious centre at Delos, where its treasury was placed and the meetings of its council were held. The most invidious task and difficult test facing Athens was to find resources for the League from common contributions. The Athenian general and statesman Aristides made an annual assessment of four hundred and sixty talents, a sum calculated to be enough to provide two hundred ships in action for a campaigning season. Aristides and Athens emerged from the assessment with an enhanced reputation and so no arguments were raised against the appointment by Athens of ten financial officials, *Hellenotamiai* or Stewards of the Greeks.

At first all went well and in the first decade notable successes were recorded in campaigns against Persia. Most allies accepted the equity of the arrangements which were made. Consultation was adequate and all allies had equal voting power. The momentum created brought in members until they totalled some two hundred. All benefited from the common successes achieved at a relatively low cost and none suffered from the ravages of the campaigns, which were fought at a distance on their behalf. Few suffered any disruption, for most allies contributed nothing except money, and Athens supplied most of the ships for expeditions, which were marine-based, together with a few allies such as Lesbos, Chios and Samos. Once a campaign had started Athens was less dependent upon her allies for the supply of men and ships than was Sparta upon the Peloponnesian allies. The nature of naval warfare was such that forces could not be levied at the start of each campaigning season. There had to be a continuing programme of procurement and construction and so Athens was more continuously dependent upon allied contributions, in money or in kind, than was Sparta in the Peloponnese. To that extent it was more difficult for Athens to keep up the momentum of an alliance, of whose members some might be only remotely concerned or involved at any given time. The problem arose in its most acute form after Athens agreed the Peace of Callias soon after 450, determining the respective spheres of Greek and Persian activities.

In most alliances there arises sooner or later the question of the right of secession. The oaths that had been sworn by the Delian confederates in 478/7 had no time limit, but c. 467 Naxos and then c. 465 Thasos attempted to withdraw. Athens, as hegemon, had sole executive authority and intervened by force to impose a settlement. Athenian initiative, too, was not merely confined to keeping wavering members in the League, for it also extended to incorporating new members. Carystus in Euboea, for example, most important strategically, was compelled by Athens to join c. 472.[635]

At no particular time was any decision taken to convert the League into a subordinate empire, but the conversion of the League into what the Athenians themselves described in a document as 'the cities over which the Athenians hold sway'[636] was a gradual and inexorable process which the Athenians did nothing to halt. Even the contributions of members were described as 'the tribute which is paid to Athens'.[637] The power of the Athenians grew whilst that of the allies in sheer military and naval terms diminished. The allies contributed to a force which was an Athenian force and could be used without any hindrance purely for Athenian benefit. The surplus from the contributions accrued to the Athenians, for nominally in the interests of safety and possibly on the proposal of the Samians, the treasury was moved from Delos to Athens. By 432 the Athenians had built up enormous financial reserves, such as no other Greek state possessed, and from them they disbursed money on civic projects in spite of opposition at home. Athens began to encroach gradually on the political life of her allies by the nature of the settlements and conditions which were imposed on rebellious states. We have seen already how régimes and forms of constitutions were imposed and supervised by the Athenians in the case of such communities as Erythrae and Miletus. Further practical limitations would be felt by allies when the Athenians established cleruchies. Groups of Athenian citizens, who retained their identity as such, were sent out and settled in such localities as Andros, Naxos and Euboea, where their first loyalty was not to the territory of their residence but to Athens. Garrisons were installed where needed. Political directives were issued, aiming at the protection or exclusion of certain categories of persons in member-states. The Athenians, for example, regularly appointed their *proxenoi* in allied communities and insisted on measures for their protection or immunity from attack or violence. As far as other aspects of members' external policy were concerned Athens tended to exercise greater control than did Sparta over her allies. When two members, for example, of the Delian League, Miletus and Samos, went to war against each other then Athens intervened,[638] although the forces of the League were not on campaign elsewhere.

The Delian League aimed to have a common external policy but it had no pretensions to federal institutions or bureaucracy. Nevertheless a surprising amount of legal activity concerning the affairs of the individual states took place in the Athenian courts. In the instances of Erythrae in 453/2 and Chalcis in 446/5 cases involving the extreme penalties of death, exile or deprivation of political rights were to be referred to Athens.[639] Other cases, as we will see, concerning appeals against financial assessments of members were heard by courts at Athens. In the case of Erythrae not only was there installed an Athenian garrison but also Athenian *episkopoi*, overseers, whose task was to supervise the regular working of the new constitutional arrangements. In addition to such control the Athenians ordered that anyone exiled from Erythrae should also be excluded from all the cities of the alliance. Increasingly the Athenians assumed the right to issue edicts concerning the whole alliance. In a decree of 447 the Athenian assembly, in conjunction with the Athenian council, devised measures to improve the collection of money and contributions through the Athenian commissioners and political residents.[640] Another decree, dating from 426, for tightening up the collection of tribute provided specific legal remedies against defaulters.[641] Allies were required to appoint collectors and any party obstructing them was to be liable to prosecution in his own city. The matter was to be referred to the appropriate Athenian officials to be brought before an Athenian court, which had discretion over the penalty. In 425/4 a new assessment of contribution was ordered by a resolution of the Athenian council and assembly to increase the annual amount raised from about four hundred and sixty to fifteen hundred talents a year.[642] A court was set up to deal with resulting cases and another court was appointed by the Athenians to hear appeals against their assessors. It was a complex task to deal with the assessment of over three hundred and fifty cities and the Athenians could claim to be acting with some sense of responsibility since disputes over administrative detail were to be referred to Athenian courts, which the Athenians regarded as capable of objective and impartial judgement. Nevertheless, the regulations emanated from Athens, and the dividing line between exercising administrative functions and imposing policy was not carefully observed. There could be few decrees more peremptory than that which was issued *c.* 450–46 ordering all members of the League to employ Athenian coins, weights and measures, to close local mints and to withdraw independent silver coinage.[643] Copies of that decree were posted in every city, and Athenian generals and governors were to supervise its imposition.

The Peloponnesian War saw the accumulated resources of the Delian League being used to reinforce the military and diplomatic efforts and interests of Athens. Those resources were not employed against the old enemy, Persia, but against Sparta, as was indeed quite permissible, for the allies had sworn to have the same friends and enemies. Sparta calculated that the Athenian allies would be straining at the leash for 'liberation', and her propaganda was directed accordingly, but with minimal effect, for the ruling factions, which were based generally on popular support, had an interest in preserving their links with Athens. Furthermore, Athens had not interfered in local affairs either constantly or with premeditation and malice: through the inertia of the allies Athens had acquired power and authority to intervene and administer. Even if Sparta could claim to have the general goodwill of the Greeks on her side in 431 it did her little good, for only when Athens began to lose the war and to lose the ability to protect her political friends did her subjects desert, only to find a more exacting overlord in their liberator, Sparta.

Athenian diplomatic authority among the allies was complete in 421 when Athens negotiated and signed the Peace of Nicias for her allies and asserted her right to negotiate any revision directly with the Spartans. The allies were not consulted when Athens and Sparta proceeded to conclude the alliance, and when Athens went on to conclude the One Hundred Year Alliance with Argos, Mantinea and Elis in the following year Athens ratified both for herself and for her allies, whereas the other three parties and their allies ratified the agreement separately. By 404, however, Athens was able to sign the Peace with Sparta on behalf of no one other than herself.

In the organization of the Second Athenian Confederacy we see a reaction to the previous experience of the Greeks under both the

Peloponnesian and the Delian Leagues. We see a serious attempt to reconcile the need for strong leadership with the susceptibilities and sovereignty of the members. We also see the creation of a league which was designed to be ever-ready for action but which was geared to the maintenance of sovereignty and freedom, not to constant campaigning.

In the period immediately following the King's Peace of 387/6, when Sparta became widely feared, several communities were anxious to place on record their alliance with Athens. The first known document in the series places on record the Athenian alliance with Chios and it was drawn up with strict regard to the preservation of the Peace to which Persia, Athens, Sparta and the rest of the Greeks had sworn. The alliance was defensive and involved chiefly a promise of assistance in case of attack; furthermore it was expressly stated to have been concluded on the basis of freedom and autonomy.[644] The formula employed in the treaty with Chios was repeated in subsequent alliances, such as that with Byzantium in 378.[645] Such allies not only concluded an alliance with Athens but they were also said to be allies of the other Athenian allies. Five members of the old Delian League, Byzantium, Rhodes, Chios, Mytilene and Methymna formed the nucleus of the new league. Old animosities of the fifth century had receded and Sparta had betrayed her assumed role as the champion of Greek freedom to such an extent that Greek public opinion was ranged against her. Spartan conduct in Thebes, which drove the Thebans back into alliance with Athens, and the unprovoked raid on Athens by the Spartan general Sphodrias in 378 were decisive events in the consolidation of the developing network of alliances into a rapidly expanding Confederacy.

Thenceforth Athens did not merely confirm existing treaties or accede to requests for alliances, for she and her allies published their manifesto, agreed principles of operation and actively sought to extend the membership by inviting new members to join on terms similar to those made by Thebes and Chios. Terms of membership were in strict conformity with the Common Peace made by Persia and the Greeks and they were offered to all, both to Greeks and non-Greeks, who were not subjects of Persia. The appeal was cast wide to inhabitants both of the mainland and the islands. Each state was to enjoy full freedom and autonomy under whatever constitution or régime it had, neither receiving garrisons or governors nor paying tribute. Furthermore private and public ownership of land or property by Athenians in the territory of the allies was forbidden. The Athenians thus offered safeguards in publicly renouncing the conduct which led to encroachments under the Delian League. The form of the alliance was defensive and the commitment of Athens and the allies was to go to the help of any member which was attacked by land or by sea. More specifically the alliance was given a sharper edge by the publication in its manifesto of its intention to compel the Spartans to allow the rest of the Greeks to live in peace and freedom. In the arrangements for determining the policy of the Confederacy more care was taken over the machinery for consultation and decision-making than was the case in the Peloponnesian and Delian Leagues. A common council, or *synedrion*, of all the allies of Athens was constituted at Athens. All members were represented by their own *synedroi*, and irrespective of the number of representatives which a state supplied it had one vote. Athens, as the accepted leader, remained outside the *synedrion*, and so the alliance functioned as what may be called a bi-cameral institution.[646]

Among those who swore the oath of alliance with Methymna at Athens were the *synedroi*, and they also administered the oaths to Methymna, which involved the presence there of *synedroi*.[647] In the alliance with Corcyra, Acarnania and Cephallenia in 373 the other allies also swore oaths; thereafter the Athenian assembly was left to elect representatives in accordance with a decree of the *synedrion* to administer oaths in the three new member-cities.[648] Then in direct contrast to Sparta and the Peloponnesians the Athenians and their allies all took the oaths separately for the Common Peace agreed at Sparta in 371. In 368 when envoys of Dionysius of Syracuse were present in Athens a resolution of the Athenian council was passed to the effect that the allied *synedrion* should first pass a resolution to form the basis of a decree of the Athenian assembly.[649] Then in 362/1 a resolution of the allies was passed on to the Athenian council for transmission to the Athenian assembly in connexion with the alliance with Arcadia, Achaea, Elis and Phlius.[650] In the inscription which gives details of the despatch of an Athenian garrison to Andros in 356 it is recorded that the garrison was to be paid from allied contributions in accordance with the decrees of the allies.[651]

The allies appear to have participated in the administration of the alliance until its end. For in 339 when the Athenians were arranging to repay help received from Tenedos they recommended that the allied *synedrion* should not exact contributions from Tenedos until repayments were completed.[652] In the document of 357/6 which records the thanks of Arcesine to Adrotion, the Athenian governor, there is a reference to a resolution of the allies.[653] Ways in which the allies were explicitly invited and empowered to act in supervising the alliance can be seen in the manifesto published in Athens in 377. For according to it, if any Athenian acquired property in an allied state, any state might report the matter to the allied *synedrion*, which would then arrange to sell the property and to divide the proceeds between the informants and the allied treasury. Furthermore the Athenian decree provided the allies with a voice in the trial of any private citizen or official who proposed any measure in breach of the terms of the alliance.

The allies had many safeguards and they had a genuine role to play in the evolution and execution of policy, but there were over seventy members and so they were not likely to combine in united or powerful opposition to Athens in the *synedrion*. Athens was expected to provide the leadership, and the initiative probably remained with her for most of the time. Invariably Athenian commanders are found in joint expeditions, even though allied officials might be present. The whole structure of the alliance assumed, and depended upon, agreement between the two sections of the Confederacy, Athens and the allies. That might have constituted a weakness in some ways but, even if it was inevitable that the Athenians took the initiative in raising issues, at least the allies could discuss matters independently before the Athenian assembly made its decision. In 368, for example, when envoys came with a letter from Dionysius of Syracuse the Athenian council resolved that the allies should present to the Athenian assembly whatever resolution they thought best. In the oaths for the alliance with Corcyra in 376 Athens guaranteed to assist her in case of attack, promising with reference to matters of peace and war to act in accordance with the majority of the allies and on other matters in accordance with their resolutions. For her part Corcyra promised to act in matters of peace and war in accordance with the resolutions of the Athenians and the majority of the allies, and in other respects to act in accordance with the decrees of Athens and the allies.

As long as the Confederacy had an immediate aim and a common interest, such as preventing Spartan encroachment, Athens' leadership was likely to be accepted without question, but Athens could hardly be expected to watch over all the individual interests of the separate states, nor could they be expected to feel immediate concern in all the vicissitudes of Athenian fortunes. Ultimately, if there was any conflict of wills the interest of Athens was likely to predominate. We have evidence of several individual states which had differences with

Athens or wished to secede from the alliance, but there is only one known instance where Athens on the one side and the allies on the other were intent on pursuing a different course. That occasion was in 346 at the time of the negotiations for the Peace of Philocrates between Athens and Philip of Macedon.

It is, of course, difficult to disentangle the narrative of the events of that crisis from the conflicting accounts of the two Athenian political rivals, Aeschines and Demosthenes. Aeschines purported to quote a resolution of the allied *synedrion* to the effect that, whereas the Athenians were deliberating about peace with Philip and whereas the return was awaited of the envoys whom Athens had sent out to summon the Greek cities to rally to the cause of Greek freedom, the allies resolved that on the return and report of the envoys to the Athenians and their allies two meetings of the Athenian assembly should be summoned to deliberate on the question of peace and that whatever was there decided should constitute the common decision of the allies.[654] Aeschines alleged that although the Athenians wished to comply with the resolution of the allies they did not in fact do so as Demosthenes managed to propose and secure action before the return of the envoys who had been sent to the Greek states. In another speech Aeschines maintained that the allies passed a resolution that the Athenians should deliberate concerning peace (as distinct from peace and alliance) with Philip and that any Greek state should be able to participate in the peace by appending its signature to that of Athens within a period of three months.[655] If it had been implemented the effect of that resolution would have been to turn a bilateral treaty of peace into virtually a multilateral Common Peace. In both respects the wishes of the allies were frustrated, as both peace and alliance were concluded and an Athenian resolution included a clause that the allied *synedroi* should give their oaths to Philip's envoys forthwith. The allies were consulted and Aglaocreon of Tenedos acted as their representative with the Athenian embassies to Philip, but they did acknowledge the realities of the situation between Athens and Philip and they had stated that the Athenian decision should be binding.

The dissolution of the Second Athenian Confederacy and the establishment of the League of Corinth mark a watershed in Greek history, and the year 338 saw the end of any pretence by the traditional Greek powers to organize grand alliances. As an institution the League of Corinth was never intended to be anything other than an instrument to further the ends of Macedonian foreign policy. Its constitution, however, was skilfully and diplomatically contrived to combine ostensibly the best of the diplomatic practices which had evolved during the fourth century. It harnessed Greek sentiment and prejudice against Persia and provided a mask of continuity of the old order of things. It also enabled the Greeks to accept a humble position in relation to Macedon without offending their susceptibilities more than was necessary.

Membership of the League of Corinth was not voluntary, for after establishing military supremacy by the defeat of Athens, Thebes and their allies Philip summoned representatives of the Greek states to a conference at Corinth and from that time they were diplomatically subordinate. Of the states which were or had been of any consequence only Sparta remained aloof but she represented such a minor problem that Philip decided that coercion was not necessary. Following precedent Philip organized the League as a bi-cameral institution, with himself acting, as Sparta and Athens had done in relation to their allies, as hegemon. Members of the League bound themselves to observe the terms of the Common Peace, guaranteeing freedom and autonomy. They swore to make no hostile move against anyone who observed the Peace and guaranteed to come to the aid of anyone who was the victim of either aggression or action which was contrary to the terms of the treaty. The decision for appropriate communal action was taken by the hegemon and the allied *synedrion*. In actual practice Philip's allies were in a weaker position in relation to him than were Sparta's allies in the Peloponnesian League, but at least they did not suffer the humiliation of signing mere bilateral treaties for both offence and defence by agreeing to have the same friends and enemies. The document recording the Athenian oath of membership, found on the Athenian Acropolis, gives a formula for taking decisions which was ostensibly similar to that used in the Second Athenian Confederacy.[656] Furthermore members swore to refrain from political interference in the internal affairs of allied communities, overthrowing neither the monarchy of Philip and his successors nor the existing constitutions of member-states. Contracting régimes would thereby gain confidence and would feel inhibited from indulging in their customary manoeuvres when the problem of Macedonian royal succession arose, and the alliance was likely to gain added stability.

All members were represented in the *synedrion*, but, whereas in the Second Athenian Confederacy each state had one vote irrespective of its size, resources and the number of representatives which it sent, a system of proportional representation seems to have been worked out in the *synedrion* of the League of Corinth. That arrangement meant at least that states such as Athens, which had been accustomed to playing a major role in inter-state affairs, would not suffer the humiliation of being treated as the equals of a humble state such as Zacynthus. Equally, Philip could concentrate his diplomatic efforts as hegemon more easily by persuading a few important states than by devoting equal attention to all communities in soliciting votes.

By reason of the circumstances of the founding of the League Philip assumed a position of greater supremacy in relation to his allies than had Athens in her Confederacy. In the oaths recorded at Athens the Athenians swore that they would not break the treaty with Philip of Macedon; there was no mention of Philip *and* the allies. The League had no common aim either of regional interest or of maritime protection, and it did not evolve in a pattern of circumstances such as had led to the creation of the Delian and Peloponnesian Leagues or the Second Athenian Confederacy. As did the Persian King in 387/6 Philip saw the maintenance of the Common Peace as something which suited his particular ends, and in the League of Corinth Philip created an instrument, albeit disguised, merely to ensure his own supremacy. In the absence of any common interest he was able to find and develop a theme which could be used to secure acceptance of his position in the Greek cities, or at least to render his policy justifiable if not justified. The theme of Panhellenic unity had been resurrected many times in Greek history and there were those in Athens, if not elsewhere, who kept it alive in the fifth and fourth centuries. The Delian League and the Second Athenian Confederacy had been precedents for alliances which spread far and wide in the Greek world, but both those alliances had been either concerned with or limited by the extent of Persia's dominions. King Agesilaus of Sparta in 396 set off for Persia in a blaze of Panhellenic propaganda and Jason of Pherae entertained similar pretensions. Orators and pamphleteers such as Lysias and Isocrates succeeded in maintaining the idea, even if they were not in the mainstream of political life. Accordingly Philip and Alexander after him were able to pursue their own ends against Persia and to provide the Greeks with a pretext for following their leadership.

In practical terms the members of the *synedrion* did have some competence in regulating their inter-state affairs. For example, when Melos and Cimolus disputed the possession of three small islands the matter was referred by a resolution of the *synedrion* of the Greeks to the arbitration of Argos.[657] Nothing, however, is known of the circumstances in which the matter was referred to the *synedrion*. In all matters the real power of decision rested with Macedon, although Macedon would have neither the time nor the inclination to decide all issues arising among the Greeks, and if acts of policy were to be represented as those of the League then there was every reason to ensure that some things were seen to be done by the League. In 336 on the death of Philip several states felt that the opportunity had arrived for secession. Alexander, however, had himself declared as the hegemon and brought Thebes and other states to heel. In 335 Thebes again seceded and technically could be regarded as a traitor to the Greek cause against Persia. On that occasion Alexander referred the matter to the League and encouraged many states to pay off old scores against Thebes, which they did, for they voted to raze the city and sell its citizens into slavery.[658] Again in 331/0 when Sparta, which was not a member, led a campaign against Macedonian influence, Alexander referred the matter to the allied *synedrion*, but the allies referred it back to him as hegemon.[659] Chios was probably a member of the League from 336 but three years later it went over to Persia at a time of oligarchic resurgence. The following year Alexander restored its democracy and re-established its membership, issuing an edict to that end. A constitutional commission was created and bidden to present its recommendations for his approval. Those who betrayed the city and escaped were to be tried according to the decree of the Greeks, whilst those who remained were to be tried before the council of the League.[660]

In its membership the League was more comprehensive than anything which preceded it. It had more effective machinery for regulating inter-state affairs than had the arrangements for the Common Peace, and its Panhellenic role was stressed, whereas the Common Peace had such obvious benefits to the interests of the Persian King, who could scarcely even pretend to have at heart the interests of the Greeks. The Common Peace and the Second Athenian Confederacy were essentially defensive in concept and aimed at preserving peace, whereas the League of Corinth from the start was geared to envisage a greater variety of activity. Ideally if there was close adherence to the terms of the League, then it was likely that there would be fewer local disputes or preoccupations to draw members apart with the passage of time. Collectively the Greeks would then find it easier to deal with their external problems.

As far as the constitutional arrangements were concerned they seem to have been taken further than in the Second Athenian Confederacy in creating not so much an inter-state bureaucracy as inter-state machinery for regulating and deciding affairs. The arrangements made in 338 could have scarcely been bettered and they made the basis for the Hellenic League, organized in 302 under Antigonus Monophthalmus and Demetrius Poliorcetes. Then, from what can be gleaned from the fragments of an inscription,[661] closer attention was paid to the duties, responsibilities and status of the allied officials and *synedroi*. Universal protection was guaranteed to envoys sent to, and despatched by, the council. In the cities the *synedroi* were to be free of the necessity to submit to a formal examination of their conduct in office. That represented a considerable shift, for whereas previously the *synedroi*, as in the Second Athenian Confederacy, had not only been elected by their cities but also felt a strong obligation both to their cities and to the League, they now were made responsible solely to the council. That tendency to create a strong and central source of direction ushered the communities farther along the road to accepting federal institutions and government. It was a tendency reinforced by several other factors, such as the institution of proportional representation and the express provision that action was to be on the basis of a resolution passed by the majority and that whatever proposal failed to gain a majority of votes lapsed. The agreement of 302 contained a clause to the effect that resolutions of the council had authority, but any notion that such a formula implied complete freedom in determining the main lines of policy should be dispelled, for the inscription records that the basic form of the alliance was an oath by which each member bound himself in alliance with Antigonus and Demetrius and agreed to have the same friends and enemies. There were no illusions about the operation of such an offensive and defensive alliance, and the 'fetters of Greece' were a constant reminder of the proper order of things.

The changes brought about by Philip and Alexander in the political complexion of Greece were irreversible. It is true that neither the League of Corinth, founded in 338/7, nor the Hellenic League, created in 302, was an institution of permanence. When, however, the Achaean League and Macedon achieved their grand alliance in 224 its principal members included leagues and federations such as those of the Boeotians, Phocians, Thessalians, Epirotes and Acarnanians.[662] Although this new alliance covered something like the extent of the old League of Corinth, except Athens, it was not in a position of having to contend directly with the problems of supervising directly a host of city-states.

Those cities still continued to exist with their own institutions and political administrations but many of them had permanently surrendered their effective sovereignty or independence in determining their external affairs. Even in the case of the Arcadian League, which was dissolved, although there continued a sense of Arcadian nationality and the cities asserted their individuality, the Achaean League assumed responsibility for their external affairs. The power of the old and major cities such as Athens, Thebes and Sparta lapsed and the new combinations superseded them in importance.

The Aetolian League provided the bulwark needed against the Celts in the hour of need in 278 and it extended its influence on the Delphic Amphictyony at the expense of Macedon. Significant developments such as the conclusion of peace or the declaration of war required the decision of the assembly of the League to bind its members, but considerable discretion in significant matters was left to the federal council or even a smaller committee of selected men, the *apokletoi*. In 192, for example, the assembly decided to invite Antiochus to liberate Greece, but the *apokletoi* were left to pursue important subsidiary initiatives to achieve that end.[663] In 190 the *apokletoi* themselves negotiated a truce for six months with the Romans without reference to the assembly.[664] In 191, however, the federal assembly repudiated the terms which had been negotiated for a peace treaty by the *apokletoi* with the Romans on account of resentment at the Roman treatment of Aetolian representatives.[665] In that case it can be seen that the assembly did assert itself but as it met regularly on only two occasions each year it is easy to see the opportunity, or tendency, to centralize the power in the hands of the authorities.

The dormant Achaean League of the northern Peloponnese was revitalized in 280 and became a major power under Aratus of Sicyon. Its power extended over the whole of the Peloponnese, superseding the old powers such as the Arcadian League, Corinth, Argos and even Sparta. The combination was so successful that the disparate elements of the Peloponnese came to be regarded as a unity and the area was eventually designated by the Romans as the province of Achaea, not so much a creation of Rome as the recognition by Rome of a reality. As in the case of the Aetolian League the principles of representative government and proportional representation are to be found. Major decisions could be taken at the periodic meetings of the assembly and council, but also a strong executive body was developed and considerable power was vested in the *strategos*, who led in war. Common decisions bound members on matters concerning finance, the army and external policy, and embassies which were sent by members to states outside the League required federal approval. Embassies that were of purely religious or ceremonial importance did not require federal permission, but as the occasions when federal approval was required were no doubt more frequent than could be handled by the periodic meetings of the federal assembly, often they reported to the federal executive. In 227 envoys proceeded from Megalopolis to seek federal permission on their way to Macedon to seek Macedonian help against Sparta, which was causing difficulty for the Achaean League. The envoys succeeded in obtaining a promise of Macedonian help from Antigonus Doson and conveyed their reply to the Achaean assembly. The episode has been used to show how speedily clearance for an embassy might be obtained from the federal executive; it can also be used to demonstrate the influence and tactical strength of the central authorities. For Aratus, the *strategos*, did not want Macedonian help for the Achaeans and thought that he could most conveniently ascertain the attitude of Antigonus Doson by arranging with associates for the despatch of a Megalopolitan embassy instead of a federal embassy. By such means he obtained what he wanted without involving the federal authorities, which decided to prosecute the war by their own efforts.[666] The tactical opportunities available to the central authorities are further illustrated by the diplomatic activities pursued at the meeting of the federal council at Megalopolis in 185. In that year Lycortas returned with an Achaean embassy to recommend renewal of alliance with the Ptolemies. Naturally enough the recommendation was supported by an accompanying Ptolemaic delegation. As the business involved discussion of existing arrangements rather than a new alliance or departure from principle it did not have to be referred to the federal assembly. Aristaenus, the *strategos*, however managed to prevent a decision approving the recommendation on the ground that there were in existence many treaties with the Ptolemies and that it could not be ascertained which particular treaty was to be renewed.[667] For Aristaenus that represented a notable victory gained on a matter of policy by procedural means. The *strategos* exercised considerable discretion in mustering troops and leading them on campaign. There was a law which compelled obedience to the general's order for mobilization, even apparently when the objective was unknown. In 208 Philopoemen assembled a considerable force but it was divulged only immediately before the attack that his destination was Tegea, where he proceeded to defeat the Spartans.[668]

If the influence and authority of the federal officials was strong, there were nevertheless some clearly defined procedures. Treaties were formally concluded by oaths which were taken by senior officials. An inscription from Orchomenus in Arcadia, recording an alliance with the Achaean League in 234, lists the participation in the ceremony of the *strategos*, *hipparch* and *nauarch* in addition to another group, probably the board of *damiorgoi*,[669] who probably were involved also on other similar occasions, such as for the oaths for an agreement with Antigonus Doson.[670] The decision to contract such an alliance would be formally made by the federal assembly, for even though the meetings of the assembly may have become less frequent Achaean envoys were able to remind the Romans in 185 that it was forbidden to summon an assembly except on matters of war or alliance.[671] In 220 even though discretion in conduct of the campaign was given to the commander and the army the actual decision to aid Messenia was taken by the assembly, and in 229 Aratus convened both the federal council and the assembly to make the decision to go to war with Sparta.[672]

The Hellenic League of 224 had some similarity to the League of Corinth in its original form of 338/7 and to its successor, the Hellenic League of 302. Yet it had relatively little effect on the course of Greek affairs, for the Aetolians held aloof and its military leader, Antigonus Doson, died within a short time. Furthermore even while the League did have life it had nothing like the hold over its members which the League of Corinth had, for although members were bound to do nothing contrary to the decision of the League they were not bound to co-operate in giving effect to any measure adopted by the League, nor were members bound by the votes which their representatives cast in the allied council.

Aetolia had interests which conflicted with those of Macedon in Thessaly and entertained ambitions on the west coast of the Peloponnese, the sphere of the Achaean League, and there was little prospect of easy resolution of the issues. To some extent the third century represented a distinct break from the traditions of the old combination of powers, but it may be argued that the old three-cornered struggle between Athens, Sparta and Thebes, with Persia as the interested onlooker, was replaced by a new three-cornered struggle between Achaea, Aetolia and Macedon, with Rome as the interested observer. On the other hand there was a greater continuity in the history of Greece, which tends to be obscured by the rise of the new Leagues. The old conflicts of previous centuries still persisted unresolved.

Sparta still had her quarrel with Messenia, Elis maintained its claim to Triphylia, Oropus was still a source of dispute between Athens and Thebes, and antagonism between Thebes and Boeotian neighbours still could be exploited. The larger combinations could not settle these issues which at one time or another became a liability to be endured by, or an opportunity to be exploited by, the new powers.

In the third century the three groups conducted their affairs with little awareness of developments outside Greece. The temporary alliance of Aetolia and Achaea, a move promising much, bore no relationship to the development of Roman interests in Italy and the Adriatic, it was aimed solely against Macedon. In 217 Agelaus of Naupactus spoke out in a Panhellenic vein and warned that neither Rome nor Carthage would confine its ambitions to Italy and Sicily.[673] Of those two powers Carthage was the more remote and Philip V of Macedon concluded with Hannibal an alliance which bound not only them but also his Greek allies to expel Roman forces from the Balkans.[674] This chapter is hardly the place to discuss Roman aims in external policy, to establish whether imperialism was the spur to Rome or to assess whether any consistent policy was pursued to gain objectives in the long term. The Greeks themselves were not in a position to assess such factors and certainly in the first half of the second century Rome annexed no Greek territory, and it was not until 148 that Macedonia became a Roman province. Furthermore the cultural and political experiences of the Greek communities of Italy and Sicily in subordination to Rome were not such as to ring the bells of alarm in Greece. Indeed early Roman essays by force into Greece involved not so much the presence of Roman legionaries as the assistance of Greek naval allies. The advance of Roman power was not a spectre to haunt the Greeks or to evoke an emotional response such as was created by the Persians.

Institutionally Rome at first attempted to avoid entanglements with the Greeks. In response to the alliance between Philip V and Hannibal Rome and the Aetolians made a pact,[675] but when the Aetolians made a separate peace with Philip in 206[676] the Romans did not exploit the opportunity for recrimination, and on many other occasions Greeks flouted the will or the advice of Rome without untoward consequences. The mere presence of Rome, however, was a constant factor in the shaping of policies by the Greeks and it did affect the actual working and conduct of Greek institutions. The proclamation of Greek freedom by Flamininus in 196 could not complete the discharge of Roman responsibility. As in the case of the Persian proclamation of 387/6 it implied some kind of continuing responsibility either for interpretation or for enforcement. Flamininus' commission was by no means the last of its kind. In 183, for example, three commissioners considered the problems of the Achaeans and Spartans[677] and in 168 ten commissioners dispensed the affairs of Greece in the wake of Pydna.[678] In dealing with the affairs of Illyria and Macedon the Roman Senate professed that it was the intention of Rome to bring freedom to the subjected – not subjection to the free.[679] Even in 146 the Governor of the province of Macedonia was detailed to supervise the affairs of what was termed 'Free Greece'. Despite the proclamations of freedom the influence of Rome, even after the legions had withdrawn following Flamininus' settlement, was such that the Aetolians mobilized in the cause of liberating Greece from Roman control.

Unless Rome intervened with a strong military presence in Greece she had to pursue her legitimate aims of policy by despatching a stream of embassies, commissioners and edicts and by co-operating with certain parties to counter the activities of others. Her strength was such that she was able to despatch the embassies and commissioners to recommend decisions and she was the recipient of appeals, not of representations. Co-operation between Rome and other, lesser powers was not as between equals. When Rome concluded the alliance with Aetolia there was no question but that a Roman should be the supreme commander in joint operations. Furthermore defeat at the hands of Rome had serious implications. The Roman victory over Aetolia soon brought the Aetolians to realize that they could not negotiate a settlement of their differences with Rome.[680] Defeat involved surrender and the dictation of terms by Rome. The Aetolians were made to promise to have the same friends and enemies as Rome, a condition commonly imposed in Greek diplomacy, but additionally they were made to promise to uphold the rule and majesty of the Roman people, a condition which effectively precluded their independence in foreign policy.

The Achaeans, too, became effectively dependent upon, and subordinate to, Rome long before the temporary dissolution of their League in 146. For from 192 they became no less dependent upon Roman support than they had been on Macedonian support. That dependence irked them at times but they found no satisfactory way in which they could assert their independence, and perhaps their subordination to Rome was to some extent masked by their ability to flatter their own vanity in the flamboyance and ceremonial of diplomatic exchanges with the court of the Ptolemies. In the conduct of the affairs of the League the Achaeans found themselves both obliged to take decisions and to breach their established rules of procedure on account of either the pressure or the presence of the Romans. In 198, for example, Philip tried to ensure the neutrality of the Achaeans whilst the Romans sought their alliance. After listening to speeches from various envoys, including a Roman delegation, in the assembly the Achaeans remained silent initially and the ten federal *damiorgoi* split equally over the question of whether to put to the vote a proposal for an alliance with Rome or to accept the correct view that it was illegal to propose, and to vote upon, any measure which contravened the alliance with Philip. The influence of Rome over-awed the Achaeans.[681] In fact the Achaeans so adapted their procedures that they permitted their federal officials to summon meetings of the primary assembly not only to consider matters of war and peace but also to discuss subjects raised in written notice by the Roman Senate. In 170 the Achaean elections were influenced by the presence of Rome. Plainly it was not possible for men to speak out openly against Rome but even those who objected to an excessive subservience to her were so muted as to permit the election of Archon as general and of Polybius as *hipparch*, men likely to be compliant in the face of Roman demands.[682] At the first regular meeting of the Achaeans for the year 168 at Corinth two proposals were considered. The first, which had the support of the majority, was to send military aid to the Ptolemies against Antiochus Epiphanes. The second proposal was to keep the forces at home ready to help the Romans who were about to mount a decisive campaign in Macedonia. The proposals were deferred to an extraordinary meeting at Sicyon, but opinion still favoured the first proposal, whereupon the Achaeans were confronted with a letter from the Romans urging them to co-operate in sending envoys to reconcile the kings in dispute.[683] To the majority discretion appeared to be the better part of valour. Achaean limitations were clearly exposed in 155 when in response to appeals by both parties to the dispute between Crete and Rhodes the Achaeans recognized that they could neither go to war nor send assistance without the approval of Rome.[684] Indeed after their victory at Pydna the Romans were less inclined to conceal their hand and in 168 they successfully demanded the extradition to Rome of those who were allegedly of an anti-Roman disposition.[685] It was of little use to the Greeks and won them little honour that embassies representing many of their states assembled at Amphipolis to offer congratulations to the Romans on their victory.

The successive elimination of the three Greek powers of Macedon, Aetolia and Achaea by no means represents the end of Greek history or diplomacy, but the external relations of communities by this point have become so inextricably bound up with Rome that the emphasis is principally on Rome in the diplomacy of the Mediterranean states and the theme should be continued by someone who is prepared to write a book on Ancient Roman Diplomacy.

APPENDIX

SELECTED DOCUMENTS IN
TRANSLATION

ALLIANCE BETWEEN ELIS AND HERAEA, *c.* 500

Bronze tablet found at Olympia[686]

This is the covenant between the Eleans and the Heraeans. There shall be an alliance for one hundred years and this year shall be the first; and if anything is needed, either word or deed, they shall stand by each other in all matters and especially in war; and if they stand not by each other, those who do the wrong shall pay a talent of silver to Olympian Zeus to be used in his service. And if anyone injures this writing, whether private man or magistrate or community, he shall be liable to the sacred fine herein written.

(following the translation of
Meiggs and Lewis, *Greek Historical
Inscriptions*, 17, p. 32).

COMMERCIAL ARRANGEMENTS BETWEEN ATHENS AND PHASELIS, *c.* 450

An Athenian decree inscribed on marble[687]

Resolved by the council and people in the prytany of the tribe Acamantis;

Onasippus was secretary, Epimodes was chairman, Leon proposed:
For the people of Phaselis to place on record the decree that whatever cause of action arises at Athens involving a man of Phaselis, the case shall be heard at Athens before the polemarch, as in the case of men of Chios. Other cases arising elsewhere shall be heard according to the existing arrangements with Phaselis. Furthermore, if any other Athenian magistrate proceeds to pass judgement then his verdict shall be void. If anyone contravenes this enactment he shall pay a fine of ten thousand drachmas to Athena. The secretary of the council is to publish this decree inscribed on stone and he is to set it up in the city at the expense of Phaselis.

RELATIONS BETWEEN ATHENS AND CHALCIS 446/5

An inscription on marble of an Athenian decree[688]

The council and people resolved, in the prytany of the tribe Antiochis, Dracontides was chairman, Diognetus proposed:

That the Athenian council and jurors swear as follows:

I shall not drive out the Chalcidians from Chalcis and I shall not raze their city. I shall deprive no individual of his political rights nor shall I punish him with exile or arrest him or put him to death or seize his money without a trial before the Athenian people, and I shall put no judgement to the vote against anyone either collectively or individually without the due issue of a summons, and whenever I hold office as *prytanis* so far as I am able I shall introduce to the council and people within ten days an embassy after its arrival. Those measures I shall guarantee to the Chalcidians for their loyalty to the Athenian people. The embassy which has come from Chalcis shall administer the oaths with the commissioners for oaths to Athenians and shall publish a list of those who swear. The board of generals is to ensure that all swear the oaths.

That the Chalcidians swear as follows:

I shall not revolt from the people of Athens by any device or stratagem either by word or by deed and I shall not obey anyone who is in revolt, and if anyone does revolt I shall denounce him to the Athenians, and I shall pay to the Athenians that amount of tribute which I can persuade the Athenians as being proper and I shall be as good and just an ally as I can, and I shall come to the assistance and defence of the people of Athens if anyone wrongs the people of Athens, and I shall obey the people of Athens.

Of the Chalcidians all those who have reached adult age are to swear the oath. Whoever fails to take the oath shall forfeit his political rights and his goods shall be confiscated by the state and one tenth shall be dedicated to Olympian Zeus. An embassy of the Athenians shall proceed to Chalcis to administer the oaths with the commissioners for oaths in Chalcis and shall publish a list of those of the Chalcidians who swear.

Anticles proposed: to the good fortune of the Athenians, that the Athenians and Chalcidians conclude the oath after the manner that the people of Athens decreed in the case of the Eretrians. The Board of generals shall ensure that this is done with the utmost despatch. The people shall elect forthwith five men who shall proceed to Chalcis and administer the oaths. And concerning the hostages the reply shall be given to the Chalcidians that for the present the Athenians have decided to let matters rest as they have been decreed. But whenever it seems appropriate they will deliberate and make such change as seems suitable to the Athenians and Chalcidians. With reference to aliens in Chalcis with the exception of as many as reside there without paying taxes to Athens, and anyone who has been granted exemption from taxation by the people of Athens, the rest shall pay tax to Chalcis in the same way as the Chalcidians. The secretary of the council shall record this decree and the oath in Athens on stone and shall erect it in the city at the expense of the Chalcidians, and the council of the Chalcidians shall record it and erect a copy in Chalcis in the temple of Olympian Zeus. That shall be decreed by the Chalcidians. The sacrifices required by the oracles on behalf of Euboea are to be performed with the utmost despatch by Hierocles and three men elected by the council from its own members, and to effect the despatch the board of generals shall give its co-operation and provide the money to that end.

Archestratus proposed: that everything shall be as Anticles proposed but that with respect to punishment that should be determined by the Chalcidians themselves in Chalcis, just as in the case of Athenians in Athens, with the exception of cases involving exile, death and deprivation of political rights. In such cases there is to be appeal to the court of the Thesmothetai at Athens in accordance with the decree of the people. And with regard to the protection of Euboea the generals are to make the best provision which they can as may be best for Athens.

THE PEACE OF NICIAS 421[689]

The Athenians and Lacedaemonians and their allies have made a treaty as follows and have sworn to it city by city.

As regards the temples shared by the Greeks whoever wishes shall offer sacrifice and have access to them and consult their oracles and send deputies to them according to their ancestral customs by land and sea without fear. The sacred area and temple of Apollo at Delphi and the Delphians shall be governed by their own laws, and be subject to their own dues and shall have jurisdiction in their own courts both of themselves and of their territory according to ancestral custom.

The peace shall be binding for fifty years on the Athenians and the allies of the Athenians and the Lacedaemonians and the allies of the Lacedaemonians without fraud or injury both by land and sea. It shall not be lawful to bear arms with intent to do injury either for the Lacedaemonians and their allies or for the Athenians against the Lacedaemonians and the allies of the Lacedaemonians by any stratagem or device.

If there is any matter of dispute between them they shall have recourse to justice and oath in the way agreed upon.

The Lacedaemonians and their allies are to deliver Amphipolis to the Athenians. As many cities as the Lacedaemonians have handed over to the Athenians, their citizens shall be free to depart whither they may wish themselves and in possession of their property. The cities are to be autonomous while they pay the tribute assessed in the time of Aristides. It shall not be lawful for Athens or her allies to bear arms to injure them, if they pay their tribute, now that the peace has come into effect. The cities referred to are Argilus, Stagirus, Acanthus, Scolus, Olynthus, Spartolus. They are to be allies neither of Lacedaemon nor of Athens. But if Athens persuades the cities, it is to be lawful for Athens to accept them as allies of their own volition. The people of Mecyberna and Sane and Singus shall inhabit their own cities, like those of Olynthus and Acanthus. The Lacedaemonians and their allies shall make over Panactum to Athens. Athens shall make over to Lacedaemon Coryphasion and Cythera and Methone and Pteleon and Atalanta and whatever Lacedaemonians are imprisoned in Athens or in any other place where Athenians hold sway. Moreover the Athenians are to release those of the Peloponnesians who are besieged in Scione and the rest of the Lacedaemonian allies in Scione and of those whom Brasidas sent out there and any of the allies of the Lacedaemonians who are imprisoned in Athens or in any other place where the Athenians hold sway. The Lacedaemonians and their allies are to restore in the same manner those of the Athenians and their allies whom they hold. With reference to Scione, Torone, Sermylium and any other city in the possession of the Athenians, the Athenians are to decide as they think fit.

The Athenians shall take an oath to the Lacedaemonians and their allies, city by city. Each of the two sides shall swear their greatest local oath, seventeen men from each city. The content of the oath is to be as follows: I shall abide by these agreements and peace conditions in justice and sincerity. The Lacedaemonians and their allies shall take the same form of oath towards the Athenians and both shall renew the oath each year. They shall set up inscribed pillars at Olympia, in Pythia and at the Isthmus, and at Athens on the Acropolis and at Lacedaemon in the temple at Amyclae.

And if anything be on either side forgotten, or shall be thought upon fair deliberations to be changed it shall be lawful for both to do this as may be thought fit jointly by both parties, the Athenians and Lacedaemonians.

The peace shall begin in Lacedaemon with the 24th day of the month Artemisium, Pleistolas being ephor, and at Athens on the 25th day of Elaphebolion, Alcaeus being archon.

(There follows the record of those who took the oath and poured the libations, with the names of the seventeen representatives of the Lacedaemonians and of the seventeen representatives of the Athenians.)

SPARTA AND ARGOS 418[690]

A.   A Spartan resolution to negotiate with Argos as follows:

The Argives are to restore to the Orchomenians their children, to the Maenalians their menfolk and to the Spartans those whom they hold in Mantinea.

The Argives are to withdraw from Epidaurus and to pull down the fortification. If the Athenians fail to withdraw from Epidaurus they are to be regarded as enemies of the Argives and of the Spartans and of the allies of the Spartans and the Argives.

If the Spartans hold any children they are to return them to all the cities.

In respect of sacrifice to the god the Argives, if they so decide, are to impose an oath upon the Epidaurians, otherwise they are to swear it themselves.

The cities in the Peloponnese, both small and large, shall all be independent according to their ancestral customs. If any party from outside the Peloponnese proceeds by land with hostile intent against the Peloponnese the contracting parties are to take counsel to repel him in concert in such a way as seems to be most just to the Peloponnesians. As many allies as the Spartans have outside the Peloponnese and as many as the Argives have shall be on the same footing as the Spartans and the Argives, in possession of their own territory. These terms are to be disclosed to the allies for their approval, and if the allies so decide they may refer them to their domestic authorities.

B. The treaty subsequently concluded:

The Spartans and the Argives decided to conclude a treaty and alliance for fifty years upon the following terms: they are to resolve their disputes by fair and impartial arbitration according to their ancestral customs; the rest of the cities in the Peloponnese may participate in the treaty and alliance in possession of their own sovereignty, independence and territory, resolving their disputes by fair and impartial arbitration according to their ancestral customs. As many allies as the Spartans have outside the Peloponnese and as many as the Argives have shall be on the same footing as the Spartans and Argives, in possession of their own territory. If there shall be needed a common expedition anywhere the Spartans and the Argives are to take counsel in what way they decide most just for the allies. If any dispute arises concerning any of the cities either within or without the Peloponnese in respect of either frontiers or any other matter it is to be settled. But if one allied city should be in dispute with another it is to be referred to a city which seems to both cities in dispute to be impartial. In respect of private citizens judgement is to be in accordance with the ancestral customs of the community concerned.

PROSPECTUS OF THE SECOND ATHENIAN CONFEDERACY 378/7

An inscription on marble from Athens[691]

In the archonship of Nausinicus

Callibius, son of Cephisophon, of Paeania was secretary. In the seventh prytany of the tribe Hippothontis; resolved by the council and people; Charinus of Athmonum was chairman; Aristoteles proposed:

For the good fortune of the Athenians and the allies of the Athenians; that the Spartans shall permit the Greeks to live at peace in freedom and autonomy and in secure possession of all their territory; and that the Common Peace, to which the Greeks and the King of Persia subscribed on the terms agreed, may prevail and endure for ever, be it resolved by the people:

If any of the Greeks or non-Greeks who inhabit the mainland or the islands, who are not subjects of the Persian king, wishes to be an ally of the Athenians and their allies, he shall be permitted to be so, retaining his freedom and independence, being governed under whatever constitution he wishes, neither receiving a garrison nor submitting to a governor, and not paying tribute, on the same terms as Chios, Thebes and the other allies. For those who make alliance with the Athenians and their allies the people shall relinquish all property held by Athenians, whether in public or private ownership, in the territory of those who make alliance with the Athenians and their allies and shall give a guarantee of that. If there happen to be in Athens public records which are prejudicial to any of the cities making alliance with Athens, the council which is in office at the appropriate time shall be empowered to remove them. From the archonship of Nausinicus it shall not be permissible for an Athenian to acquire either publicly or privately, by purchase or by mortgage or by any other means any house or land in allied territory. But if anyone should purchase, acquire or take on mortgage any such property in any way it shall be permissible for any of the allies who wishes to lay the matter before the council of allied representatives. Those representatives shall dispose of the property and give one half to the informant, and the other half shall be the common property of the allies. If anyone proceeds with hostile intent against those who have made the alliance either by land or by sea, the Athenians and their allies are to come to their aid by land and by sea with all their force to the utmost of their ability. Moreover if any private citizen or official proposes or puts to the vote in contravention of this decree any measure to rescind any of the provisions of this decree he may suffer deprivation of his political rights and his property shall be publicly confiscated, one tenth being dedicated to the goddess Athena. He shall be tried by the Athenians and the allies for subverting the alliance and they shall punish him with death or exile from the territory under the control of the Athenians and their allies. If he is condemned to death he shall not be buried in the territory of Attica or the allies. The secretary of the council shall publicly inscribe this decree on stone and set it up alongside the statue of Zeus the god of Freedom; the Treasurers of the goddess Athena shall disburse sixty drachmas for the inscription of the stone from their fund of ten talents. On the stone shall be inscribed the names of the cities which are allies and of any other which becomes an ally. That shall be inscribed.

ALLIANCE BETWEEN ATHENS AND CORCYRA 375[692]

Alliance of Corcyraeans and Athenians in Perpetuity

If anyone proceeds with hostile intent against the territory of Corcyra or against the people of Corcyra the Athenians are to come to their aid with all their might and to the utmost of their ability accordingly as the Corcyraeans may request. And if anyone proceeds with hostile intent against the people of Athens or against the territory of Athens either by land or by sea, the Corcyraeans are to come to their aid with all their might and to the utmost of their ability accordingly as the Athenians may request. It shall not be permissible for the Corcyraeans to make war or peace without the Athenians and the majority of the allies. In all other respects conduct will be in accordance with the resolutions of the allies.

The Oath:

I shall come to the aid of the people of Corcyra with all my might and to the utmost of my ability accordingly as the Corcyraeans may request if anyone proceeds with hostile intent against the territory of Corcyra either by land or by sea, and with respect to war and peace I shall act in accordance with the decisions of the majority of the allies, and in all other respects I shall act in accordance with the resolutions of the allies. I swear this by Zeus, Apollo and Demeter. May much good fortune attend me if I abide by the oath, may the opposite befall me if I fail.

I shall come to the aid of the people of Athens with all my might and to the utmost of my ability accordingly as the Athenians may request if anyone proceeds with hostile intent against the territory of Athens either by land or by sea, and with respect to war and peace I shall act in accordance with the decisions of Athens and the majority of the allies, and in all other respects I shall act in accordance with the resolutions of Athens and the allies. I swear this by Zeus, Apollo and Demeter. May much good fortune attend me if I abide by the oath, may the opposite befall me if I fail.

OATH TAKEN BY THE GREEK STATES ON JOINING THE LEAGUE OF CORINTH 338/7[693]

The Oath:

I swear by Zeus, Gê, Helios, Poseidon, Athena, Ares and all the gods and goddesses. I shall abide in peace and I shall not infringe the treaty with Philip of Macedon. Neither by land nor by sea shall I bear arms with injurious intent against any party which abides by the oath, and I shall refrain from the capture by any device or stratagem of any city, fortification or harbour of the parties who abide by the Peace. I shall not subvert the monarchy of Philip and his successors nor the constitutions existing in each community at the time when the oaths for the Peace were sworn. I shall refrain from contravening the terms of the agreement and I shall not allow another so to do as far as I am able. If anyone perpetrates any act in contravention of the terms of the agreement I shall render assistance accordingly as the wronged party may request and I shall make war upon him who contravenes the Common Peace accordingly as the Allied Council may resolve and as the hegemon may command, and I shall not fall short . . .

EXCHANGE OF RIGHTS (ISOPOLITEIA) BETWEEN MILETUS AND CYZICUS

Part of an inscription on marble from Miletus[694]

The people resolved on the recommendation of the council: Philiscus proposed.

The Milesians and Cyzicenes made the following agreement, for the Milesians Philiscus, son of Anaxileos, Theognetus, son of Demosthenes, Demarchus, son of Athenaeus, Mikkos, son of Antiphon, Philip, son of Philinus, for the Cyzicenes Ariston, son of Athenaeus, Proxenos, son of Athenaeus, Axes, son of Ephesius:

That the cities shall be friends in perpetuity according to their ancestral customs: any Cyzicene in Miletus is to be a Milesian and any Milesian in Cyzicus is to be a Cyzicene . . .

ALLIANCE BETWEEN CARTHAGE AND PHILIP V OF MACEDON, 215[695]

This is a treaty sworn on the one side by Hannil al the general, Mago, Myrcanus, Barmocar, all those members of the Carthaginian council who were present and all Carthaginians serving in his army and on the other side by Xenophanes, son of Cleomachus, the Athenian envoy whom King Philip despatched to us representing himself, the Macedonians and their allies.

In the presence of Zeus, Hera and Apollo: in the presence of the God of the Carthaginians and of Heracles and Iolaus: in the presence of Ares, Triton and Poseidon: in the presence of the gods who fight on our side and of the Sun, Moon and Earth: in the presence of rivers, lakes and waters: in the presence of all the gods who rule Carthage: in the presence of all the gods who rule Macedonia and the rest of Greece: in the presence of all the gods of the army who are witnesses to this oath.

Hannibal the general and all the Carthaginian councillors who are with him and all the Carthaginians serving in his army, subject to our mutual consent, propose to make this sworn treaty of friendship and honourable good-will. Let us be friends, comrades and brethren on the following conditions:

1) That King Philip, the Macedonians and the rest of the Greeks who are their allies shall support the Carthaginians, as supreme, Hannibal their commander and those serving with him, and all those who live under the same laws in the dominion of the Carthaginians, as well as the people of Utica and the cities and tribes subject to Carthage, and their soldiers and allies, and all the cities and tribes in Italy, Gaul and Liguria with whom we have a compact of friendship

and with whomsoever in this country we may hereafter conclude friendship and alliance.

2) For their part also King Philip and the Macedonians and such other Greeks as are his allies shall be supported and protected by the Carthaginians who are campaigning with us, and by the people of Utica and by all cities and tribes subject to Carthage, both soldiers and allies, and by all allied cities and tribes in Italy, Gaul and Liguria, and by all others who may become allies of Carthage in the region of Italy.

3) We will not make plots against, nor be in ambush for, each other; but in all sincerity and good-will, without reserve or secret design, will be enemies to the enemies of the Carthaginians saving those kings, cities and ports with which we have sworn agreements and friendships.

4) And we too will be enemies to the enemies of King Philip saving those kings, cities and tribes with which we have sworn agreements and friendships.

5) You will be allies to us in the war which we are now fighting against the Romans until such time as the gods give to us and to you the victory: and you will assist us in all ways that may be needed and in whatsoever way we may mutually determine.

6) And when the gods have given us victory in our war against the Romans and their allies if the Romans ask us to conclude terms of friendship, those terms shall include the same friendship with you, made on the following conditions: *a*) that the Romans may never make war upon you, *b*) that the Romans are not to have power over Corcyra, Apollonia, Epidamnus, Pharos, Dimale, Parthini or Atitania, *c*) that the Romans also restore to Demetrius of Pharos all those of his friends now in the dominion of Rome.

7) If ever the Romans make war on you or on us we will aid each other according to the need of either.

8) Likewise if any other nation whatever does so, always excepting kings, cities and tribes with whom we have sworn agreements and friendships.

9) If ever we decide to take away from, or add to, this sworn treaty, we will so take away, or add thereto, only as we may both agree.

ROME AND THE AETOLIAN LEAGUE

A. Alliance concluded in 211 on the following terms:[696]

That forthwith the Aetolians should wage war by land against Philip; that the Romans should provide naval assistance with not less than twenty-five quinqueremes; that of the cities from the Aetolian frontier as far as Corcyra the land, including walls, buildings and estates, should belong to the Aetolians and all the rest of the spoils to the Romans, and the Romans should ensure that the Aetolians have possession of Acarnania. If the Aetolians concluded peace with Philip they were to add the condition that the peace would be considered valid only if Philip refrained from war with the Romans, their allies and their subjects. Correspondingly if the Roman people' concluded a treaty with Philip it should be on the condition that he should have no right to invade Aetolia and its allies.

(There was an addition that if they so wished and decided Elis, Sparta, Attalus, Pleuratus and Scerdilaidas should enjoy the same rights of friendship, Attalus being king of Asia and the last two named being kings of Thrace and Illyria.

Such was the compact and after a delay of two years copies were deposited at Olympia by the Aetolians and in the Capitol by the Romans.)

B. Peace concluded in 189:[697]

The people of Aetolia shall uphold faithfully the rule and dominion of the Roman people. They are not to permit the passage through their territory and cities or the supply by public consent of enemies proceeding against the Romans or their allies and friends. They shall consider as their own enemies the enemies of the people of Rome and they shall make war upon those against whom the Romans make war. The Aetolians shall return all the deserters, fugitives and captives of the Romans and their allies, with the exceptions of those prisoners of war who escaped to their own country and were subsequently recaptured and of those who were enemies of Rome at the time when Aetolia was fighting on the same side as the Romans. The return is to be effected to the prefect of Corcyra within one hundred days after that on which the oaths are sworn. But in the event of any not being discovered in that time whenever they come to light they are then to be handed over without fraud, and in such cases no return to Aetolia shall be permitted after the oaths have been taken. The Aetolians shall pay forthwith to the consul in Greece two hundred Euboeic talents of silver, of a standard not less than the Attic, paying if they wish one third in gold instead of silver at the rate of one mina of gold for ten minae of silver, and annually for the first six years from the date of the conclusion of the oaths fifty talents, and they shall deliver that sum in Rome. The Aetolians shall give to the consul forty hostages, aged between twelve and forty years, for six years. The selection of the hostages shall be at the discretion of Rome but will not include a strategus, hipparch or public secretary or anyone who has previously been a hostage in Rome. The hostages too are to be delivered in Rome and if anyone of them should die he is to be replaced. With reference to Cephallenia, it shall not be included in the treaty. Of the territories, cities and population which belonged to Aetolia but which subsequently either were captured by, or went over as friends to, the Romans from the consulship of Lucius Quinctius or Gnaeus Domitius, the Aetolians shall effect no recovery. Moreover the city and territory of Oeniadae shall belong to Acarnania.

GREECE AND ROME IN 196

A. Peace between Philip V of Macedon and Rome[698]

The Ten Commissioners arrived from Rome and on their advice peace was granted to Philip on the following terms: that all the Greek cities in Europe and Asia should enjoy freedom under their own constitutions: that Philip should withdraw the garrisons from those cities which he controlled and that he should hand over those cities ungarrisoned to the Romans before the Isthmian Games: that he should also withdraw from the following cities in Asia, Euromum, Pedasa, Bargylia, Iasus, Myrina, Abydos, Thasos and Perinthus (for it was decided also that they should be free); that with respect to the liberation of the Ciani Quinctius should communicate by letter to the King of Bithynia the decision of the Senate and the Ten Commissioners; that Philip should return to the Romans the captives and deserters and surrender all his warships except five and one royal galley of almost unmanageable size which was propelled by sixteen banks of oars; that he should have no elephants and no more than five thousand men under arms; that he should not wage war beyond the boundaries of Macedonia without orders from the Senate; that he should pay an indemnity of a thousand talents to the Roman people, one half immediately and the other half by instalments over the years.

(The terms presented above are given as the standard version by Livy, who next proceeds to list variants and additions which appear in the accounts of the annalists Valerius Antias and Claudius Quadrigarius as follows: Valerius Antias records that an annual tribute of four thousand pounds of silver was imposed upon the king for a term of ten years; Claudius records an immediate payment of twenty thousand pounds followed by thirty annual instalments of four thousand and two hundred pounds. The same author writes that it was specifically added that Philip should not wage war against Eumenes, the son of Attalus, who had then newly acceded to the throne. Hostages, including Demetrius, the son of Philip, were taken against the fulfilment of those conditions. In addition Valerius Antias states that the island of Aegina and the elephants were presented as a gift to Attalus in his absence and that Stratonicea and the other cities of Caria which Philip had held were similarly presented to Rhodes, whilst the islands of Paros, Imbros, Delos and Scyros were assigned to Athens.)

B. The Roman edict on the 'Liberation' of Greece, announced at the Isthmian Games in 196:[699]

'The Roman Senate and Titus Quinctius, the commander, following the defeat of King Philip and the Macedonians bid Corinth, Phocis, and all the Locrians and the island of Euboea, Magnesia, Thessaly, the Perrhaebians and the Phthiotic Achaeans to be free, exempt from tribute, and subject to their own laws.'

ATHENIAN PROXENY FOR COROEBUS OF SPARTA 367[700]

In the archonship of Nausigenes, in the seventh prytany of the tribe Aiantis, Moschus, son of Thestius, of Kudathene was secretary, the council and people resolved. The tribe Aiantis presided, Paramuthos of Otryne was chairman, Moschus, son of Thestius was secretary, Diophantus proposed: that concerning the report of the envoys who have come from Sparta, it be decreed by the council that those who happen to be presiding at the appropriate time should make consultations in the assembly concerning them and introduce the recommendation of the council to the assembly, that whereas Coroebus of Sparta is a good man to the people of Athens both at present and in former time, the council resolves that the title of Proxenos and Benefactor of the Athenian People be granted to him and to his descendants. The secretary of the council shall inscribe this decree on stone and shall set it up on the Acropolis. For the inscription the Treasurer of the people shall give twenty drachmas from the funds disbursed by the people in connection with decrees.

NOTES

The notes consist principally of references to the source material. In order to contain the length of the notes references to articles and modern works generally have been omitted. The reader will be able to pursue certain topics further by consulting the standard commentaries on such works as those of Herodotus, Thucydides, Xenophon and Polybius. Additionally the relatively recent appearance of the second and third volumes of *Die Staatsverträge des Altertums* provides an extensive bibliography on most of the relevant treaties and diplomatic documents.

The most comprehensive work on the inter-state relations of the Greeks from the sixth to the fourth century, published in French, is:

V. Martin   *La Vie Internationale dans la Grèce des Cités*, Paris 1940.

The fullest work to appear in English is:

Coleman Phillipson   *The International Law and Custom of Ancient Greece and Rome*, 2 vols., London 1911.

Other relatively recent studies on certain aspects are:

E. Badian   *Foreign Clientelae 264–70 B.C.*, Oxford 1958.

G. E. M. de Ste Croix   *The Origins of the Peloponnesian War*, London 1972.

R. M. Errington   *The Dawn of Empire: Rome's Rise to World Power*, London 1971.

P. Gauthier   *Symbola: les étrangers et la justice dans les cités grecques*, Nancy 1972.

A. J. Graham   *Colony and Mother City in Ancient Greece*, Manchester 1964.

J. A. O. Larsen   *Representative Government in Greek and Roman History*, Berkeley 1955.

J. A. O. Larsen   *Greek Federal States*, Oxford 1968.

L. A. Losada   *The Fifth Column in the Peloponnesian War*, Leiden 1972.

R. Meiggs   *The Athenian Empire*, Oxford 1971.

D. J. Mosley   *Envoys and Diplomacy in Ancient Greece*, Wiesbaden 1973.

L. Piccirilli   *Gli Arbitrati Interstatali Greci*, vol. I Dalle Origini al 338 a.C., Pisa 1973.

T. T. B. Ryder   *Koine Eirene: general peace and local independence in ancient Greece*, London 1965.

C. G. Starr   *Political Intelligence in Classical Greece*, Leiden 1974.

Since the text of this book was written two comprehensive entries of fundamental importance have appeared in Pauly-Wissowa's *Realencyclopädie der classischen Altertumswissenschaft, Supplementband XIII* (Munich 1973), as follows:

F. Gschnitzer   *Proxenos* col. 629-730.
D. Kienast   *Presbeia* col. 499-628.

The following abbreviations have been used:

ATL	B. D. Meritt, H. T. Wade-Gery and M. F. McGregor, *The Athenian Tribute Lists*, 4 vols. (i, Cambridge, Mass., ii–iv Princeton, 1939-53).
CQ	*Classical Quarterly.*
FGH	F. Jacoby, *Die Fragmente der griechischen Historiker*, (Berlin and Leiden 1923-).
FHG	Th. Müller, *Fragmenta Historicorum Greacorum*, (Paris 1878-85).
IG	*Inscriptiones Graecae*, (Berlin 1873-).
M & L	R. Meiggs and D. M. Lewis, *A Selection of Greek Historical Inscriptions to the end of the Fifth Century B.C.*, (Oxford 1969).
OGI	*Orientis Graeci Inscriptiones Selectae*, (Leipzig 1903-5).
SEG	*Supplementum Epigraphicum Graecum.*
SIG³	W. Dittenberger, *Sylloge Inscriptionum Graecarum*, (third ed. Leipzig 1915-24).
St.	H. Bengtson, *Die Staatsverträge des Altertums* vol. II, (Berlin and Munich 1962).
*St.*III	H. H. Schmitt, *Die Staatsverträge des Altertums*, vol. III, (Munich 1969).
Tod I²	M. N. Tod, *A Selection of Greek Historical Inscriptions*, vol. I, second ed., (Oxford 1946).
Tod II	M. N. Tod, *A Selection of Greek Historical Inscriptions*, vol. II, (Oxford 1948).

Conventional or, it is hoped, readily intelligible abbreviations of ancient authors are given, e.g., Th. for Thucydides, Hdt. for Herodotus, Plb. for Polybius. All references to Xen., Xenophon, are to the *Hellenica* unless otherwise indicated.

1 All dates are BC unless otherwise indicated
2 Th.1,9
3 Hom. *Il.* 3,222
4 *St.*112
5 Th. 1,18,1
6 Hdt. 5,66
7 *id.* 6,77f.
8 *id.* 6,127 f.
9 *id.* 7,148 f.
10 Th. 5,14,4
11 *id.* 1,24 ff.
12 *id.* 1,126
13 *id.* 1,103,4
14 *id.* 1,67,4; 1,139
15 Hdt. 5,49-50

16 *id.* 6, 105 f.
17 Th. 1,18,2
18 *id.* 1,91,3 f.
19 See Hdt. 1,61 f.; 5,63; 94. See also W. W. How and J. Wells, *Commentary on Herodotus* (Oxford 1912) vol. II p. 344-5
20 Hdt. 5,73 f.; 97 f.
21 *id.* 7,144
22 Th. 2,65,9
23 Arist. *Ath. Poi.* 23,5; Plut. *Arist.* 25
24 Th. 1,100
25 *id.* 1,96
26 *id.* 1,98
27 *id.* 1,100 f.

28 *id.* 1,102
29 A. *Eum.* 757-80
30 Th. 2,13
31 *id.* 1,104
32 *id.* 1,103,4
33 *id.* 1,107
34 *id.* 1,105
35 M&L 33, where 460 or 459 is suggested as the date. Tod I² gives 459 or 458. Adcock put down 457
36 Th. 1,107 f.
37 Alliance with Segesta in 458/7, *St.*139. Treaties with Leontini (*St.*163) and Rhegium (*St.*162) are dated 433/2 but have been thought on the basis of Th. 3,86,3 to be renewals of earlier treaties. For the literature see *St.* notes *ad loc.* and M&L commentary to no. 63
38 Th. 1,112,1; Plut.*Cim.*18,1; *St.* 143, where the date is given as '453?'
39 Th. 5,14,4
40 Plut. *Arist.* 25,3
41 *id. Per.*11,5-6
42 *St.*151, M&L 43
43 M&L 40
44 Diod. Sic. 11,88,3; Paus. 1,27,5
45 Th. 1,19
46 See Th. 1,116,1 where seventy Samian ships are mentioned
47 M&L 45, *ATL* ii D 14
48 *St.*152. See especially Diod. Sic. 12,4,4-5
49 Th. 1,112,5
50 Plut. *Per.*17,3
51 Th. 1,113 f.
52 *St.*156, Th. 1,115,1
53 Th. 1,140,2
54 Plut. *Per.*14,16
55 Th. 1,115,2
56 *id.* 1,40,5
57 *id.* 1,24 f.
58 *id.* 1,66 f.
59 For the views of Archidamus see Th. 1,80 ff. and for those of Sthenelaidas *id.* 1,86 ff.
60 Th. 1,73
61 *id.* 1,125
62 *id.* 1,126 f.

63 *id.* 1,139, 1-2
64 *id.* 1,139,3
65 *id.* 2,12,3
66 *id.* 2,35 ff.
67 *id.* 2,47 ff.
68 *id.* 2,70
69 *id.* 3,2 f. It is instructive to read Thucydides' account of the appeal of the Mitylenian envoys to the Peloponnesians (Th. 3,9 f.) and of the speeches of Cleon and Diodotus (*id.* 3,42 f.) at Athens
70 Th. 3,86
71 *id.* 4,3 ff.
72 *id.* 4,89 ff.
73 *id.* 4,78 ff.
74 *id.* 4,118; *St.*185
75 Th. 4,58 ff.
76 *id.* 5,4,1
77 *id.* 5,16
78 *id.* 5,18, *St.*188. A translation is given on p.257. The Peace was followed by an alliance, Th. 5,23,4, *St.*189
79 Th. 5,27 ff.
80 *id.* 5,39 f.
81 *id.* 5,43
82 *St.*193, IG I² 86. *cf.* Th. 5,47
83 Th. 5,57 f.
84 *St.*194, Th. 5,77;79. *See* p.258 for a translation of Thucydides' account of the draft proposals and of the terms concluded
85 Th. 5,84. As in the case of the debate on Mytilene Thucydides' 'Melian Dialogue' is instructive reading
86 Th. 6,1 ff.
87 *id.* 7,87,5
88 *id.* 7,18
89 *id.* 7,18,2
90 *id.* 8,96,5
91 *St.*183, And. 3,28-9
92 For documents in Spartan negotiations with Persia see *St.*200-2, Th. 8,18; 37;58
93 Th. 8,6,3
94 *id.* 8,2,2
95 Diod.Sic. 13,52,2

96 Arist. *Ath. Pol.* 34,1
97 Xen. 2,1,21 f.
98 *id.* 1,5,1 f.
99 *id.* 2,2,3
100 *id.* 2,2,19-20
101 *St.*211. See especially Xen. 2,2,20
102 Xen. 2,4,1
103 *id.* 3,4,2 f
104 *id.* 4,3,12 f.
105 *St.*223. See especially *IG* II² 14; Xen. 3,5,16. See also Diod. Sic. 14,82,1 for the alliance of others including Corinth and Argos
106 Xen. 4,2,11-12
107 *id.* 4,8,12 f.
108 And. 3 (*On Peace*) purports to be Andocides' Statement to the Athenian people
109 *FGH* III B 328 (Philoch.) F 149
110 Xen. 5,1,29
111 *id.* 5,1,31;35-6. *St.*242
112 Xen. 5,1,36
113 *id.* 5,2, 1-10
114 *id.* 5,2, 11 ff.
115 *id.* 5,2,25 ff.
116 *id.* 5,3,27
117 *id.* 5,4,1
118 *IG* II² 40. On relations between Athens and Thebes see *St.*254/5
119 *St.*248, *IG* II² 34
120 *St.*257, *IG* II² 43. A translation is given on p.259
121 It has been argued on the basis of Diod. Sic. 11,47,1 that the Delian League had been a bi-cameral institution
122 Xen. 5,4,64 f.
123 *id.* 6,2,1; Diod. Sic. 15,38; *St.*265
124 *St.*269. Xen. 6,3,18; Diod. Sic. 15,50,4
125 Th. 2,2
126 *id.* 3,52,1
127 *id.* 5,32,5 f.
128 Xen. 2,4,2
129 *id.* 5,4,2 f.
130 *id.* 6,4,1 f.
131 *id.* 6,4,28

132 *St.*270, Xen. 6,5,1 f.
133 For Thebes' alliance with Arcadia see *St.*273, Diod. Sic. 15,62,3. See also Xen. *op. cit.*
134 *St.*274, Xen. 7,1,1 ff., Diod. Sic. 15,67,1 f.
135 *St.*283, Xen. 7,1,42
136 Diod. Sic. 15,79,2
137 Athens made an alliance with Dionysius in 367 (*St.*280) but complimentary exchanges took place by summer 368 (*IG* II² 103)
138 Xen. 7,1,27
139 *St.*282, Xen. 7,1,36-7; Plut. *Pel.*30
140 *IG* VII 2408
141 *St.*289, *IG* II² 111
142 *St.*284, Xen. 6,4,2
143 *St.*290, *IG* II² 112; *St.*291, Xen. 7,5,1
144 Xen. 7,5,27
145 *St.*292, *IG* IV 556, Tod II 145
146 Some of Ephorus' work survives by incorporation in the history of Diodorus Siculus
147 Diodorus used more extensively the work of Theopompus on Philip, but only excerpts and fragments survive of Theopompus' fifty-eight books of *Philippics*
148 Arist. *Oec.* 2,1350a 16
149 Diod. Sic. 15,67,4; Plut. *Pel.* 29,9; Paus. 9,15,1-2
150 *St.*298. Diod. Sic. 16,4,1; *Dem.* 23,121; *id.* 2,6-7
151 Dem. 1,5
152 *St.*314, Diod. Sic. 16,34,5
153 Tod II 150
154 See *St.*315 for Philip in Thessaly in 353
155 *St.*293, *IG* II² 116
156 *St.*308, Tod II 158
157 *St.*309, *IG* II² 127
158 *St.*313. See especially Diod. Sic. 16,22,2
159 Isoc. 8 (On Peace)
160 Diod. Sic. 16,8,5
161 For the treaty of *c.* 352/1 see *St.*318, Dem. 18,87

162 For the alliance of Athens and Olynthus see *St*.323, *FGH* III B 328 (Philoch.) F 49
163 *St*.329. See esp. Dem. 19,48,143
164 For the partisan accounts of the proceedings see Aeschines' speeches 1–3 and Demosthenes' 18 and 19
165 [Dem.] 12
166 See [Dem.] 7 (Hegesippus' speech on Halonnesus)
167 For the Athenian alliance in 342 with Achaea, Arcadia, Argos, Megalopolis and Messenia see *St*.337
168 For the Athenian alliance with Thebes in 339 see *St*.345, Aeschin. 3,141 f.
169 *St*.III 403, Tod II 177
170 For the bilateral arrangement between Athens and Philip after Chaeronea see *St*.III 402, Diod. Sic. 16,87,3
171 Isoc. *Philippus*
172 In 343. *St*.333, Arr.2,14,2
173 For renewal of arrangements see *St*.III 403 II
174 Arr. 1,4,6–8
175 *id*. 1,9,9–10
176 *id*. 1,17,9–13
177 *id*. 2,14 ff.
178 *id*. 2,25,1–3
179 *id*. 3,18,11–12
180 *St*.III 415, Diod. Sic. 18,18,3
181 *St*.III 421, Diod. Sic. 18,74,2
182 *St*.III 428. *OGI* 5=Welles *Royal Correspondence in the Hellenistic Period* (Newhaven 1934) No. 1. Diod. Sic. 20,19,3
183 *St*.III 433/4. Suda s.v. Δημήτριος and Diod. Sic. 20,37 give their statements on Greek freedom
184 *St*.III 446, *IG* IV² 1,68
185 Diod. Sic. 22,9. Paus. 10,19,7 f.
186 For the alliance of Athens and Sparta at the instigation of Ptolemy II in the Chremonidean War against Antigonous Gonatas see *St*.III 476, *IG* II² 686/7
187 Plut. *Arat*. 33,1–2; Plb. 2,44,1
188 *St*.III 520, Plb. 5,103,7 f.

189 *St*.III 500, Plb.2,12,3
190 *St*.III 506. Plb. 2,52,3 f. Plut. *Arat*.38,9 f.
191 *St*.III 507. Plb. 2,54,3; *id*. 4,9,4
192 Plb. 4,69,4 f. Plut. *Cleom*.30,1
193 *St*.III 520. Plb. 5,103,7 f.
194 Plb. 5,104
195 *St*.III 528; Plb. 7,9,1 f. Livy, 23,33,9 f. Polybius' version is a translation of the Punic text. For an English translation see p.262
196 *St*.III 536. Livy 26,24,1 f.
197 *St*.III 543. Livy 29,12,11
198 For the terms of the Peace between Rome and Carthage see Plb.15,18
199 *St*.III 547. Plb. 15,20,2 f.
200 Plb. 18,22 f. Livy 33,10
201 Livy 33,12–13; 24,5–7;30. For a translation of the terms see p.265
202 Livy 33,31,1 – 32,9. A translation is given on p.265
203 Livy 34,48,3; 49,4–52,1
204 *id*. 37,38–44
205 Plb. 21,32. *cf.* Livy 38,11. See p. 264 for a translation
206 Livy 37,45,10–21; 55,1–56,1; *id*. 38,38. Plb. 21,42
207 Plb. 25,3,1–4. Livy 42,13,8–9; 30,6
208 *SIG*³ 643. *cf.* Livy 42,11–13
209 Livy 45,29
210 Plb. 29,27
211 Livy 45,24,9 – 25,4
212 Paus. 7,16,7–10
213 Arist. *Pol*. 7,10
214 *St*.188, Th.5,18,10
215 *St*.III 446, *IG* IV² 1,68
216 *SIG*³ 643
217 *IG* II² 106, Tod II 135. For a translation see p.266
218 Livy 42,11–13
219 Th. 5,47
220 *St*.193, *IG* I² 86
221 Xen. 6,3,1–17
222 Th. 1,32 f.
223 *St*.III 528; Plb. 7,9,1 f.
224 Plb. 21,32
225 Livy 38,11

226 Plb. 21,42. Livy 37,45,10–21; 55,1–56,1
227 Livy 33,12–13; 30
228 *IG* II² 114, Tod II 146
229 *IG* XII 7,5, Tod II 152
230 Xen. 1,1,35; 3,15
231 *id.* 2,3,13–14
232 *id.* 5,2,25 f.
233 Diod. Sic. 18,74,2
234 Th. 1,24,2
235 *id.* 1,56,2 f.
236 *id.* 6,104
237 Diod. Sic. 16,88,3
238 Th. 1,32,4
239 *id.* 2,9,2
240 *id.* 1,35,2; 40,2
241 Xen. 3,5,3 f.
242 Th. 1,40,5; 41–2
243 *St.*161. Th. 1,44,1
244 *St.*223. *IG* II² 14; Xen. 3,5,16
245 The phrase in Plut. *Arist.*25 is that Aristides bound the *Greeks* by oaths and he himself swore on behalf of Athens. *St.*132
246 *St.*113; Hdt. 1,69,1–3
247 Th. 1,3 f.
248 Xen. 3,1,3
249 *id.* 5,2,11 f.
250 e.g. in 431, Th. 2,7,2
251 e.g. in 421 (Th. 5,21,1; 46,2), 366 (Dem. 19,137) and 346 (Dem. 19,253)
252 And. 2,11; 20
253 Th. 1,67,4
254 Diod. Sic. 16,74 f. See also Dem. 8 and 9
255 Xen. 3,2,21 f.
256 *St.*144; Th. 5,14,4
257 *St.*195. Th. 5,81,1; Xen. 5,2,2
258 *St.*193. *IG*² 86, Th. 5,47
259 *St.*217; Xen. 2,2,30–1
260 Th. 7,18,2
261 Dem. 9,26
262 Arr. 1,9,9–10
263 Diod. Sic. 19,53,2; Paus. 9,7,4
264 Diod. Sic. 19,52,2
265 Xen. 2,2,19 f.
266 See the classic description of the effects of war in Th. 3,82–3

267 *St.*189. Th. 5,23–5
268 *St.*329; Aeschin 3,54; Dem. 19,48
269 *St.*192. Th. 5,41,2–3
270 Xen. 5,2,25 f. *Hell. Ox.* 12,1 f; 13,1 f.
271 Xen. 3,5,1; Paus. 3,9,8; *Hell. Ox.*2,2
272 Hdt. 9,2
273 Th. 1,126,2
274 *IG* I² 10; M&L 40
275 *St.*159; *IG* I² 50; *id.* 102; Diod. Sic. 12,28,3
276 *IG* II² 1; M&L 94
277 Th. 8,73 f.
278 *id.* 8,64
279 *St.*289; *IG* II² 111, Tod II 142
280 See for example *IG* II² 6 and 9
281 Xen. 4,8,34. *Hell. Ox.*2,3
282 Xen. 5,2,1–10
283 *id.* 3,2,27 f.
284 Th. 3,70 f.
285 Hdt. 8,144
286 *St.*105. Hdt. 1,22,3–4
287 *St.*115. Hdt. 1,141,4
288 *St.*113. Hdt. 1,69,1–3
289 *IG* II² 43,line 16
290 Th. 2,9,4 in the list of the principal allies of Athens gives the Ionians of Asia Minor and their *Dorian* neighbours of Caria
291 Th. 6,46,2. The connection of the communities was with Euboean Chalcis, *FGH* 555 (Antiochus of Syracuse) F 9
292 Th. 1,107
293 Xen. 6,4,1
294 Hdt. 7,145,1
295 Xen. 3,4,3
296 *id.* 6,1,4 f.
297 Th. 2,8,4. *cf.* the arguments of Corinth (Th. 1,124,3)
298 Xen. 4,8,12 f.
299 *St.*242. Xen. 5,1,31
300 *St.*292. *IG* IV 556
301 Th. 1,53
302 Aeschin. 2,109
303 Th. 4,118,6
304 *id.* 2,12,2

305 Xen. 5,4,22
306 Th. 2,67
307 *Hell.Ox.*2,1
308 Th. 5,45
309 Xen. 5,4,22
310 *id.* 7,1,33
311 *id.* 6,3,2 f.
312 Aeschin. 2,91-2. Dem. 19,58.
313 Aeschin. 2,19
314 [Plut.] X Or. 841e (Lycurgus)
315 Dem. 9,72
316 *id.* 18,178-9
317 [And.] 4,41
318 Xen. 4,8,12. Plut. *Art.* 22,3-4
319 Xen. 7,1,33. Arr. 2,15,2
320 Th. 4,119,2
321 *id.* 5,19,1; 24,1
322 *id.* 5,44,3; *FGH* III B 324 (Androtion) F 44
323 Diod. Sic. 12,4,4. For a fine after an earlier visit see Dem. 19 273; see also Hdt. 7,151
324 Xen. 6,3,4
325 Aeschin. 3,138-9
326 Th. 1,91
327 *id.* 5,44,3
328 Diod. Sic. 15,28,1
329 Th. 5,46,1
330 Heracleides Ponticus ap. Th. Müller *FHG* vol ii p. 222 F 31
331 *IG* I² 57, M&L 65
332 Th. 1,91,3; Plut. *Arist.* 10,7
333 Dem. 18,282; 285. Nep. *Phoc.* 1,3
334 See *St.*III 476 Syll.³ 434/5, for the decree proposed by Chremonides for the alliance of Athens and Sparta in the Chremonidean War
335 Plut. *Cim.*17
336 *St.*143. Plut. *Cim.*18,1; *FGH* 115 (Theopompus) F 88
337 Plut. *Nic.*10; *id. Alc.*13; Th. 5,46,1
338 Xen. 6,3,1 f. He had taken the lead in the prosecution of Andocides in 392/1 for advocating peace with Sparta
339 Dem. 18,178-9; 219. Plut. *Dem.*18,1

340 Dem. 19,166-8; 191
341 *FGH* 115 (Theopomp.) F 88; Plut. *Cim.*14
342 Xen. 6,3,4, Alcibiades aimed to revive the Spartan proxeny held by his grandfather at Athens as it had lapsed (Th. 6,89,2)
343 Xen. 4,5,6
344 *id.* 5,4,22
345 Plut. *Cim.*14
346 *id.* 10,5. Th. 5,76,3
347 Diod. Sic. 13,27,3
348 Xen. 6,1,4
349 *id.* 3,2,27. Paus. 3,8,4
350 *St.*289; *IG* II² 111
351 *IG* II² 33
352 *id.* 6, Tod II 98
353 Xen. 2,2,13 f.
354 Hdt. 9,5
355 Xen. 6,4,20
356 [Dem.] 7,20
357 Dem. 15,22
358 *St.*139, M&L 37, *IG* I² 19
359 *St.*207, M&L 87, *IG* I² 116
360 Aesch. 2,55; 110
361 Plut. *Pel.*30; Ath. 6,229 f.
362 Dem. 19,31; 137. Xen. 7,1,33 f.
363 *IG* II² 141, Tod II 139
364 *IG* II² 207
365 *St.*155, *IG* I² 39, M&L 52
366 *St.*264, *IG* II² 102, Tod II 129
367 *IG* II² 107, Tod II 131
368 Arist. *Ath. Pol.*43,4
369 *St.*293, *IG* II² 116
370 *IG* XII 7,5, Tod II 152
371 *IG* II² 107, Tod II 131
372 *IG* II² 226, Tod II 173
373 Th. 2,21,1
374 *id.* 2,13. *cf.* Justin 3,7
375 Th. 5,43; 46,5; 61,2; *id.* 6,61,3
376 *St.*193. Th. 5,47,8; *IG* I² 86
377 Aeschin. 3,95-6
378 Th. 5,59,5 f.
379 *id.* 1,101 f.
380 *id.* 1,58,1
381 Plb. 4,16,5. See G.E.M. de Ste. Croix, The Alleged Secret Pact between Athens and Philip II, CQ NS 13 (1963) p. 118-9

382 *St*.III 428. *OGIS* = C. B. Welles
*Royal Correspondence in the Hellenistic
Period* (Newhaven 1934) No. 1;
Diod. Sic. 20,19,3
383 *IG* II² 128 (Tod II 159). *cf. IG*
II² 96 (*St*.262)
384 *Hell.Ox*.1,1 f.
385 Xen. 5,4,20 f.
386 Aeschin. 3,194
387 *FGH* 328 (Philoch.) F 149
388 Dem. 19,116; Aeschin. 2,6; *id.*
3,79; 81. Din.1,28
389 Nep. *Phoc.* 1,3. Dem. 18,282
390 Th. 5,36,1
391 Xen. 6,1,17
392 Th. 2,21,1
393 *id.* 5,63
394 Xen. 3,5,25
395 See the remarks of Th. 6,1. *cf.
id.* 6,6,3 and 6,8,1–4
396 Th. 8,6,4
397 Xen. 3,4,1
398 Th. 2,67,1
399 *id.* 4,50,1
400 *Hell.Ox*.2,1
401 Xen. 4,8,13
402 *id.* 7,1,33
403 *St*.134; *IG* I² 10
404 *St*.139; *IG* I² 19. *IG* I² 1 refers
to cleruchs sent to Salamis in the late
sixth century
405 *St*.155, *IG* I² 39
406 *St*.149; *IG* I² 16
407 *St*.111. W. Dittenberger and
K. Purgold *Die Inschriften von
Olympia* (1896 repr. Amsterdam 1966)
No. 10
408 *St*.110, M&L 17
409 Th. 5,18,10. The subsequent
alliance provided for the deposit of
copies on the Acropolis and in the
Temple of Amycla (Th.5,23,5)
410 Th. 5,47,11
411 *IG* II² 6, Tod II 98
412 *St*.257, *IG* II² 43
413 *St*.262/3, *IG* II² 96/7
414 Th. 8,1 f.
415 Dem. 18, 169–72
416 Hdt. 3,38

417 *id.* 8,144
418 *id.* 7,136
419 Plut. *Sol*.10; Paus. 1,35,2
420 Aeschin.3,31
421 Diod. Sic. 15,79,5–6. More
recently Theban dissidents had plot-
ted with the knights of Orchomenus
422 Th. 8,10
423 *St*.104. Aeschin. 2,115. *cf. id.*
3,109; 110
424 *St*.149, *IG* I² 16 (Phaselis, with
reference to Chios. For a translation
see p.255). *St*.169, *IG* I² 60 (Mytilene).
St.207, *IG* I² 116 (Selymbria).
St.209, *IG* II² 1 (Samos). The neuter
plural *symbolă* is used for *an* agreement. Alternatively *symbolê* (sing.) or
symbolai (plur.) can be used.
425 *St*.235, *IG* II² 46 (Troezen).
St.294 (Siphnos). *St*.296 (Crete)
426 *St*.321, *IG* II² 179
427 Th. 5,79,4
428 *St*.228, *IG* XII 2,1
429 *St*.231, Tod II 111
430 *St*.322, Tod II 165
431 *St*.320, Tod II 162
432 *St*.289, *IG* II² 111
433 *St*.306; Dem. 20,29–31; 36–7
434 *IG* II² 212, Tod II 167
435 *St*.146, *IG* IX 1,333
436 *St*.232, *SEG* XIV 530
437 *St*.III 508, *IG* XII 5,532
438 *St*.III 495, *IG* V 2,419
439 *St*.III 492, *OGI* 229
440 *St*.132; Arist. *Ath. Pol*.23,5
441 *St*.187, *IG* I² 90
442 Th. 3,70,3
443 Xen. 2,2,20
444 *id.* 3,5,16. The Thebans were
represented as appealing to the
Athenian sense of grandeur. Thrasybulus assured the Thebans merely
that Athens would offer support after
any Spartan attack. For the defensive
form see *St*.223, *IG* II² 14
445 Xen. 5,3,26
446 Plut. *Pel*.27,3
447 *St*.III 446, *IG* IV² 1,68
448 Th. 1,44,1

449 *id.* 1,53
450 *id.* 5,31,6
451 *St.*193. *IG* I² 86, Th. 5,47
452 Xen. 7,5,4
453 Th. 5,23,1 f.
454 *St.*224, *IG* II² 15
455 *St.*248, *IG* II² 34
456 *St.*256, *IG* II² 41
457 *St.*263, *IG* II² 97 (Corcyra). *St.*280, Tod II 136 (Dionysius). *St.* 293, *IG* II² 116 (Thessaly). *St.*340, *IG* II² 230 (Eretria). *St.*307 (Illyria and Chalcis)
458 Xen. 7,4,2 f.
459 *St.*290, *IG* II² 112
460 *St.*291, Xen. 7,5,3
461 Xen. 7,1,1 f.
462 Aeschin. 3,143
463 *St.*313. Dem. 15,26; *schol.*Dem. 3,28
464 *St.*134, *IG* I² 10
465 *St.*145, M&L 47
466 *St.*154, *ATL* ii D 16
467 *St.*155, *IG* I² 39
468 *St.*159, M&L 56. Diod. Sic. 12,28,3-4
469 Th. 1,101,3
470 *id.* 1,117,3
471 *id.* 4,69,4
472 Xen. 2,2,20 (12); Diod. Sic. 13,107,4 (10)
473 Diod. Sic. 16,34,5
474 Th. 7,83,2
475 *id.* 4,54,3-4. Subsequently Th. 4,57,4 reports that the Athenians left them in possession of their own land
476 Th. 4,105,2
477 Diod. Sic. 18,18,4
478 Th. 4,57,4
479 Diod. Sic. 16,59,3
480 Xen. 2,3,6
481 *id.* 2,3,7
482 Th. 3,28,1
483 *id.* 7,82,2
484 *id.* 3,52,1
485 *id.* 4,88
486 *id.* 1,29,5
487 *id.* 4,69,3
488 *id.* 4,105,2

489 *id.* 2,70,3
490 *id.* 1,103,1; Diod. Sic. 11,84,8
491 Paus. 9,1,7
492 Diod. Sic. 16,34,5
493 Isoc. 4,43
494 Th. 3,56,2
495 *id.* 3,65
496 *id.* 5,49
497 Tod II 137
498 Hdt. 7,206; 9,11
499 Th. 5,54
500 Xen. 4,7,2
501 *id.* 3,5,23-4. Diod. Sic. 14,81,3 uses the term *anochai* for this truce
502 Plut. *Pel.*29, where the word *anochai* is used
503 Diod. Sic. 11,80,6
504 Xen. 3,4,25; Diod. Sic. 14,80,8
505 Th. 4,15,2; 16,2
506 *id.* 4,117 f.
507 *id.* 5,59,5
508 Xen. 3,2,19-20; Diod. Sic. 14,39,5-6
509 Th. 5,26,2
510 *id.* 5,32
511 *id.* 4,97 f.
512 *id.* 2,12,2
513 *id.* 2,22,2
514 *SIG*³ 110
515 Th. 4,16,3 f.
516 Xen. *An.*3,3,5
517 Plut. *Per.*30,2 f.
518 Aeschin. 2,80
519 Hdt. 7,9,2
520 Th. 1,29
521 Plut. *Pyrrh.* 26,11
522 Th. 1,53
523 *id.* 1,146
524 Arist. *Ath. Pol.*23,5
525 The references are collected in *St.*242
526 *St.*III 403, Tod II 177
527 *St.*110, M&L 17. See *St.*120, M&L 10, for the sixth century alliance concluded between Sybaris and Serdaioi ἐπὶ φιλότατῃ πισταῖ κἀδόλοι
528 *St.*231, Tod II 111
529 *St.*328, *IG* II² 213

530 *St.*187, *IG* I² 90
531 *St.*243, Isoc. 14,27
532 *St.*186, *IG* I² 71
533 *St.*208, *IG* I² 47
534 *St.*236, Aristoph. *Plut.*178
535 *St.*248, *IG* II² 34
536 Th. 5,44,1
537 *id.* 2,67
538 *id.* 5,112
539 *id.* 2,72
540 *id.* 1,35,2; 40,2
541 *id.* 5,18,5
542 *id.* 3,70,2
543 *St.*167, *IG* I² 53
544 *St.*280, Tod II 136
545 *St.*184, *IG* I² 87
546 *St.*111. W. Dittenberger and K. Purgold *Die Inschriften von Olympia* (1896 repr. Amsterdam 1966) No. 10
547 Th. 1,78,4. *cf. id.* 1,140,2
548 *id.* 7,18,2
549 *id.* 1,86
550 [Dem.] 7,36; *id.* 12,11
551 Aeschin. 3,83
552 Hdt.5,95
553 Plut. *Them.*23
554 Plut. *Ap. Lac.* 215c
555 Dem. 3,27
556 Th. 5,31,4
557 *Hell.Ox.*13,4
558 Paus. 3,9,11
559 *IG* XII 3,1259, Tod II 179
560 *IG* IV 926
561 Tod II 113
562 Plut. *Sol.*10
563 Hdt. 6,108
564 Plut. *Pel.*26
565 Aeschin. 3,122 f. Dem. 18, 149 f.
566 *St.*292, *IG* IV 556
567 Xen. 4,5,6 f.
568 Aeschin. 2,18
569 Th. 4,118 f.
570 *St.*258, *IG* II² 42
571 *St.*293, *IG* II² 116
572 *St.*205, *IG* XII 9,188
573 Th. 5,41
574 Diod. Sic. 12,75,4

575 *St.*263, *IG* II² 97
576 *St.* 293, *IG* II² 116
577 *St.*187, *IG* I² 90
578 *St.*289, *IG* II² 111
579 *St.*186, *IG* I² 71 (Macedon). *St.*184, *IG* I² 87 (Halieis). *St.*289, *IG* II² 111 (Ceos). *St.*307 (Chalcis and Grabus of Illyria), D. M. Robinson *Transactions of the American Philological Assn.* 69 (1933) pp. 44 f. No. 2. *St.*308, Tod II 158 (Chalcis and Philip)
580 *St.*322, Tod II 165
581 *St.*309, *IG* II² 127. The treaty was between Athens, Cetriporis of Thrace, Lyppeus of Paeonia and Grabus of Illyria
582 *St.*340, *IG* II² 230 (341); *St.*229, *IG* II² 16 (394)
583 *St.*260. E. Nachmanson *Historische Griechische Inschriften* (Bonn 1913) 31
584 Dem. 19,151; 158–9; 278
585 Aeschin.2,85
586 Xen. 6,3,19
587 *St.*262, *IG* II² 96
588 *St.*120, M&L 10
589 *St.*162, *IG* I² 51 (Rhegium); *St.*163, *IG* I² 52 (Leontini)
590 Th. 4,63,1
591 *St.*110, M&L 17
592 *St.*193, *IG* I² 86
593 Th. 3,114,3
594 *St.*195. Th. 5,81,1; Xen. 5,2,2
595 *St.*263, *IG* II² 97
596 *St.*290, *IG* II² 112
597 See Isoc. 8 (On Peace)
598 *FGH* III B 328 (Philoch.) F 55
599 *St.*293, *IG* II² 116
600 Dem. 20,37
601 Paus. 5,23,4
602 Th. 5,56,3
603 *id.* 5,43
604 Xen. 4,6,1 f
605 *St.*205, *IG* XII 9, 188
606 Dem. 15,3; Diod. Sic. 16,7,3; Isoc. 8,16
607 Th. 5,78
608 Dem. 16,27
609 Xen. 7,4,2

610 *id.* 6,3,18
611 *id.* 6,5,2
612 *IG* I² 108
613 Th. 5,32
614 Paus. 1,25,3
615 Lys. 26,23
616 Th. 1,118,3
617 Hdt. 6,106
618 *id.* 7,206
619 *id.* 9,6–7
620 Xen. 4,5,11
621 Dem. 18,134
622 Aeschin. 2,116
623 *St.*112. *Plut. Quaest. Graec.* 292b, *Plut. Quaest. Rom.* 277c
624 Hdt. 5,91–3
625 Th. 1,88
626 *id.* 1,119–25
627 *id.* 2,6 f.
628 *id.* 3,2,1 f.
629 *id.* 4,21 f.
630 *id.* 5,17,2
631 Xen. 2,2,19
632 *id.* 6,3,19
633 *id.* 6,5,3
634 Plut. *Arist.*25
635 Th. 1,98,3 f. (Naxos, Carystus); *id.* 1,100,2–3 (Thasos)
636 See the commonly accepted restoration of lines 1 and 3 of *IG* I² 86 (*St.*193)
637 *IG* I² 65, M&L 68
638 Th. 1,115,2
639 *IG* I² 10 (Erythrae); *St.*155, *IG* I² 39 (Chalcis)
640 *IG* I² 66, M&L 46
641 *IG* I² 65, M&L 68
642 *IG* I² 63, M&L 69
643 M&L 45, *ATL* ii D 14
644 *St.*248, *IG* II² 34
645 *St.*256, *IG* II² 41
646 Diod. Sic. 11,47,1 might be taken to imply that the Delian League too was bi-cameral
647 *St.*258, *IG* II² 42
648 *St.*262, *IG* II² 96
649 *IG* II² 103, Tod II 133
650 *St.*290, *IG* II² 112
651 *SIG*³ 192, Tod II 156

652 *IG* II² 233, Tod II 175
653 *IG* XII 7,5,Tod II 152
654 Aeschin. 2,60
655 *id.* 3,69 f.
656 *St.*III 403, *IG* II² 236
657 *IG* XII 3,1259, Tod II 179
658 Arr. 1,9,9
659 Diod. Sic. 17,73,5
660 *SIG*³ 283, Tod II 192
661 *St.*III 446, *IG* IV² 1,68
662 Plb. 4,9,4. For the alliance of the Achaeans and Antigonus of 224 see *St.*III 506, and for its subsequent extension to a wider alliance see *St.*III 507
663 Livy 35,33; 34,2
664 *id.* 37,6–7; Plb. 21,4–5
665 Livy 36,26–9; Plb. 20,9–10
666 Plb. 2,48,8; 50 f.
667 *id.* 22,7–9
668 Paus. 7,12,6
669 *St.*III 499, *IG* V 2,344. In the inscription '*synedroi*' is a less probable restoration than '*damiorgoi*'.
670 Aratus had ten *damiorgoi* with him when he went to meet Antigonus and concluded agreement (Plut. *Arat.*43,1; 44,1)
671 Plb. 22,10,10–12; 12,5–7
672 *id.* 2,46,6; 4,7,1–7
673 *id.* 5,104
674 *St.*III 528, Plb. 7,9,1–16
675 For translations of the two treaties see p.263
676 Livy 29,12,1
677 Plb. 23,4,7
678 Livy 45,28
679 *id.* 45,18,1–2
680 For a translation of the treaty imposed by Rome on Aetolia in 189 see p. 264
681 Livy 32,19–23
682 Plb. 28,6
683 *id.* 29, 23–5
684 *id.* 33,16
685 *id.* 30,6,5 f. Livy 45,31,4 f.
686 *St.*110. M&L 17
687 *St.*149, M&L 31
688 *St.*155, M&L 52

689 *St.*188, Th. 5,18 f.

690 *St.*194, Th. 5,77; 79

691 *St.*257, *IG* II² 43

692 *St.*263, *IG* II² 97

693 *St.*III 403, *IG* II² 236

694 *St.*III 409, dated to the late fourth century. *Milet.* I, 3,137

695 *St.*III 528, Plb. 7,9,1 f. (text

based on Carthaginian document)

696 *St.*III 536, Livy 26,24,10–13. For part of the documentary record see *IG* IX, 1³,2,241

697 Plb. 21,32. Livy 38,11

698 Livy, 33,30. *cf.* Plb. 18,44

699 Livy 33,32,5

700 *IG* I² 106, Tod II 135

INDEX